MILITARY AND VETERAN ISSUES

HIRING VETERANS INTO CIVIL SERVICE POSITIONS

PRACTICES, COMPLEXITIES, AND PROTECTION ISSUES

MILITARY AND VETERAN ISSUES

Additional books in this series can be found on Nova's website under the Series tab.

Additional e-books in this series can be found on Nova's website under the e-book tab.

MILITARY AND VETERAN ISSUES

HIRING VETERANS INTO CIVIL SERVICE POSITIONS

PRACTICES, COMPLEXITIES, AND PROTECTION ISSUES

SERGIO RUIZ
EDITOR

nova publishers
New York

Library of Congress Cataloging-in-Publication Data

ISBN: 978-1-63484-436-9

Published by Nova Science Publishers, Inc. † New York

CONTENTS

PREFACE

The laws and regulations regarding the preferences in hiring that can or must be given to veterans and certain family members are extremely complex. The preferences vary by the specific circumstances of the veterans and the hiring authorities being used. Some veterans can be non-competitively appointed, while other veterans may not be eligible for that same hiring authority, and the availability of an authority may depend on the grade of the position being filled. The right of a veteran to have his or her application considered for a position may depend on whether an agency is considering applicants who are internal to Government but outside the agency's own workforce. The degree of preference owed can vary by agency or position being filled. Under certain circumstances, the mother of a veteran may be eligible for preference, whereas the father would not be eligible. There are many other examples of how veterans may be treated differently under the law, but to put the message more simply: the laws relating to veterans' preference invite misunderstandings, confusion, perceptions of wrongdoing, and possibly actual wrongdoing—whether intentional or inadvertent. This book discusses hiring authorities pertaining to veterans, the hiring of veterans under those authorities, and employee perceptions about veteran hiring. It also describes the statutes and pertinent case decisions for two laws designed to protect the employment rights of veterans in the civil service.

In: Hiring Veterans into Civil Service Positions
Editor: Sergio Ruiz

ISBN: 978-1-63484-436-9

Chapter 1

VETERAN HIRING IN THE CIVIL SERVICE: PRACTICES AND PERCEPTIONS*

U.S. Merit Systems Protection Board

EXECUTIVE SUMMARY

The laws and regulations regarding the preferences in hiring that can or must be given to veterans and certain family members are extremely complex. The preferences vary by the specific circumstances of the veterans and the hiring authorities being used. Some veterans can be non-competitively appointed, while other veterans may not be eligible for that same hiring authority, and the availability of an authority may depend on the grade of the position being filled. The right of a veteran to have his or her application considered for a position may depend on whether an agency is considering applicants who are internal to Government but outside the agency's own workforce. The degree of preference owed can vary by agency or position being filled. Under certain circumstances, the mother of a veteran may be eligible for preference, whereas the father would not be eligible. There are many other examples of how veterans may be treated differently under the law, but to put the message more simply: the laws relating to veterans' preference invite misunderstandings, confusion, perceptions of wrongdoing, and possibly actual wrongdoing—whether intentional or inadvertent.

This report discusses hiring authorities pertaining to veterans, the hiring of veterans under those authorities, and employee perceptions about veteran hiring. Data from a survey conducted by the U.S. Merit Systems Protection Board ("MSPB" or "The Board") indicate that Federal employees perceived inappropriate favoritism towards veterans more frequently than they perceived denials of veterans' preference rights, with 6.5 percent of respondents reporting they observed favoritism towards veterans compared to 4.5 percent reporting they observed a denial of veterans' preference rights. Both sets of perceptions are problematic as such conduct is not in keeping with the merit system principles (MSPs) and the responsibility of agencies to avoid prohibited personnel practices (PPPs). Additionally, the survey data

* This is an edited, reformatted and augmented version of a report to the President and Congress, issued August 2014.

showed that employees are less likely to be engaged and more likely to want to leave their agencies if they report having observed either of these two types of conduct.

Agencies must operate within the laws enacted by Congress and regulations promulgated by the Office of Personnel Management (OPM). Many of the challenges discussed in this report can be addressed only by Congress, OPM, or both. However, agencies can do the following: (1) ensure that agency officials act appropriately within the laws and regulations; (2) educate the workforce about the rules regarding veterans; and (3) provide greater transparency about what is being done and why it is being done in a particular manner.

Perceptions of inappropriate favoritism towards veterans are particularly an issue in the Department of Defense (DoD), where 8 percent of DoD employees responding to the survey reported having seen this behavior. Additionally, while only 3 percent of DoD supervisors and 2 percent of managers reported perceiving violations of preference rights, 7 percent of supervisors and 4 percent of managers reported perceptions of inappropriate favoritism towards veterans.

Some of the perceptions of inappropriate favoritism may have been a result of the complex hiring process and a proliferation of hiring authorities, which can invite misunderstandings and provide opportunities for suspicion. However, in two other MSPB surveys, some DoD respondents wrote in comments to express that they had observed manipulations of the hiring process to favor individuals who were retiring from military service. These alleged improprieties included: (1) writing job descriptions specifically for retiring military members; (2) military or former-military colleagues of retirees hiring those retirees without regard for which applicant was better qualified; and (3) holding jobs vacant until the desired military retiree became available. Additionally, DoD's own hiring data indicates that large numbers of retirees are being hired with little or no break in service between its military and civilian service, supporting perceptions that the hiring process was manipulated to ensure employment of those retirees. It is important that DoD address these perceptions and any underlying causes.

There is a statute, codified at 5 U.S.C. § 3326 (known as the 180-day rule), designed to prevent such occurrences by providing oversight for the hiring of recently retired military members into DoD. However, the issue of where the responsibility for oversight may rest is complicated (as discussed in the report) and, due to an exception in the law, the oversight has not been in effect for 13 years.

Because of the seriousness of the survey respondents' perceptions and allegations, the extent to which the negative perceptions are held by supervisors and managers, the supporting data from hiring records, and the allegations' relationship to the MSPs and PPPs, we recommend resuming oversight of the hiring of military retirees. In the alternative, if Congress determines that the law is no longer needed, the law should be repealed.

SECTION ONE: INTRODUCTION

"They will not be persuaded to sacrifice all views of present interest, and encounter the numerous vicissitudes of War, in the defence of their Country, unless she will be generous enough, on her part, to make a decent provision for their future support[.]" [1]

— George Washington

The history of veterans' preference in Federal hiring and retention predates the foundation of the modern, merit-based civil service in the Pendleton Act of 1883.[2] The Pendleton Act itself contained a provision to expressly protect preferences that had previously been granted to "those honorably discharged from the military or naval service[.]"[3] As the civil service was modified and reformed in the 130 years following the Pendleton Act, Congress continued to make provisions for various forms of preference for those who served the Nation as a member of the armed forces. The result today is an assortment of rights scattered throughout several titles of the U.S. Code and the Code of Federal Regulations.[4]

There is no question that Congress has the power to create such rights regarding Federal employment or that there is a legitimate public policy purpose in protecting and rewarding those who risked their lives or dedicated their time in the uniformed services.[5] Under Title 5 of the U.S. Code, agencies have an obligation to both: (1) observe all legally required preferences for veterans; and (2) ensure that selections are "determined solely on the basis of relative ability, knowledge, and skills, after fair and open competition which assures that all receive equal opportunity."[6] Balancing these two objectives can be challenging.[7] Additionally, there are policy objectives that strongly encourage the hiring of veterans into the civil service.[8] Survey responses indicate that some employees perceive that agencies may have failed to adequately balance these obligations.[9]

Purpose

This report discusses various forms of preference for veterans permitted or required in Federal hiring as well as employee perceptions of how agencies are using those authorities.

The report's goals include:

- Informing policymakers about the complexities of the existing system;[10]
- Educating all readers to help them understand that the civil service is designed to increase hiring opportunities for veterans while simultaneously ensuring that hiring is based upon an individual's merits as they relate directly to the job in question; and
- Helping agencies to recognize and address possible sources for improprieties and perceptions of improprieties with regard to the hiring of veterans

Defining a Veteran

The Merriam-Webster Dictionary defines a veteran as "an old soldier of long service" or "a former member of the armed forces."[11] However, the definition of a veteran for purposes of civil service law is not as simple as the dictionary might imply. Black's Law Dictionary defines a veteran as "a person who has been honorably discharged from military service."[12] Title 38 of the U.S. Code, which deals with veterans' benefits, defines a veteran as "a person who served in the active military, naval, or air service, and who was discharged or released therefrom under conditions other than dishonorable."[13] However, Title 5 of the U.S. Code, which applies to hiring in the civil service, contains its own definition of veteran, which incorporates some of Title 38 and then provides other language that Title 5 accepts as meeting the definition of "veteran."[14] The full definition of "veteran" from Title 5 contains approximately 250 words and can be found in the glossary at Appendix F. The glossary also provides the Title 5 definitions for disabled veteran and preference eligible.

The preferences due to an individual as a result of military service will often have additional requirements or restrictions beyond being a "veteran." Some hiring preferences given to veterans require that the veteran have served for a set period of time.[15] Others are predicated upon the extent of the sacrifices made by the veteran in service to the Nation.[16] Additionally, *under certain conditions*, the preference earned by the veteran may be used by someone other than the veteran, such as a spouse, widow(er), or mother.[17] Thus, the term "preference eligible" is not interchangeable with "preference eligible veteran."[18] A veteran is not "preference eligible" unless he or she retired below the rank of Major or its equivalent—with an exception for those who are disabled.[19] Furthermore, according to the so-called "180-day rule," a retired member of the armed forces cannot be appointed to a position in DoD (including non-appropriated fund instrumentalities) for 180 days after retirement, unless one of three exceptions applies.[20] Because of all the caveats and exceptions that apply to the hiring of veterans, it is understandable that misunderstandings will arise.

Methodology

This study relies primarily upon a review of Federal laws and regulations as well as data from three surveys conducted by the MSPB: (1) the 2010 Merit Principles Survey (MPS); (2) the 2011 Federal Merit Systems Survey (FMSS); and (3) the 2011 Fair and Open Competition Survey (FOCS).[21] We also sent questionnaires to OPM and DoD, and invited the Department of Labor (DOL) and veterans' organizations to comment on the complexity in veterans' hiring laws and how they might be improved. DOL and the veterans' organizations declined to respond; OPM and DoD submitted responses which are discussed within the report. Additionally, this report uses data from OPM's Central Personnel Data File (CPDF) regarding the full-time, permanent Federal workforce.[22]

We also provided both OPM and DoD with a draft copy of this report and an opportunity to comment. We have considered those comments and the report includes clarifications and technical corrections based on those comments. However, the report's broad findings and conclusions remain essentially unchanged. A brief discussion of OPM's response is in Appendix A. A copy of OPM's full response is in Appendix B and a copy of DoD's full response is in Appendix C. We thank both agencies for their input.

Section Two: Veterans' Preferences in Hiring for Competitive Service Positions

"Resolved by the Senate and House of Representatives of the United States of America, in Congress assembled, [t]hat persons honorably discharged from the military or naval service by reason of disability resulting from wounds or sickness incurred in the line of duty, should be preferred for appointments to civil offices, provided they shall be found to possess the business capacity necessary for the proper discharge of the duties of such offices."

—March 3, 1865[23]

The competitive service consists of all civilian positions in the Federal Government that are not specifically excepted by law, executive order, or OPM regulation.[24] As explained in Section Three, veterans' preference also applies to the excepted service, although it may take a different form than in the competitive service. However, the Senior Executive Service (SES) is a separate service and is not addressed in this report because veterans' preference does not apply to the SES.[25]

Before discussing some of the authorities that may be used to hire an individual into positions that are in the competitive service,[26] it is important to note that agencies often solicit candidates using multiple authorities at the same time. "Agencies may use a variety of appointing authorities to hire job applicants."[27] An agency may conduct "simultaneous parallel procedures under the competitive examination and merit promotion processes to fill the same position."[28] For example, an agency may select a candidate from a list of reinstatement eligible applicants (which does not use veterans' preference), even if there is another referral list containing preference eligibles.[29]

Competitive Examining

Competitive examining, while the most open of all hiring authorities, is used to appoint less than one-third of new Federal hires.[30] Competitive examining allows all qualified U.S. citizens to apply for a vacancy.[31] By law, under competitive examining, individuals who meet certain criteria related to military service receive a form of preference when being considered for positions. This is known as "veterans' preference."[32]

In FY 2010, the year the MPS was conducted, only 27 percent of the positions in the civil service that were filled with an external hire were filled using a competitive examining hiring authority.[33] One possible reason why agencies may use alternatives to competitive examining may be the sheer complexity of the process and the labor involved in adhering to all of its rules. Another possible reason is that agencies may want to be presented with as many different options as possible from which to select a new employee.[34]

There is no unified test covering admission to all civil service positions.[35] Most competitive examinations are conducted by Delegated Examining Units (DEUs), which consist of human resources (HR) staff in the hiring agency who have been authorized by OPM to conduct examinations in accordance with OPM's rules.[36] There are two statutorily authorized methods to conduct competitive examining: (1) the rule of three; and (2) category rating.[37] As discussed below, they share some commonalities, yet differ at an important stage in the process.

The Rule of Three

Although a 2010 executive memorandum instructs agencies not to use it, the rule of three remains in the statute.[38] We discuss the rule of three below because it: (1) was still in use a few months before our survey was conducted in 2010; (2) remains in statute; (3) has been used in the past; (4) may be used in the future; and (5) some of the rules used when hiring through this method also apply to category rating.

Under the rule of three, when a candidate met the minimum qualification requirements for a position, the candidate would be assigned a numeric score.[39] Points would then be added to this score if the individual was entitled to veterans' preference.[40] Veterans' preference points were assigned as follows. Five points were added to the passing examination score or rating of a veteran who served:

- During a war;
- During the period April 28, 1952 through July 1, 1955;
- For more than 180 consecutive days, other than for training, any part of which occurred after January 31, 1955, and before October 15, 1976;
- During the Gulf War from August 2, 1990, through January 2, 1992;
- For more than 180 consecutive days, other than for training, any part of which occurred during the period beginning September 11, 2001, and ending on the date prescribed by Presidential proclamation or by law as the last day of Operation Iraqi Freedom; or
- In a campaign or expedition for which a campaign medal has been authorized. Any Armed Forces Expeditionary medal or campaign badge, including El Salvador, Lebanon, Grenada, Panama, Southwest Asia, Somalia, and Haiti, qualifies for preference.

Ten points were added to the passing examination score of:

- A veteran who served at any time who has a compensable service-connected disability rating of at least 10 percent but less than 30 percent;
- A veteran who served at any time who has a compensable service-connected disability rating of 30 percent or more;
- A veteran who served at any time and has a present service-connected disability or is receiving compensation, disability retirement benefits, or pension from the military or the Department of Veterans Affairs but does not qualify under a different item in this list;
- A veteran who received a Purple Heart; or
- A spouse, widow(er), or mother[41] of a veteran who meets certain criteria related to the veteran's death or disability.[42]

In addition to the application of points, a minimally qualified veteran with a compensable, service-connected disability of 10 percent or more would automatically be placed at the top of the list, even if other candidates scored much higher after the addition of the 10 extra points. This elevation was known as "floating" to the top of the list.[43]

Once veterans' preference was applied to whomever met the criteria, the top three candidates would then be referred on a certificate in order of their adjusted scores. On a rule of three certificate, a supervisor was prohibited from selecting a non-veteran if there was a veteran higher on the list. In other words, a supervisor could not hire the second person on the list if the first person was a veteran and the second was not, even if the second person had a higher score before the scores were adjusted for points and floating occurred.[44] This was known as "blocking" the list.[45]

If a selecting official concluded that that the veteran blocking the list was not qualified, the official could submit a "pass over" request to the examination unit.[46] The pass over process is the same under category rating, which is discussed in the next section. Examples of acceptable reasons to request a pass over include: a prior history of performance issues; medical inability to perform the duties; or an intentional false statement made in the examination process.[47] DEUs are delegated the authority to decide to pass over a veteran, unless the individual is a 30 percent compensable veteran, in which case, OPM retains the authority to make the pass over determination.[48] If the pass over request is denied, the agency is not permitted to select a lower-ranking non-preference eligible.[49]

Category Rating

In 2002, Congress authorized the Government-wide use of category rating as an alternative approach for competitive examining.[50] On May 11, 2010, the President directed agencies to stop using the rule of three and instead to only use category rating for competitive examining.[51] One of the most important differences between the rule of three and category rating is that category rating does not use a point-based system, and thus veterans' preference takes a different form.

Under category rating, applicants who meet minimum qualifications are grouped into categories, such as "best qualified" and "well qualified."[52] The Delegated Examining Operations Handbook explains that agencies must establish and define the categories *prior to announcing the job*.[53] This timing is critical, because: (1) the rules require it; and (2) any attempt to tailor the criteria for a category after receiving applications could create an opportunity for real or perceived manipulation of the process. If the proper sequence of events is not followed, allegations can arise that an agency sought to deliberately exclude candidates by placing the dividing line between categories (known as the cut-off) based on knowledge of where the candidates would be in relation to that line.[54]

Once the candidates have been placed in their categories, a form of veterans' preference is applied. In category rating, *there are no points added to any scores*.[55] Instead, qualified preference eligibles designated as having a 10 percent or more compensable disability float to the top of the list just as in the rule of three. All other preference eligibles float to the top of the category in which they were placed. A selecting official may select any eligible candidate(s) in the highest quality category, but cannot bypass a preference eligible for a non-preference eligible.[56] However, other than veterans' preference, all candidates in the referred category are on an equal footing—there is no requirement to select from the first three candidates.[57]

Before category rating was enacted, it was tested as a demonstration project. In our 1995 report, *The Rule of Three in Federal Hiring: Boon or Bane*, we compared the rates at which a selection was made from a rule of three certificate for a single vacancy (called case examining) versus a certificate using category rating. We found that 65 percent of category rating certificates resulted in a selection, compared to only 57 percent of case examining certificates.[58] A different report evaluating the demonstration project stated that one of the strengths of the program was "a manager's ability to review and have access to more than three candidates."[59]

The test agency found that veterans had a greater likelihood of being hired under category rating than under the rule of three.[60] One possible explanation for this outcome may be that an agency is no longer limited to selecting from among only three candidates. For example, if the top category contains eight veterans with 5-point preference, all eight will be referred. This may increase the potential that one of the referred veteran candidates will impress management sufficiently to be selected; whereas if management is not impressed with the three candidates referred under the rule of three, management may opt not to take anyone from that certificate and instead use a different hiring authority or select no one at all.[61]

It is possible for a veteran who would have been referred under the rule of three to not be referred under category rating. Under category rating, a veteran with preference points but no disability who just misses the cut-off line will not be referred, while a non-veteran who scores just above the cut-off line will be referred and can be selected, if not blocked by a veteran. While category rating overall appears to benefit veterans, for a preference eligible who is not placed in a referred category, this process can seem unfair because the preference applies only within a category—not in relation to all other applicants.

Additional Competitive Examining Provisions for Veterans

For certain positions with an age requirement, the agency may be required to waive that condition for a preference eligible.[62] If a non-veteran who is 38 years old is told that an application will not be accepted because 38 years is too old to apply, but the application of a preference eligible who is 39 years old is accepted, the non-veteran may question whether this is proper.

Furthermore, there are a few jobs that are set aside for which a preference eligible must be selected unless no preference eligible veterans are available.[63] An applicant who is not aware of this law may believe that an inappropriate preference has been given.[64]

Additionally, depending on the nature of an individual's preference, certain preference eligibles are entitled to be placed on a "register" even if the register is closed to others. (Registers are used to establish a list of qualified applicants for positions that are frequently vacant so that the agency need not issue a new vacancy announcement each time it intends to hire.) Veterans who are unable to file an application at the time of the announcement due to military service, reserve duties, or hospitalization may also be able to file late.[65] If someone unfamiliar with the rules learns that an individual was allowed an exception to the closing date, the observer may perceive the lawful action as improper.

Limitations on the applicability of preference within competitive examining also may create misunderstandings. Under category rating, any individuals with a 10 percent or more service- connected disability do not automatically float to the top of the list *if the position is scientific or professional at the grade GS-09 (or equivalent) or above*. For example, a hypothetical person, Jessie, is a 30 percent disabled veteran with a degree in engineering who is minimally qualified to be an engineer as well as an engineering technician. Jessie applies for a GS-09 engineer position and a position as a GS-09 engineering technician position. Jessie will automatically float to the top of the technician certificate, but not the engineer certificate. If Jessie does not understand this part of the veterans' preference rules, Jessie may assume that a preference granted in one case has been unlawfully withheld in the other, when, in fact, the law would not permit the agency to grant this preference for an engineering position because it is considered a "professional" or "scientific" position.[66]

As long as it is the policy of the Federal Government to recognize military service by providing preferential treatment in the civil service, any agency to which the rules apply has a responsibility to educate people about veterans' preferences. Such education for managers and HR staff is necessary to ensure that the authorized preferences are given, but the education is also needed to ensure that those who observe the preferences are not demotivated or disengaged by perceptions of inappropriate favoritism. For external applicants in particular, agencies may find it helpful to refer interested parties to sources of information such as OPM's *Vet Guide*. Of course, internal and external education would be easier if the rules were simpler.[67]

Veterans Applying for Competition that is Internal to the Government

As stated earlier, an agency has the discretion to fill a vacant position by selecting one specific type of hiring authority over another.[68] One of the most commonly used authorities to select an individual for a position is the use of "merit promotion procedures" (MPP).[69] Among other things, MPP permits agencies to hire individuals who already work for the Government into other positions without any requirement to offer external applicants the opportunity to be considered through competitive examining. However, as with so many issues involving veterans, there is a caveat.

If an agency's area of consideration is limited to individuals already in the agency's own workforce, then veterans and other preference eligibles[70] have no special right to apply and have their applications considered. But, under the Veterans Employment Opportunities Act of 1998 (VEOA),[71] if the agency considers applicants internal to the Government from outside its own workforce, then any veteran who was honorably discharged after three years of service, and any preference eligible, is entitled to have his or her application considered.[72]

For example, if the General Services Administration (GSA) announces an MPP vacancy with an area of consideration limited to current GSA employees in the competitive service, no one outside of GSA has a right to apply and be considered for the position. But, if GSA's area of consideration is all current Federal employees in the competitive service, then veterans and other preference eligibles are entitled to apply and be considered for the position.

However, the definition of "agency" can be complicated when dealing with DoD, because according to Board case law the military departments within DoD are each considered individual agencies.[73] For other cabinet departments, the Board has found that subordinate bureaus are considered part of the same agency—namely the department that runs them.[74] This is pertinent because the right to apply under VEOA is based on recruitment occurring outside the "agency." So, to determine whether there is a right to consideration, one must first determine what entities are a part of the hiring agency and whether any other agencies are in the area of consideration.[75]

For example, if the sole area of consideration for a vacancy is competitive service Army employees, then veterans and preference eligibles who do not already work for the Army in such positions are not entitled to consideration for the vacancy.[76] But if the area of consideration encompasses all competitive service DoD employees, then more than one agency is in the area of consideration, so a qualifying veteran or preference eligible is entitled to also be considered, even if the individual has never worked in the civil service.[77]

In contrast, Customs and Border Protection (CBP) and Immigration and Customs Enforcement (ICE) are two separate components within a single agency—the Department of Homeland Security (DHS).[78] Thus, an MPP vacancy open only to employees of CBP and ICE involves only one agency's workforce and would not create a VEOA entitlement for external veterans or preference eligibles to be considered for the position.

One of the most important features of MPP and the VEOA hiring authority is that, under these authorities, veterans and individuals with preference are not given any advantage in selection over other qualified candidates.[79] Many preference eligibles understand that they are entitled to preference in selection for Federal jobs; some may not understand that the type of vacancy announcement for which they apply will determine not only whether their application can be considered, but also whether any selection preference can be used. Competitive examining *requires* the application of preference in selection from a referral list; MPP *prohibits* it.[80]

If an agency announces a competition using both competitive examining and MPP open to the entire Government (which automatically means considering VEOA applicants), and a qualified preference eligible applies for all announcements, the preference will be applied on the competitive examining list but not on the VEOA list.[81] Preference eligibles who know (or believe) that they have blocked a list may believe something improper occurs when someone who has been blocked on the competitive examining list is nevertheless selected over the preference eligible via the MPP list.

In DoD, in every year from FY 2005 to FY 2010, a larger percentage of external hires were brought in under VEOA (an authority that can be used only by veterans and preference eligibles) than under competitive examining (open to all qualified U.S. Citizens).[82] As discussed in Section Four, in the 2010 MPS, DoD had a higher rate of perception of favoritism towards veterans than the rest of Government. The high use of VEOA in DoD may be one of many factors that influence perceptions in DoD regarding the treatment of veterans.

Veterans Recruitment Appointment

The Veterans Recruitment Appointment (VRA) is a hiring authority established by law that enables agencies to appoint eligible veterans *without competition* to positions at any grade level through GS-11 or its equivalent.[83] A VRA appointment is an appointment into the excepted service to serve in a position that is otherwise in the competitive service.[84] Upon completion of a probationary/trial period, the individual is eligible for conversion to the competitive service.[85] Unlike VEOA (if the agency uses MPP), agencies are never required to consider applicants under VRA. It is simply an option that may be used at the agency's discretion. However, when a competition does occur under VRA, an additional set of rules for veteran's preference in the excepted service can come into play.[86] In FY 2010, 5 percent of external hires Government-wide were brought in under VRA (7 percent in DoD).[87]

Some individuals may perceive a non-competitive hiring authority that deprives other veterans of the opportunity to apply as a violation of veterans' preference—particularly if the other veterans are entitled to a level of preference that would place them above the selectee on a referral list.[88] At the same time, other observers may perceive it as a deprivation of an opportunity for non-veterans to compete and therefore an improper preference. However, the agency is under no obligation to make the opportunity public to solicit such applications.[89]

Additionally, VRA contains different requirements for eligibility than competitive examining or VEOA. Only some veterans are eligible for VRA, based on factors such as when they served, precisely where they served, and whether they were injured.[90] As OPM's *Vet Guide* explains, under competitive examining, if a veteran served during the Gulf War from August 2, 1990, through January 2, 1992, that individual would be eligible for veterans' preference solely on the basis of that service. However, this veteran would not be eligible for a VRA appointment unless the veteran served in the actual campaign or suffered from a service-related disability.[91]

Another element of VRA with the potential for misunderstandings is the expiration date for eligibility if the veteran did not serve in a conflict and was not injured. Such a veteran may be eligible for a VRA appointment if his or her service was within the prior three years, while veterans who served in a war/campaign or who are disabled do not have their eligibility expire. In contrast, VEOA eligibility does not expire with the passage of time for any veteran.[92] An individual who is eligible for VRA one month, but not eligible the next, may become confused about the expiration provisions and suspect that some impropriety has occurred—especially if he or she is still being referred for VEOA announcements.

The VRA law also requires that veterans with less than 15 years of education hired under VRA receive training, regardless of the skills of the veteran or the needs of the position into which the veteran is hired.[93] A veteran who is ordered to attend training, while others in the exact same position (with perhaps less knowledge) are not required to attend, may perceive the order as an implication that veterans are considered less capable than their peers.[94] Conversely, when other civilian employees see that only the veteran is being given the training, they may see that use of resources as a form of favoritism.

VRA can be a helpful authority for agencies to hire veterans quickly. However, because VRA offers so many opportunities for perceptions of improprieties—and those perceived improprieties appear particularly serious because of the non-competitive nature of the authority—it is important that agencies use this authority with caution and transparency. When using VRA, agencies should take steps to help those who observe the process to understand the unique attributes of this law.

Agencies also should remind their decision-makers that the PPPs apply to the excepted service as well as to the competitive service.[95] It is a PPP to knowingly violate a veteran's preference right.[96] Thus, deliberately ignoring an application from a veteran with preference is as improper for a VRA application as it is for a competitive examining application. Furthermore, it is a PPP to "define the scope or manner of competition or the requirements for any position for the purpose of improving or injuring the prospects of any particular person for employment."[97] Thus, the reason why management chooses to use the VRA authority is pertinent to the propriety of the action.[98]

Prior research conducted by MSPB indicates that the use of VRA frequently has not been the result of a deliberative process. In the survey conducted for our 2008 report, *Appointment Authorities: Cutting through the Confusion*, we asked supervisors who reported being involved in the hiring process from which authorities they had accepted candidates. For VRA appointees, 39 percent of their supervisors stated they did not accept VRA applications. This means that approximately 4 out of every 10 supervisors who were involved in the selection process for a VRA hire may not have known that they were using an authority that had a severely limited applicant pool.[99]

Thirty Percent Disabled Veterans Appointment

The law permits an agency to "make a noncompetitive appointment leading to conversion to career or career-conditional employment of a disabled veteran who has a compensable service- connected disability of 30 percent or more."[100] As with VRA, this authority is an option for agencies, but its use is never required by law (unlike preference in competitive examining or the consideration of VEOA applicants when hiring from outside the agency).

Unlike VRA, which involves permanent appointments and requires the completion of a probationary/trial period before conversion to the competitive service, the 30 percent disabled veteran authority (DVA) appointment begins as a time-limited appointment, but the individual may be converted to the competitive service "at any time."[101]

However, as with VRA, because the 30 percent DVA process is non-competitive, it may provide opportunities for perceptions of improprieties, including perceptions that other preference eligibles have been denied an opportunity to compete for a position. Additionally, because this authority begins as a temporary or term appointment, and then non-competitively becomes a permanent appointment, it may appear as if the agency engaged in a subterfuge. Because the individual will be on board when converted to the permanent position, there may be more opportunities than with other external appointment authorities for co-workers to witness the unusual nature of the appointment and draw conclusions about its propriety. As with all of the hiring authorities, education may be needed to counter those perceptions. And, as with the other hiring authorities, agencies should be vigilant to ensure that the motives behind the use of this authority do not constitute the commission of a PPP.

Certified from a Training Program

Under 5 C.F.R. § 315.604, when a disabled veteran has satisfactorily completed an approved course of training conducted under Chapter 31 of Title 38, any agency may appoint the veteran non-competitively to the position or class of positions for which the veteran was trained. The individual then may be converted to the competitive service.

This hiring authority was among the first exceptions to competitive examining made by OPM following the Civil Service Reform Act of 1978 (CSRA).[102] Unlike competitive examining, VEOA, and VRA, this hiring authority cannot be explicitly found in the U.S. Code, but Title 5 does—with certain limitations—grant OPM the authority to promulgate regulations for the excepted service.[103] We asked OPM to identify which statute authorizes the regulation at 5 C.F.R. § 315.604; OPM declined to do so.[104]

Section Three: Veteran Hiring in the Excepted Service

"When considering civil service reform, it is useful to remember that the federal government is not the 'single employer' it is widely reputed to be."[105]

A substantial portion of the civil service operates under a variety of exceptions to Title 5, creating a complex patchwork of rules separate from the already complicated rules that apply to the Title 5 competitive service.[106]

The "excepted service" can refer to agencies, positions, or hiring authorities.[107] Certain agencies, such as the Central Intelligence Agency (CIA), are excepted from the rules for veterans' preference.[108] Some positions, such as chaplains or attorneys, are in the excepted service regardless of the employing agency.[109] Additionally, as explained in Section Two, there are authorities that have been used to hire individuals under excepted service rules into positions that would otherwise belong in the competitive service.[110] This Section discusses exceptions to the competitive service based upon the hiring agency or position being filled.

As shown in Figure 1 below, from FY 2000 to FY 2012, traditional competitive examining was used for less than a third of new appointments to permanent, full-time positions. The addition of the VEOA and VRA authorities—discussed in Section Two—brings the percentage to about half of new hires. For all the complexities of the statutes, regulations, and rules discussed in Section Two, they leave a large portion of Government hiring unaddressed.

Examples of Agency-Based Statutory Hiring Authorities

Section Two addressed hiring into positions that are in the competitive service, even if the hiring authority is not in the competitive service and may come from a different title of the U.S. Code. However, some agencies in the executive branch have positions that—by statute—are not covered by all of the Title 5 hiring laws discussed in Section Two. Yet, in many of these agencies, there is still some form of preference that is given to veterans.

For example, the Department of State has its own appointment process for the Foreign Service. When seeking a position as a Foreign Service Officer, applicants first take an exam. If the individual passes the Foreign Service Officer's Test, then an oral assessment is performed. If the individual also passes that assessment, then points are added to the register score—but not the same points as were used in the rule of three.[112]

For positions in the Department of Veterans Affairs, Veterans Health Administration (VHA), the VHA has *discretionary* authority to appoint health care personnel under 38 U.S.C. § 7401(1) without regard to Title 5 civil service requirements, including veterans' preference.[113]

The practice of the VHA has been to "give preference to qualified disabled veterans and preference eligibles when qualifications of candidates are approximately equal."[114] In other words, veterans' preference serves as a tie-breaker.

Not every agency with exceptions to Title 5 rules has the flexibility to decide what form of preference it will grant. For example, Congress authorized the Department of Transportation to establish a personnel system for the Federal Aviation Administration (FAA) that is not subject to the provisions of Title 5, with certain enumerated exceptions.[115] Because veterans' preference is one of the enumerated exceptions, Title 5 veterans' preference for competitive examinations applies to the selection of candidates for positions in the FAA personnel system.[116]

Examples of Position-Based Regulatory Hiring Authorities

An agency can be covered by competitive examining rules but have specific categories of positions that are excepted from the competitive service, such as chaplains and attorneys.[117] When hiring for such positions, veterans' preference applies "to the extent that it is administratively feasible to do so."[118] The U.S. Court of Appeals for the Federal Circuit has explained that "where positions are entirely exempt from the usual appointment process, it is more likely that the detailed requirements of [veterans' preference] will prove to be infeasible."[119] Thus, the use of excepted service authorities for positions has an important effect on the preferences a veteran may use when seeking employment in a particular field.

Some regulations that place positions in the excepted service have been litigated and have case law to support their use. For example, 5 C.F.R. § 213.3202(d) places all Federal civil service attorneys in the excepted service. In *Jarrard v. Department of Justice*, the Federal Circuit discussed at length the reasons why attorneys are in the excepted service and held that traditional veterans' preference, such as the use of points, does not apply to such positions. The court held that, because of the nature of attorney hiring, there was no obligation for an agency to consult OPM before passing over a veteran for a non-veteran when hiring attorneys.[120]

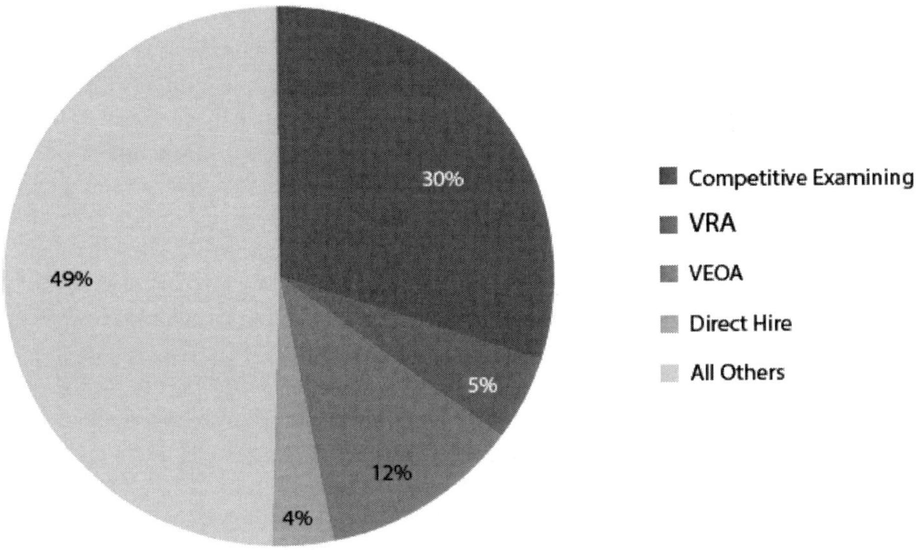

Figure 1. Percent of Hiring by Authority (FY 2000-2012).[111]

Other Excepted Service Hiring Authorities

There are other situations in which hiring may occur in the excepted service—this report does not contain an exhaustive list. For some of these excepted service hiring situations, the rules for veterans' preference can closely resemble those used in competitive examining.[121] For example, when numerical scores are assigned, then 5 or 10 points may be added, as under competitive examining.[122] OPM's regulations contain instructions for three different ways in which the referral list may then be ordered (labeled Order A, B, or C). In addition to these three orders, the regulations also have instructions for ordering an excepted service professional positions list. Lastly, there are two options offered for ordering an unranked applicant list.[123]

This Section does not list every way in which veterans' preference may apply in the excepted service. However, it illustrates how challenging it may be for a veteran (or agency) to identify the preference that may be owed to an individual and to determine how that preference should be applied.

The different sets of rules for positions within the competitive service, with the excepted service rules added to that, results in a patchwork of laws and rules that are challenging to understand. There are so many factors about the person applying, the position for which he or she is applying, the authorities being used, and the agency in which the positions exist, that the system is beyond unwieldy.[124]

Which preferences a veteran should have and when they should be given are questions for Congress and the President. However, we recommend that the system be made simpler for veterans and non-veterans to understand and for agencies to administer.

SECTION FOUR: PERCEPTIONS REGARDING VETERAN HIRING

> *"Veterans' hiring preferences represent an awkward—and, many argue, unfair—exception to the widely shared view that merit and merit alone should prevail in the employment policies of government. After a war, such laws have been enacted virtually without opposition. During peacetime, they inevitably have come to be viewed in many quarters as undemocratic and unwise. Absolute and permanent preferences. . . have always been subject to the objection that they give the veteran more than a square deal."*[125]

There is a saying that "perceptions shape reality." A better way to put it might be that perceptions shape how people view events, and those views affect the decisions that people may make in response to those events as well as to future events. Perceptions are also one potential indicator of reality. If many people have the same perception, they may not all be correct, but the accuracy of a conclusion held by multiple witnesses may be much greater than that of a single individual.[126] As a result, employee perceptions of inappropriate actions related to veterans matter because: (1) they may indicate that actual improprieties have occurred; and (2) those perceptions—regardless of their accuracy—may affect the viewers' relationships with their employer.

Federal Employee Perceptions of Improprieties

In our MPS 2010, we asked respondents whether they had observed, been personally affected by, or had not observed: (1) a knowing violation of veterans' preference or protection laws; or (2) inappropriate favoritism towards a veteran.

The answer options were:

- I was personally affected by this;
- I observed this but was not personally affected;
- This did not occur; or
- Don't Know/Can't Judge

The responses of "Don't Know/Can't Judge" have been removed from the data to allow for comparisons of responses from those who had perceptions. Except where otherwise indicated, the responses "I was personally affected by this," and "I observed this but was not personally affected," have been combined into a single category to indicate a perception of an occurrence.[127]

As can be seen in Table 1 below, more respondents reported perceptions of inappropriate favoritism towards veterans than reported perceptions of knowing violations of veterans' preference or protection laws.[128] The total difference between these two questions was outside the margin for error.[129]

Readers should bear in mind the relatively small number of respondents that perceive either inappropriate favoritism towards veterans or violations of veterans' preference rights.[131] As shown in Figure 2 below, knowing violations of a veterans' preference requirement had one of the lowest perception rates of all the PPPs, and inappropriate favoritism toward veterans—while not a direct PPP—was also less common than most of the PPPs.[132] However, these negative perceptions are important for the merit principles and prohibited personnel practices and can have a real effect on a workforce of more than a million people.

When examining this data, it is important to recognize that a perception is not the same as a proven fact. In general, it is difficult to use perception data to determine actual rates of PPPs because most PPPs require an element of motive, and while observers can use circumstantial evidence to reach assumptions about motive, such assumptions may be erroneous. Additionally, the veterans' preference PPP requires that the offender's violation be done knowingly. In many cases, it may be unrealistic to expect an observer to have a complete understanding of the perceived offender's knowledge level.[134]

Table 1. Perceptions of Violations of Veterans' Preference/Protection or Favoritism towards Veterans[130]

An official in my organization has…	*Happened to me*	*I saw this*	*Total*
…knowingly violated a lawful form of veterans' preference or protection laws.	1.4%	3.1%	4.5%
…inappropriately favored a veteran.	1.5%	5.0%	6.5%

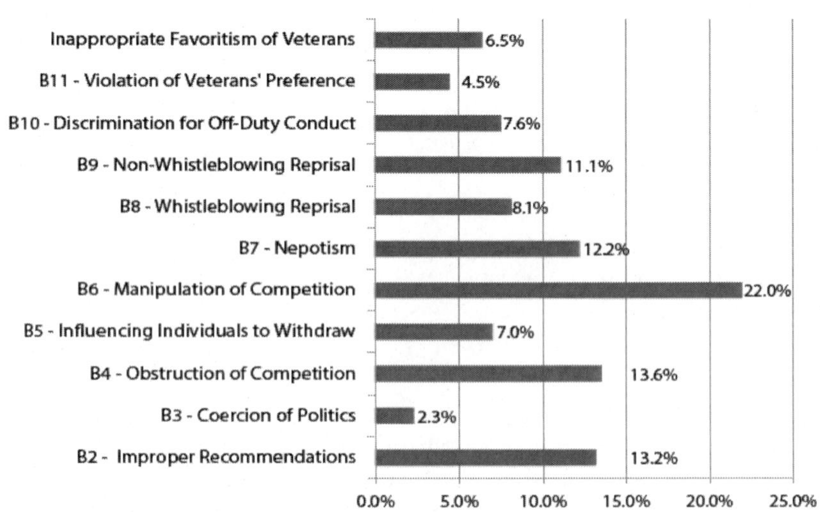

Figure 2. Percent of Respondents Reporting Perceptions of Particular PPPs.[133]

Additionally, as explained in the previous Sections of this report, veterans' preference laws are exceptionally complex and many people, both veterans and non-veterans, may misunderstand how and when these laws apply, which in turn may lead to misperceptions. Therefore, we cannot establish the actual frequency of these alleged abuses to a certainty using only perception- based data. Furthermore, even a review of a multitude of actual recruitment cases would not answer this question because such files could not tell us the motives behind the decisions or the knowledge level of the individuals making the decisions. Thus, a paper record often cannot prove either deliberate favoritism or a knowing violation of veterans' preference.

However, these perceptions are nevertheless important because they may affect other issues, such as employee engagement levels. Employee engagement is a heightened connection between employees and their work, their organization, and/or the people they work for or with. The greater an employee's level of engagement, the more likely it is that the employee will go beyond the minimum required and expend discretionary effort to provide excellent performance.[135] As explained in our report on the PPPs, the more that an individual believes he or she has observed or been affected by a PPP, the more likely it is that the individual will be disengaged.[136] As can be seen in Figure 3 below, this pattern held true for the question on the 11th PPP and also for the question on favoring a veteran, which is not directly a PPP but can take the form of various actions that are PPPs.[137]

Of those who perceived a violation of veterans' preference/protection rights, 48 percent were not engaged, and of those who perceived inappropriate favoritism towards a veteran, 40 percent were not engaged. In contrast, in the MPS 2010 survey population as a whole, only 15 percent of respondents were not engaged.

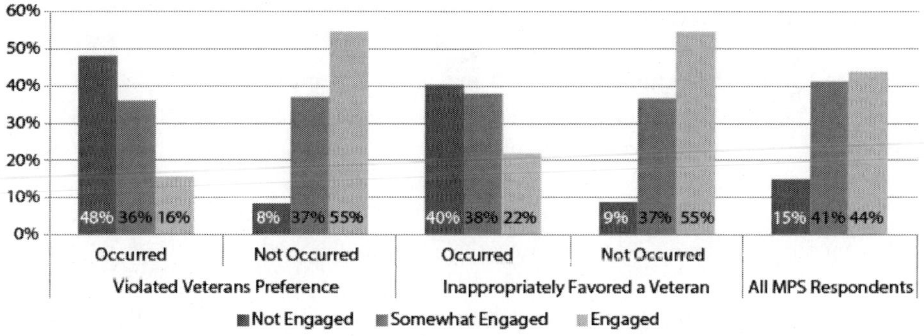

Figure 3. Observations of Veterans-Related Conduct and Engagement Levels.[138]

Motivation is one aspect of engagement. Motivation drives *what* employees do, *how* they do it, *how hard* they will try, and *how long* they will persist in a given endeavor.[139] We asked employees if they agreed that they felt highly motivated in their work. While 71 percent of respondents overall agreed that they felt highly motivated, only 50 percent of those who perceived a knowing violation of veterans' preference/protection agreed they were highly motivated. Of those who perceived inappropriate favoritism towards a veteran, only 53 percent agreed that they were highly motivated.

Observers of knowing violations of preference rights or favoritism towards veterans were also more inclined to report that it was likely they would leave their agency.[140]

As explained in our report on the PPPs, one of the best ways to address perceptions of management improprieties is with greater transparency by management.[141] The extent of these perceptions of inappropriate actions regarding veterans might be reduced if management did a better job of explaining what they do and why they do it.[142] This does not necessarily mean discussing the matter with employees who show no interest in the matter, but rather means being alert for signs of interest and making it clear to employees that they are welcome to ask questions about what happened and why.

Not all employees trust the explanations that they are given, but, in the absence of such explanations, the influence of conjecture becomes more powerful.[143] Additionally, the knowledge that officials can be called upon to explain what has occurred may dissuade some officials who might be tempted to deliberately engage in inappropriate processes.

However, when engaging in such communications, management must be cognizant of the provisions of the Privacy Act and its limitations on releasing information about individuals. "No agency shall disclose any record which is contained in a system of records by any means of communication to any person, or to another agency, except pursuant to a written request by, or with the prior written consent of, the individual to whom the record pertains," with certain enumerated exceptions, such as situations covered by the Freedom of Information Act (FOIA).[144] Thus, management must be careful to discuss what it did without going into detail about the specific history of individuals to which it applied what it did—unless the information is considered to be in the public domain or the agency first obtains permission in writing from those individuals.[145]

Department of Defense Employees' Perceptions

DoD employees have slightly different perceptions from most other Federal employees with regard to how well their officials ensure that veterans receive the preferences to which they are entitled and avoid inappropriate favoritism.[146] Also, as explained in Section Five, DoD operates under a special law—that applies only to DoD—which places restrictions on the hiring of newly-retired military members. For DoD, perceptions regarding the restriction law are a part of the larger story of how the treatment of veterans in the civil service is perceived.

As noted earlier, Government-wide, 4.5 percent of survey respondents indicated that they observed or were affected by an official knowingly violating a lawful form of veterans' preference or protection laws. At the same time, 6.5 percent reported that they observed or were affected by inappropriate favoritism towards a veteran.

However, as shown in Table 2 below, DoD employees are more likely than others to believe that they have observed or been affected by a violation of preference, and also are more likely than others to report observing or being affected by inappropriate favoritism of a veteran.

It is important to recognize that in DoD, a greater percentage of the civilian workforce are veterans compared to the composition of most agencies, and thus it is to be expected that there would be more opportunities for employees to form a perception regarding how veterans are treated.[147] However, it is problematic that favoritism perceptions are disproportionate to perceptions of violations of veterans' preference.

A survey respondent's place within the chain of command appears to bear a relationship to his or her perceptions of both inappropriate favoritism and knowing violations of veterans' rights. As can be seen in Figure 4 below, in DoD, non-supervisors have negative perceptions of these issues more often than team leaders, who have them more often than supervisors, who, in turn, perceive improprieties more often than managers. However, the rate at which the perceptions drop differs greatly for these two issues.

The rate of perceptions of a violation of veterans' preference rights are cut in half between the percentage of non-supervisors who see it and the percentage of team leaders who see it. One possible explanation for this steep drop in perceptions above the non-supervisory level may be the complexity of the veterans' preference laws and the extent to which those with the responsibility to manage the workforce understand the laws. A lack of understanding by line employees as to what is being done and why may lead to assumptions of improprieties.

Table 2. Comparison of Perceptions Regarding Treatment of Veterans in DoD and Non-DoD Agencies

An official in my organization has…	*Non-DoD*	*DoD*
…knowingly violated a lawful form of veterans' preference or protection laws.	4.0%	5.3%
…inappropriately favored a veteran.	5.5%	8.0%

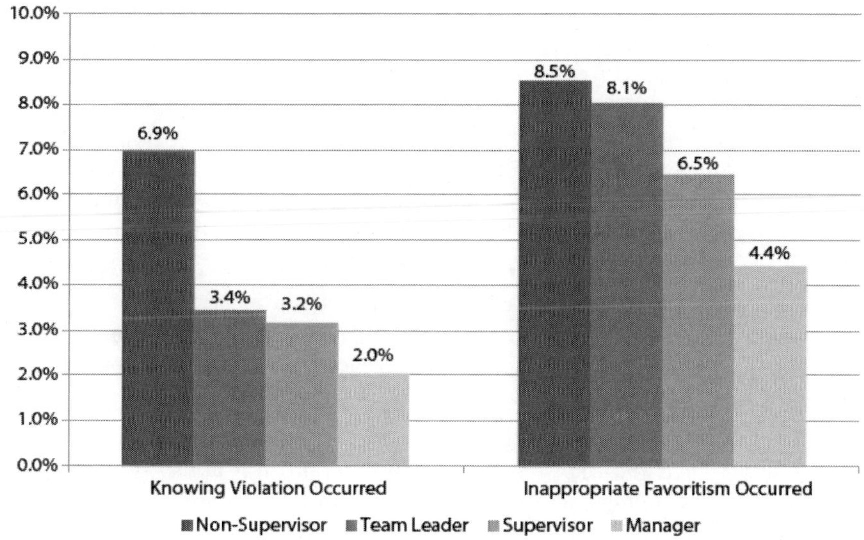

Figure 4. Perceptions of DoD Respondents by Supervisory Status.[148]

Yet, for inappropriate favoritism towards veterans within DoD's civil service, the drop in perceptions is much less dramatic, with both team leaders and supervisors perceiving it almost as often as non-supervisors. Because supervisors are responsible for implementing many personnel decisions, their perceptions that such decisions may be based upon inappropriate favoritism are particularly disconcerting. Additionally, as shown in Figure 4, both supervisors and managers in DoD perceive inappropriate favoritism at twice the rate that they perceive knowing violations of veterans' preference. Thus, it seems plausible that something other than misunderstanding of the rules may be a cause for some of these perceptions. The people in the best position to know what the agency is doing and why are saying there is a problem.

We cannot determine from multiple choice survey questions precisely why these perceptions regarding inappropriate favoritism towards veterans exist or why they continue so far up the chain of command in DoD. We are also unable to firmly establish the extent of any connection between these perceptions of inappropriate favoritism and the long-term use of the national emergency exception to the 180-day rule for hiring retired service members discussed in Section Five.[149]

However, it is important for DoD to explore why some of their employees perceive inappropriate favoritism towards veterans at these rates.[150] We recommend that, moving forward, DoD agencies regularly use their own surveys, exit interviews, and personnel action databases to monitor the situation and measure the effects of any changes in policies or practices.

Human Resources Perceptions

As a part of our recent study into the extent to which competition for Federal positions is fair and open, we asked HR staff about their experiences, including those related to hiring veterans. This data helps shed some light on the issue of perceptions of denials of veterans' preference rights.

In the fair and open competition survey (FOCS), we asked HR staff how important various priorities were in their work unit. As shown in Figure 5 below, of those who had an opinion regarding their organizations' hiring priorities, 79 percent stated that hiring veterans was important, whereas only 50 percent stated the same emphasis was placed on internal hiring, and 41 percent indicated that level of emphasis was placed on external hiring. The most common priority, however, was to hire the "best candidate" (92 percent).

For internal candidates, the greater emphasis placed on hiring veterans may not seem fair. At the same time, preference eligibles may infer that inadequate importance was given to protecting veterans' preference, because hiring the "best" candidate was important to more HR offices than hiring a veteran. Any set of priorities may be subject to favor or disfavor depending on how those priorities affect the observer.

Given the importance that was placed on hiring veterans, it is not surprising that guidance regarding veterans' preference was the most common type of guidance that HR specialists reported giving to managers, with 71 percent of HR survey respondents stating that they "always" or "most of the time" gave such guidance.[152]

Yet, educating managers regarding veterans' preference may not have always worked in the veterans' favor. When asked why more vacancies were not open to all sources, 28 percent of HR specialists agreed that a factor may have been concern that a veteran might prevent the hiring of a different candidate by "blocking" the list.[153] In a 1992 report on hiring veterans, the Government Accountability Office (GAO) reviewed 1,136 certificates, of which 357 had a veteran at the top of the list. GAO reported that 71 percent of the certificates with a veteran at the top were returned without a selection, while only 51 percent were returned with no selection when a non-veteran topped the list.[154]

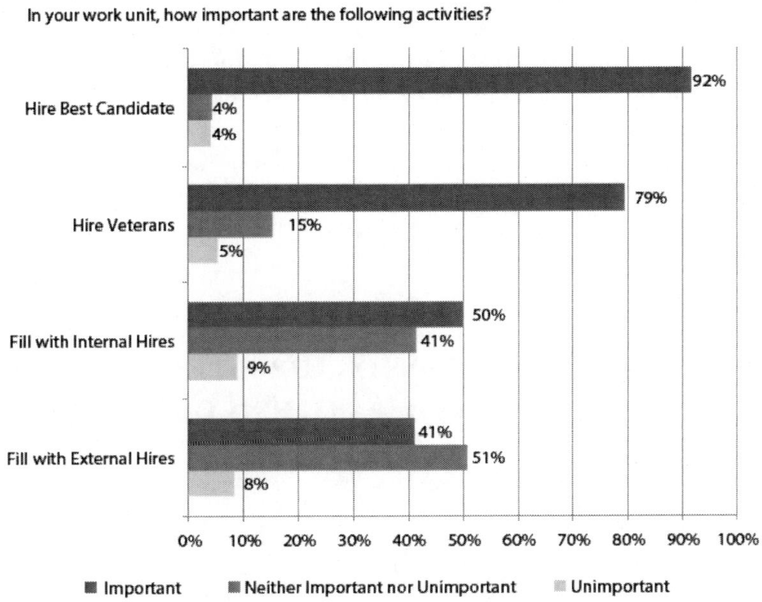

Figure 5. Hiring Priorities Reported by HR Offices.[151]

Agencies have the responsibility to ensure that lawful preferences are not deliberately withheld, unauthorized advantages are not granted, and that the process is as transparent as possible to reduce any perceptions that may not be accurate. Agencies should ensure that job descriptions accurately describe what is needed for their positions and include in their vacancy announcements any selective factors.[155] Qualifications should be assessed fully and fairly using valid testing methods.

If this is done properly, then a veteran who is able to block the list should also be able to perform in the position. If for any reason the veteran cannot perform in the position, the rules have a "pass over" procedure to address such situations.[156] However, the extent to which veterans should be given preferences in hiring is a public policy question that belongs to Congress and the President—not individual managers.[157]

Hiring Practices Strategies

There is no ideal solution to prevent real and perceived discrimination through the use of multiple lists under the current laws, other than for management to explain the choices they made. To recruit one list at a time would unreasonably delay management's ability to hire, and to select only one hiring authority for each recruitment action could restrict management's ability to obtain a quality pool of applicants. Unless Congress chooses to change how recruitment occurs in the Federal Government, using multiple lists with greater transparency may be the best solution. Even with reformed hiring authorities, we expect that transparency would be desirable.

We encourage agencies to: (1) avoid PPPs by preventing actions based on improper motives; and (2) ensure that people understand why the agency is doing what it is doing as well as informing concerned observers of the specific hiring authority being used so that interested individuals can see the rules for themselves. The mere act of indicating the source of the authority—even if employees do not choose to read the laws or regulations for themselves— may be sufficient to assure some employees that management is following legitimate rules for conducting their activities. Achieving perfect trust and understanding in all cases may not be a reasonable expectation. But, given that honest communication can sometimes help, we encourage agencies to try.

SECTION FIVE: RESTRICTIONS ON HIRING RETIRED SERVICE MEMBERS INTO THE DEPARTMENT OF DEFENSE

"In the Department of Defense. . . we have a special obligation to assure that consideration of retired military personnel for civil service positions is extended on an equitable basis and that there is strict compliance in spirit and in procedure with the fundamental merit system principle of open public competition. Such an approach is essential not only in the interests of the public and of career civil service employees, but in order to protect retired military personnel from unwarranted allegations that they obtained their positions through influence based upon prior military service."[158]

Most laws pertaining to hiring veterans in the Federal Government are designed to provide a preference to the veteran or a relative of the veteran in recognition of the service that the veteran provided to the Nation. There is one law that is a notable exception and it applies only to DoD. This Section discusses that law and its application. Our goal is to note the extent to which provisions in the law have not been active, the perceptions that may have been influenced by that lack of operation, and recommendations for moving forward.

For 50 years, there has been a law that restricts the appointment within DoD of a retired member of the armed forces within 180 days of his or her retirement—the so-called "180-day rule."[159] However, this law contains exceptions to its restrictions.[160]

To understand this law and its intent, it is necessary to understand its history. The law began as a policy memorandum within DoD. The Gilpatric memorandum (named for the Deputy Secretary of Defense who signed it) was issued in 1961 in order to ensure that retired military members were not given civil service positions for reasons other than merit. The Gilpatric memorandum instructed, among other things, that any "[a]ction to employ a retired military person at an installation at which he was stationed for duty within the 6 months' period immediately preceding the proposed appointment will require prior approval by the Secretary of the military department concerned or his designee for the purpose."[161] A request for such approval had to be accompanied by a statement that management had: (1) given full consideration to career employees before selecting the recently retired service member; (2) applied veterans' preference laws to any selection from a civil service register; (3) made reasonable efforts to seek applicants from all possible sources and not written the qualification requirements in a manner designed to provide an advantage to the individual; and (4) not held the position vacant pending the retirement of a preferred individual.[162]

In 1963, Congress considered a law to codify the principles of the Gilpatric memorandum. During hearings on the bill, the House heard testimony regarding abuses within DoD, which included allegations of management:

- Creating a hostile environment to force civilians out of positions so that the jobs could be given to desired military retirees;
- Abolishing positions to remove their civilian incumbents and then re-establishing them soon thereafter to place retired military into those same positions;
- Re-writing civil service position descriptions to ensure that only prior military members could qualify; and
- Holding positions vacant until desired military candidates retired.

One Congressman stated that he "heard it said that often the retiree writes the specifications to fit himself and then applies for the job."[163]

In 1963, the Chairman of the Civil Service Commission (CSC) testified that he believed the Gilpatric memorandum was "sound public policy" and favored "reinforcing" it but also explained that he preferred to keep it as an "executive action" rather than a law.[164] Despite this recommendation, Congress chose not only to codify the Gilpatric memorandum in 1964 but to expand it.[165] Where the Gilpatric memorandum gave Department secretaries or their designees the authority to waive the restriction on hiring a recently retired military member, the statute assigned this authority to the CSC for any position in the competitive service, and following the CSRA, to OPM. The law also applied the restriction to the entirety of DoD and not just to installations where the retiring military member had served recently.[166]

As explained in the legislative history of the 180-day law, the purpose of this section of P.L. 88-448 was to:

> Incorporate the principle of the Gilpatric Memorandum into the law, and expand it to prohibit the employment of such a person anywhere in the Department of Defense for a period of 6 months unless the criteria in section 204(b) are satisfied and the permission of the appropriate Secretary [is obtained], and if the office is in the competitive service, after the approval of the Civil Service Commission is secured."[167]

In other words, the Gilpatric memorandum's requirement for approval by the Secretary remained, and a second level of review in the form of the CSC (later OPM) was added by this statute.

As shown in Table 3, the law also modified the conditions under which a retiring service member could be hired within 180 days of his separation from service.

Changes in hiring authorities—most notably the addition of VEOA—have made the review provisions even more important than they were at the time of enactment.[168] As discussed earlier, in DoD, in every year from FY 2005 to FY 2010, a larger percentage of external hires were brought in under VEOA than under competitive examining.[169]

Both VEOA and competitive examining require that the selection be made from among the "best qualified" candidates—with the agency determining the criteria for that category provided that minimum qualifications have been met.[170] However, unlike competitive examining, in which the list may be blocked by a preference eligible, any VEOA candidate who is "best qualified" may be selected. Thus, it is possible that an agency may set the bar much lower for VEOA without fear that it will result in the agency being forced to hire someone other than the desired candidate. Without further study, we cannot state the extent to which this may occur.[171]

Table 3. Comparison of 5 U.S.C. § 3326 and Gilpatric Memorandum

5 U.S.C. § 3326 Exception to Prohibition	*Criteria*	*Comparison to Gilpatric Memorandum*
Waiver authorized by OPM and Secretary of the service	1. Full consideration, in accordance with placement and promotion procedures of the department concerned, was given to eligible career employees; 2. When selection is by other than certification from an established civil service register, the vacancy has been publicized to give interested candidates an opportunity to apply; 3. Qualification requirements for the position have not been written in a manner designed to give advantage to the retired member; and 4. The position has not been held open pending the retirement of the retired member.*	Similar to Gilpatric memorandum, but with the added requirement for CSC/OPM approval.
Hard-to-fill jobs	Special pay tables that have already been created for the position because of difficulties hiring for such positions.**	Similar to Gilpatric memorandum.
National emergency	DoD is not prohibited from making such hires if "a state of national emergency exists."***	This exception is not in the Gilpatric memorandum.

* 5 U.S.C. § 3326(c).

** Compare 5 U.S.C. § 3326(b)(2) ("the minimum rate of basic pay for the position has been increased under section 5305 of [Title 5]") with Roswell L. Gilpatric, Memorandum: Employment of Retired Military Personnel, Jul. 5, 1961, available in Hearings Before the Committee on Post Office and Civil Service, H.R. 7381, Jul.-Aug. 1963 at 149 ("[e]xception to this requirement for prior clearance may be made for shortage category positions for which advanced in-hiring rates have been approved.") Section 5305 of Title 5 allows for special pay rates at a higher than normal level for positions where OPM has determined that a higher rate is necessary for reasons such as "rates of pay offered by non-Federal employers being significantly higher than those payable by the Government within the area, location, occupational group, or other class of positions under the pay system involved[.]"

*** 5 U.S.C. § 3326(b).

VEOA was intended to produce more opportunities for veterans to enter the civil service, but, as with any flexibility, how it is used determines the extent to which it advances the goals of other civil service laws. VEOA can create the opportunity for highly qualified veterans to be selected for civil service positions. However, VEOA can also be misused by a supervisor to hire less-qualified compatriots—including recent military retirees—at the expense of better-qualified applicants, who may include preference eligible veterans who applied under a competitive examination.[172] The waiver requirement in the DoD law, with its imposition of an outside layer of review, acts as a protection against blatant abuses of VEOA with respect to recent retirees. However, the effectiveness of such a review requirement depends upon the review actually occurring and the impartiality of the reviewer.

Delegation of the Waiver Authority

While the DoD law explicitly moved the final waiver authority for competitive service positions from the DoD departments to OPM, and the legislative history indicated that Congress intended that the Secretary's approval be separate from the approval of the CSC (later OPM), OPM delegated this authority to DoD in 1979. The 1979 Federal Register notice gives no explanation of the reason behind OPM's decision and merely states that with respect to the 180-day rule, "Prior OPM approval on competitive jobs is removed." The Federal Personnel Manual (FPM) Bulletin on this subject issued at the time repeats the words providing the delegation, but adds no explanation of OPM's reasoning other than the overarching goal of decentralization.[173] There was no expiration date placed on this delegation of authority.[174]

We asked OPM to explain its reason for delegating to DoD the authority to immediately hire retired military (which P.L. 88-448 removed from DoD jurisdiction and placed instead with CSC/OPM). We also asked OPM to tell us if it believed that such a delegation to DoD comports with the intent of the statute, and if so, why it had reached this conclusion. However, OPM declined to discuss the reasoning behind its delegation of authority to DoD.[175] The authority to grant such a waiver has been re-delegated within DoD by a DoD policy. For SES and equivalent senior expert positions, the selecting official has the authority to grant the waiver. This means that he or she is giving permission to himself or herself to make the appointment.[176] OPM must approve an individual's entry into the SES, so there will be some external assurances that such an individual is qualified for employment at the executive level.[177] However, because such recruitment actions are managed by the agency, opportunities for perceived or actual manipulation of the recruitment process may remain.[178]

For positions equivalent to the GS-14 and GS-15 levels, review cannot be delegated below the Major Commands or Deputy Directors of the sub-agency.[179] While this is not the same as having an external agency such as OPM reviewing the waiver request, it is preferable to giving the selecting official the authority to waive the hiring prohibition.

For positions below GS-14 and all wage grade positions, the DoD policy does not limit how low the authority can be re-delegated, only that it be "appropriate to meet operational and organizational needs."[180] This condition is remarkably subjective and depends heavily on the integrity and commitment of those making the delegation decisions. If Congress in 1964 had such trust and faith in DoD managers, it is unlikely that the Gilpatric memorandum would have become law in the first place.

The National Emergency

The statute allows for the hiring of retired service members in less than 180 days of their retirement without an assessment of the particular hiring case when a state of national emergency exists. In its response to a draft copy of this report, OPM repeatedly referred to the national emergency exception as a "flexibility" and indicated that its use by DoD was optional.[181] The statute does not expressly state whether the emergency declaration *permits* or if it *mandates* that DoD bypass the 180-day restriction on hiring.[182] While noting OPM's position, because the Board is prohibited from expressing an advisory opinion on matters that may come before it in the future, we take no position at this time as to whether the statute permits or mandates that the exception be used.[183]

The 180-day rule was suspended in September of 2001 because of the terrorist attacks on September 11th.[184] The suspension of the 180-day rule remains in place to this day. As explained in the President's most recent notification of the extension of the state of national emergency:

> Because the terrorist threat continues, the national emergency declared on September 14, 2001, and the powers and authorities adopted to deal with that emergency must continue in effect beyond September 14, 2013. Therefore, I am continuing in effect for an additional year the national emergency that was declared on September 14, 2001, with respect to the terrorist threat.[185]

Whether a state of national emergency exists, and for how long, are questions in which the Board has no role.[186] Nevertheless, such a declaration has a real effect on a civil service law that was passed for the express purpose of fostering the health of the civil service.

Survey Data for the 180-Day Rule

We cannot determine the extent of any connection between the inactivation of the 180-day rule and employee perceptions of inappropriate favoritism towards veterans in DoD. However, we note that the Gilpatric memorandum and the hearing transcripts for 180-day law make clear that concerns about perceptions or the reality of such favoritism were the reasons the rule was originally issued by DoD and why the law was subsequently enacted by Congress.[187]

We recently conducted a study about favoritism, titled *Preserving the Integrity of the Federal Merit Systems: Understanding and Addressing Perceptions of Favoritism.* The survey (FMSS) used to support this study did not mention the hiring of retired military service members but asked Federal employees the following open-ended question: *If you have witnessed favoritism in your organization within the past two years, what are the most common ways that supervisors demonstrate favoritism?*

Some of the narrative responses that we received alleged that job descriptions were being written specifically for retiring members of the armed forces, that the retired military were being hired by their friends without regard for which applicant was best qualified, and that there was a repeated pattern of a person being in the work unit as an active military service member on a Friday and reporting as a civilian the following Monday—timing that appeared very suspicious to the respondents and implied that the job had been held for the military retiree. Some respondents expressed concerns that the hiring of retired military into highly-graded positions has become so pervasive that it has created a "glass ceiling" for career employees.[188]

Similarly, in our FOCS, we asked the HR respondents who reported that they had witnessed favoritism in their agency to "briefly describe the most common ways that supervisors demonstrate favoritism." The responses we received indicated that some HR specialists, much like the Federal employees surveyed in the FMSS, believed the same concerns that led to the 180-day waiting period being created in the first place had become a problem once again (or never ceased to be a problem). For instance, some respondents stated they had observed the writing of positions descriptions (PDs) with a particular retiring officer in mind and the re- announcing of vacant positions that already had highly-qualified applicants in order to delay the process until a retiring service member was available for selection.

Perceptions that managers are writing PDs for their retiring friends (or even for themselves as their own retirement approaches) have led to the term "no Colonel left behind" being added to the Federal HR lexicon.[189] We heard this phrase used on many occasions before the FOCS was conducted, and on this survey it was used once again by the HR respondents. One HR respondent described the situation as follows:

> Due to [the] National Emergency, the 180-day waiting period for hiring retired military has been lifted[. T]his has caused the most favoritism in hiring and payout of [multiple] incentives. Going on terminal leave on Friday and [being] hired as a civilian on Monday [has become common] for many high level management positions. [190]

We asked OPM if it had performed any oversight of how the delegated authority had been used, and OPM replied that it had no records of its actions prior to 2001 and had performed no oversight since then due to the national emergency.[191]

We requested information from DoD to see if these perceptions of individuals were supported by hiring data. As explained below, we found there was a basis for reasonable observers to become suspicious of DoD's hiring practices concerning recently retired service members, although the data cannot establish impropriety in specific cases.

According to the database provided by DoD, from the start of FY 2002 to the end of FY 2012, DoD hired 40,449 individuals within 180 days or less of their retirement from active duty ("180-day veterans"). In this same period, DoD hired a total of 480,174 full-time, permanent, external employees.[192]

To examine the "glass ceiling" question raised by some respondents, we also investigated the positions being filled by these military retirees. In the General Schedule, from FY 2002-FY 2012, less than a third of external hires in DoD were at grades GS-11 through GS-15. However, in the population of 180-day veterans hired during the same period, more than half of the GS hires were for positions graded GS-11 through GS-15.[193] Because many of these military retirees would likely have 20 or more years of service, it is reasonable that they would be candidates for the higher-graded positions more often than entry- or journeyman-level positions.[194] Yet, the perceived consequence—a "glass ceiling"—remains a serious problem even if there is no impropriety behind it. A lack of advancement opportunities, whether actual or merely perceived, can make it more difficult for an agency to attract and retain qualified candidates at the entry- and journeyman-level.[195]

Perceptions that the system has been manipulated to favor the retired military may also be shaped by the extent to which these 180-day veterans are placed in civilian positions with little or no break in service following their active duty service. Between September 14, 2001 and January 28, 2013, DoD hired 41,630 180-day veterans. As shown in Figure 6, below, more than one-third of these appointments took effect prior to the effective date of the individuals' retirement from the armed forces and more than half occurred within a pay period or less from the date of retirement from the armed forces.[196]

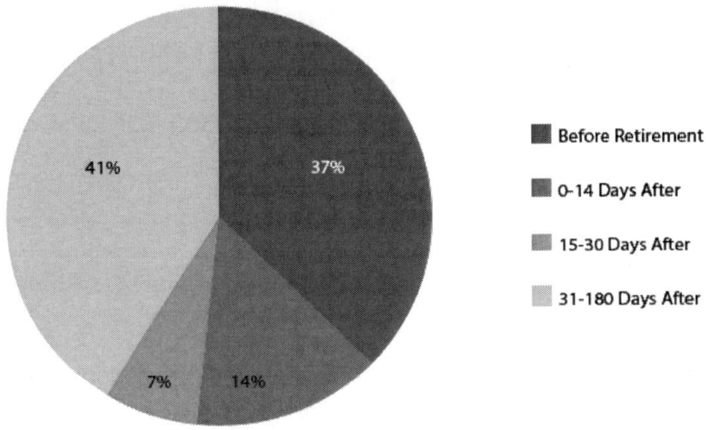

Figure 6. Time Period Between Military Retirement and Civilian Appointment.[197]

That so many retiring service members were able to be appointed on or before their retirement dates is not necessarily proof that the positions were deliberately being held vacant pending the availability of the service members. These individuals may have been retirement-eligible for some time and waited for a job offer before submitting their paperwork to leave military service.

In any event, when there is so little time between an individual's separation from the military and the start of a civilian career, and no review of whether improprieties occurred such as holding the position open for the military retiree, it may create suspicion.

Supervisors and other agency officials need to understand that, even if the 180-day prohibition is temporarily suspended, the crafting of PDs to favor an individual or delaying recruitment in order to wait for the availability of an individual are PPPs under 5 U.S.C. § 2302(b)(6), which the President has not ordered waived.

Management officials are not allowed to "grant any preference or advantage not authorized by law, rule, or regulation to any employee or applicant for employment (including defining the scope or manner of competition or the requirements for any position) for the purpose of improving or injuring the prospects of any particular person for employment[.]"[198] Thus, even if 5 U.S.C. § 3326 does not prohibit hiring recently retired service members, the conduct described by respondents in both the FMSS and FOCS is still prohibited by law. As stated earlier, a perception is not necessarily proof that an event occurred, but it can be a warning sign that warrants investigation to ensure that either: (1) the conduct is stopped if it has been happening; or (2) the environment that has led to faulty perceptions is addressed to reduce such harmful impressions. Respondents in *three different surveys* reported perceptions of inappropriate actions by DoD managers to provide advantages to veterans not permitted by law, and DoD's own hiring data indicates there may be a basis for some of these perceptions.[199]

Recommendations for the Future of the 180-Day Rule

The concerns expressed in both the FMSS and FOCS are precisely the same issues that the 180- day waiver requirement was intended to address when Congress enacted it into law in 1964.[200] Fifty years later, reports of the same problems persist. When we asked the HR respondents in the FOCS what could be done to decrease the practice of favoritism, responses again reflected the respondents' concerns about the drafting of PDs in a manner designed to benefit retiring military and the holding open of vacancies pending the eligibility of a retiring service member to apply. Some HR staff called for the reinstitution of the 180-day waiting period for the express purpose of addressing these issues, which may indicate that they believed the requirement for a waiver was successful in limiting abuses when the requirement was in place. We respectfully recommend that Congress revisit 5 U.S.C. § 3326. The data from three different surveys and the hiring data provided by DoD appear to indicate that the problems that section 3326 was intended to address remain serious concerns. If Congress is persuaded that the health of the civil service must be protected through some level of additional review before a DoD official hires a military service member at the same approximate time as his or her retirement from service, the law should be amended.[201]

In particular, the ongoing use of the national emergency provision for at least 13 years (more than a quarter of the life of the law) may be a concern because of its cumulative effect over time. If Congress determines that the 180-day rule should not be in effect as long as the United States faces any terrorist threats, we must consider the possibility that the law has become obsolete.[202] If Congress desires that the law have effect, the national emergency provision may need to be removed or rephrased in a more limited way.

In its reply to a draft copy of this report, DoD indicated that it continues to support the national emergency exception as currently codified. DoD also stated its belief that, at the least, the Secretary of Defense should have "the discretion to utilize the national emergency exception on a DoD-wide or targeted basis when it is determined necessary for accomplishing the Department's mission."[203] While a targeted use of the emergency exception for specific positions or missions would be more appropriate than applying the exception to the full range of defense agencies for a period of over 13 years, we remain concerned that such exceptions could be vulnerable to abuse. In order to protect the merit systems, it would be best if any inactivation of the waiver requirement be narrow and brief. The larger the number of positions excepted from review, and the longer the period in which waivers are not required, the greater the scope of the potential harm.

We also recommend that Congress examine the issue of OPM's delegation of the waiver authority. While we have not used the studies function to issue a determination as to whether OPM had the authority to delegate its responsibilities regarding the waiver authority, we have concerns about the effect such a delegation has on the health of the civil service and the opportunities it may create for the commission of PPPs.[204]

We believe it is in the best interest of the civil service and the Nation it serves for there to be some mechanism by which waivers may be obtained to enable DoD to hire recently retired (or soon to be retired) service members. The retiring service members may have valuable skills that cannot be easily found in the applicant pool or may be substantially more qualified than other candidates. However, opportunities for favoritism need to be restricted to ensure that: (1) the duties of the position are needed for the mission; and (2) the person selected is the candidate who is most likely to excel in the position. Additionally, Federal employees should not be given reason to believe that their advancement cannot be earned on merit. Lastly, it is crucial that the American people have trust that the civil service does not permit money to be wasted or important work left undone so that Government officials can abuse the system to favor their friends. Such perceptions do their own harm, apart from that caused by mismanagement of human capital.

The law establishing the 180-day rule stated that there would be an outside review of such hiring actions by the CSC, and later by OPM when it inherited a portion of the duties that had belonged to the CSC. While OPM's review of DoD's hiring actions is not the only possible means by which to ensure the integrity of the system, that approach is far better than the delegation and re-delegation of the review authority into the hands of the very people upon whom it was meant to serve as a check.[205] We cannot endorse such a process and strongly advise against it. We ask Congress, OPM, and DoD to recognize the discouraging effects of promising oversight in statute while providing little or no oversight in practice.

SECTION SIX: FINDINGS AND RECOMMENDATIONS

"For it has been said, all that a man hath will he give for his life; and while all contribute of their substance, the soldier puts his life at stake, and often yields it up in his country's cause. The highest merit, then, is due to the soldier."

—Abraham Lincoln[206]

Summary of Veterans' Hiring Authorities Findings and Recommendations

One role of the MSPB is to study the civil service's merit systems and advise Congress and the President of its findings. However, the extent to which the law should give a preference based on military service is a public policy question that remains solely with Congress and the President. Accordingly, we have made no recommendations for specific changes to the veterans' appointment authorities, but rather discuss the system as it exists today. Over the years, Congress has enacted many provisions designed to promote the employment and retention of veterans and preference eligibles in the Federal Government. For example, the longstanding principle of veteran's preference in examining is now accompanied by veteran hiring authorities such as VEOA, VRA, and DVA. Individually, all of these provisions were designed and implemented to achieve a particular purpose. Collectively, they make Federal recruitment a complex process affecting the health of the civil service by inviting opportunities for misperceptions, confusion, or intentional abuses.[207]

The more complicated the laws, the more opportunities there are for agencies to make mistakes, veterans to misunderstand their rights, and observers to assume that something improper has occurred. It may be easier to hide inappropriate conduct if the rules are perceived as so convoluted that it is possible for a rational person to believe a manager's claim that the law permitted a preference that it does not actually allow. Additionally, a complicated system places an extra burden on those charged with managing that system, especially in a time of limited resources where job applications may abound but employees to assess them are scarce. The challenges and burdens of managing this system fall particularly hard upon OPM. Many of the requirements for veterans' preference are spelled out in a variety of different laws with varying degrees of clarity. OPM has the responsibility to write regulations and policies to give effect to these laws and to form a cohesive system, a responsibility further complicated by the existence of agency-specific personnel systems and rules over which OPM has little or no control. Just as the system of hiring preferences does not lend itself to short or easy explanations, a system this detailed and complex cannot be easy to manage or update as case law evolves or new statutes are enacted.

If Congress chooses to examine hiring laws in the future, we recommend that it consider the benefits of creating a simpler system that would be easier to manage, apply, and explain to those who will be affected by the decisions made under that system.

In the meantime, we recommend that agencies make every effort to explain to employees at all levels, whether veterans or non-veterans, what the rules are and why certain decisions were made. Education of supervisors and HR staff may reduce errors, transparency may reduce opportunities for abuse, and openness may reduce misperceptions.

Summary of the 180-Day Hiring Prohibition Findings and Recommendations

The data provided by DoD show that since 2001 there have been over 41,000 appointments of retired service members for whom a waiver would have been required if the 180-day rule was in effect. The data also show that a majority of the hires were to the upper-level grades and that for many of these appointments, there was little or no break in time between the military and the civilian service.

Respondents in three different surveys indicated that inappropriate favoritism towards veterans was a problem. In the surveys that permitted respondents to identify the source of the problem, some respondents alleged that there had been improper manipulations of the system for the purpose of benefiting retiring military members.

We have concluded that the law prohibiting the hiring of recently retired veterans has two major problems and several additional areas in need of attention. First, the national emergency exception has essentially rendered the law meaningless in a post-9/11 world. Second, the delegation and re-delegation of the waiver may be contrary to Congress' expressed intent and, when in use, may greatly weaken the law's effectiveness.

Additionally, there are word choices in the statute that could be clearer in order to ensure that the statute: (1) applies to those whose retirement from military service is pending; and (2) addresses whether the exceptions from the 180-day rule give DoD the *option* to hire or if they *require* that DoD disregard the retirement status issue entirely.

We respectfully recommend that Congress revisit 5 U.S.C. § 3326. If Congress finds there is no longer a need for a restriction on the process by which DoD appoints recently retired military service members, then the law should be repealed. If, however, like some of our survey respondents and the Congress of 1964, Congress remains concerned that inappropriate favoritism by manipulating positions and recruitment activities will occur in the absence of oversight, then the law could be strengthened by amending it in two ways.

First, we recommend that Congress examine whether the effect of the national emergency exception in the 21st century is consistent with Congress's goals for the merit systems. Second, we recommend that Congress consider what role it wants OPM to have in the waiver process and ensure that the statutory language reflects that intent. If Congress finds it acceptable for DoD to perform the oversight function, we recommend that the law contain a restriction on the level to which this authority can be re-delegated and a requirement that the official granting a waiver cannot be the same person as the official who requests that waiver.

Until such time as the law is amended or repealed, we recommend that OPM and DoD re-examine how DoD has used its delegated authority and the emergency exception to the 180-day waiver. The restrictions of that law—when in effect—do not prevent the hiring of retired service members; they merely ensure review of the hiring action to confirm that the selection was based on merit and not favoritism. Such measures may help not only to prevent actual favoritism but also to reduce perceptions that favoritism has prevailed over merit. If OPM declines involvement, one possible solution may be for DoD to independently reinstate the Gilpatric memorandum, a copy of which is in Appendix D of this report.[208]

If OPM and/or DoD conclude that the law has become unnecessary, one or both agencies should ask Congress to repeal it. But, as long as the 180-day rule is in the law, we recommend that it be given a practical effect.

APPENDIX A: DISCUSSION OF THE RESPONSE

As a result of issues raised in OPM's reply we made modifications to this report; but, as explained below, for some issues raised by OPM we determined that changes were not warranted. In its reply, OPM expressed concern that our earlier draft did not provide an adequate discussion of how veterans' preference applies in the excepted service and instead focused too heavily on the issue of those situations where the nature of the position may limit the administrative feasibility of the application of preference. We have modified the report to provide a more in- depth discussion of the application of veterans' preference in the excepted service. However, we found some of OPM's other comments less persuasive. For example:

1. OPM objected to what it perceived as a call for sweeping changes to the rules governing hiring and particularly veterans' preference based upon 11 percent of survey respondents reporting negative perceptions regarding the treatment of veterans. OPM is mistaken; the report does not ask for sweeping changes to veterans' preference or an overhaul of the hiring system. Rather, the report describes the system as it currently functions for readers to assess the complexities of the process for themselves. The survey data serves to add another layer of information, namely, how employees perceive that system. Our recommendation regarding changes to the rules for veterans' preference is that *if* Congress opts to make changes to the laws in the future, it may be beneficial for Congress to consider how complex the system has become and the potential advantages of simplifying the system.
   Additionally, OPM noted that while 4.5 percent of respondents perceived that veterans were denied their preference rights, 6.5 percent perceived inappropriate favoritism towards veterans. OPM stated that these seemingly opposing views made it difficult to draw clear conclusions from the survey data. However, the finding that more than one out of every ten employees in a workforce of approximately 1.7 million people has a negative perception regarding the treatment of veterans remains pertinent, even if the nature of that negativity may differ.
2. OPM expressed concern that it may be inappropriate for the Board to comment on 5 U.S.C. § 3326 because it interacts with a declaration of a National emergency. The

report clearly states that whether a state of national emergency exists, and for how long, are questions in which the Board has no role. Nevertheless, such a declaration has a real effect on a civil service law that was enacted for the express purpose of fostering the health of the civil service.

Title 5, section 1204(a)(3) authorizes the Board to "conduct, from time to time, special studies relating to the civil service and to other merit systems in the executive branch."[209] We believe that studying the effect of 5 U.S.C. § 3326 on the civil service and informing Congress and the President of our findings is fully consistent with our statutory powers and Congress's intent when establishing the Board as a bi-partisan, independent agency with the responsibility to perform studies and report upon its findings.

APPENDIX B: RESPONSE BY THE OFFICE OF PERSONNEL MANAGEMENT

UNITED STATES OFFICE OF PERSONNEL MANAGEMENT
Washington, DC 20415

Employee Services

MAY 09 2014

James M. Read
U.S. Merit Systems Protection Board
Office of Policy and Evaluation
1615 M Street, N.W.
Washington, DC 20419-0002

Dear Mr. Read,

I write in response to your request that OPM read and review an advance copy of the report, *Veteran Hiring in the Civil Service: Practices and Perceptions* (draft provided March 2014). As you know, OPM has previously provided information and data responding to your written questions and requests. We appreciate your courtesy in extending the time for us to respond to your latest request.

As an overarching comment, OPM does not concur in your somewhat negative assessment of the statutory and regulatory framework that Congress and the President have created in their effort to meet the needs of the federal workforce and to sustain veterans who have served our nation. Given the length and density of this report, we are not able to provide you with a line-by-line response to this draft, or even to assess fully all of the draft's implications. We would, however, like to identify a few concerns that are significant enough, in our view, to warrant your immediate consideration. We continue to review the report, and carefully consider the ramifications of the draft's recommendations.

First, the data cited as support does not, in our view, provide a sufficient foundation for the conclusions drawn in the report. For example, the report recommends sweeping changes both to the rules governing veterans' preference and the rules governing hiring more generally based on "perceptions" about favoritism held by only 11 percent of those who responded to the MSPB survey. The conclusions to be drawn from such data are even less clear in light of the fact that 4.5 percent believe the favoritism tends in one direction and 6.5 percent believe it tends in an opposite direction. Veterans' preference is an important part of the comprehensive statutory and regulatory framework for federal hiring and represents a considered policy choice exercised by Congress. The report's implication that agencies may be doing too much to assist preference eligibles seems to be an indirect repudiation of the choices made by Congress and the President – consistently exercised since the Civil War – to recognize the sacrifices made by those who have served in our military.

Second, the discussion of the rules applicable to the excepted service is, at times, confusing and, in certain respects, inaccurate. For example, the report states, "[w]hen a position in a competitive service agency is excepted from the competitive service, veterans' preference applies 'to the extent that it is administratively feasible to do so.'" This language does not accurately reflect how veterans' preference is generally applied to positions excepted from the competitive service. If a position is excepted from the competitive service by the President or OPM, then veterans' preference must generally be applied, and the choices concerning how it may be applied are rigorous, and set out very specifically in part 302. *See, e.g.*, 5 C.F.R. §§ 302.201, 302.302, and 302.304. Contrary to what is reported in the draft, the applicability of the separate "administratively feasible" standard is limited to the short list of positions enumerated at section 302.103(c)(1) through (7), which have been exempted from the requirements in part 302 that would otherwise apply. These exemptions arise from a variety of sources. (For example, in the case of attorney positions, the exemption arises from the language in OPM's yearly appropriations statute, which prohibits OPM, and thus agencies with examining authority derived from an OPM delegation, from examining for attorney positions.) The report, as currently drafted, thus creates a misleading impression about the rigor with which veterans' preference is generally applied in the excepted service. In reality, for excepted service positions over which OPM has regulatory authority, it is applied in a manner that is quite similar to the available applications for the competitive service. Further, and with regard to note 96, OPM regulations at part 302 apply if the position has been excepted by the President or OPM. If the position has been excepted by statute, then the rules that will apply turn exclusively on the specific language of the statute. If the statute indicates that the agency may fill a position without regard to title 5, then part 302 does not apply. *See* 5 C.F.R. § 302.101(a).

Third, the draft report appears to take issue with the manner in which the Department of Defense (DoD) and OPM interpreted 5 U.S.C. § 3326 some 13 years ago. As the draft report acknowledges, however, DoD's current ability to conduct hiring free from the constraint set out in section 3326 arises automatically from an exception established by Congress in section 3326(b)(3). Indeed, the Department's ability to hire without regard to section 3326 has derived from this section for the past 13 years, because of the successive declarations of emergency issued by two different Presidents following the events of September 11, 2001. The report appears to be criticizing DoD for using an exception that Congress expressly provided. It is not entirely clear to OPM why it is appropriate to suggest that DoD should not use a flexibility that Congress apparently intended it to have under the circumstances of a national emergency. It seems likely this flexibility was useful to DoD in meeting the many challenges it faced following 9/11. Moreover, the draft report's suggestion that former President Bush's and President Obama's "ongoing use of the national emergency provision for at least 13 years . . . is problematic," and that Congress, therefore, should remove the national emergency exception seems to touch upon presidential prerogatives arising under Article II of the Constitution. Once the final declaration of emergency has expired, OPM will have a new opportunity to consider whether a continued delegation to DoD is appropriate. In the meantime, this question seems somewhat beyond what would be an appropriate scope for this report.

In sum, in addition to the issues identified above, we are troubled by the fact that this report, while purporting only to be addressing veterans' preference, seems really to be taking aim at the entire civil service system in its current form. Although the report's main recommendation – simplification of veterans' preferences – is worthy of careful consideration, the report fails to take into account the organic development of the civil service and the underlying reasons and policies that caused Congress and the President to create differing authorities. While OPM is always interested in considering proposals to make our current system better, we cannot agree with the more sweeping conclusions and recommendations offered by the Board in this report. And while OPM takes seriously the concern that the current system is perceived to be unfair by some, the Board's own data seem to suggest that this view is held only by a small minority (with internally conflicting views). Data such as these do not, in our view, demonstrate a need to undertake a major overhaul of civil service hiring authorities.

Sincerely,

Mark Reinhold
Associate Director, Employee Services
and Chief Human Capital Officer

APPENDIX C: RESPONSE BY THE DEPARTMENT OF DEFENSE

OFFICE OF THE ASSISTANT SECRETARY OF DEFENSE
4000 DEFENSE PENTAGON
WASHINGTON, D.C. 20301-4000

READINESS AND FORCE
MANAGEMENT

MAY 9 2014

Mr. James Read
Director
U.S. Merit Systems Protection Board, Office of Policy and Evaluation
1615 M Street, NW
Washington, DC 20419-0002

Dear Mr. Read:

This is in response to your letter dated March 18, 2014, regarding the U.S. Merit Systems Protection Board draft report, *Veteran Hiring in the Civil Service: Practices and Perception.* We appreciate the opportunity for the Department of Defense (DoD) to review.

The enclosure to this letter lists our specific comments. In particular, the discussion about "agency" in Chapter 2, "Veterans Applying for Competition that is Internal to the Government," is not consistent with our understanding of how the term "agency" for the Veterans Employment Opportunity Act (VEOA) is defined by the Office of Personnel Management in its implementing regulations contained in section 315.611 of title 5, Code of Federal Regulations. As detailed in the enclosure, the regulatory "agency" for DoD purposes is the executive agency, which is the entire Department and not the individual DoD Components. As a result, the discussion of "agency" conflicts with the regulatory guidance and has the potential to confuse readers in determining when VEOA candidates must be considered under merit promotion procedures.

Your letter also refers to your request last year for information relating to section 3326(b)(3) of title 5, United States Code, which restricts appointment of retired members of the Armed Forces to positions in the DoD within 180 days of retirement, unless one of three exceptions in the statute is used. As stated in our response last year, DoD supports this law. However, if you choose to recommend a change, we encourage you to provide the Secretary of Defense the discretion to utilize the national emergency exception on a DoD-wide or targeted basis when it is determined necessary for accomplishing the Department's mission.

DoD is the leader in the Executive Branch of Federal Government in hiring veterans and disabled veterans. While the report outlines many perceptions related to Veterans Preference and hiring practices, the DoD views the hiring of veterans as positive – bringing highly-skilled, well-trained individuals into the DoD workforce.

Thank you for the opportunity to review and provide comments on this report. Should you have any questions concerning our comments, my point of contact is Ms. Kerrie Tucker, whom you may reach at (571) 372-1535, or kerrie.tucker@cpms.osd.mil.

Sincerely,

Paige Hinkle-Bowles

Paige Hinkle-Bowles
Deputy Assistant Secretary
Civilian Personnel Policy

Enclosure:
As stated

DEPARTMENT OF DEFENSE
Comments on Draft MSPB Report
Veteran Hiring in the Civil Service: Practices and Perception

(1) Page 18, Chapter 2.

The last paragraph talks about the definition of "agency" when dealing with Department of Defense (DoD), which contradicts the "agency" definition in title 5, part 315, section 611(b), Code of Federal Regulations. As stated in the second page of your Executive Summary, "Agencies must operate within the laws enacted by Congress and regulations promulgated by the Office of Personnel Management." However, the draft report is not in compliance with this requirement. The federal statutes and regulations relating to the Veterans Employment Opportunity Act (VEOA) and "agency" are as follows:

5 U.S. CODE § 3304 - COMPETITIVE SERVICE; EXAMINATIONS

(1) Preference eligibles or veterans who have been separated from the armed forces under honorable conditions after 3 years or more of active service may not be denied the opportunity to compete for vacant positions for which the agency making the announcement will accept applications from individuals outside its own workforce under merit promotion procedures.

(2) If selected, a preference eligible or veteran described in paragraph (1) shall receive a career or career-conditional appointment, as appropriate.

(3) This subsection shall not be construed to confer an entitlement to veterans' preference that is not otherwise required by law.

(4) The area of consideration for all merit promotion announcements which include consideration of individuals of the Federal workforce shall indicate that preference eligibles and veterans who have been separated from the armed forces under honorable conditions after 3 years or more of active service are eligible to apply. The announcements shall be publicized in accordance with section 3327.

(5) The Office of Personnel Management shall prescribe regulations necessary for the administration of this subsection. The regulations shall ensure that an individual who has completed an initial tour of active duty is not excluded from the application of this subsection because of having been released from such tour of duty shortly before completing 3 years of active service, having been honorably released from such duty.

Title 5, Code of Federal Regulations for VEOA

§315.611 Appointment of certain veterans who have competed under agency merit promotion announcements.

(a) *Agency authority.* An agency may appoint a preference eligible or a veteran who has substantially completed at least 3 years of continuous active military service provided

(1) The veteran was selected from among the best qualified following competition under a merit promotion announcement open to candidates outside the agency's workforce; and

(2) The veteran's most recent separation from the military was under honorable conditions.

(b) *Definitions.* "Agency" in this context means an executive agency as defined in 5 U.S.C. 105. The agency determines in individual cases whether a candidate was released "shortly before" completing the required 3 years and should therefore be eligible for appointment.

5 U.S.C. § 105: Executive agency

For the purpose of this title, "Executive agency" means an Executive department, a Government corporation, and an independent establishment. (Note: The definition of executive agency excludes 5 U.S.C. § 102, which is the military departments).

5 US Code - Chapter 1: ORGANIZATION

5 U.S.C. § 101: The Executive departments are:

The Department of State.
The Department of the Treasury.
The Department of Defense.
The Department of Justice.
The Department of the Interior.
The Department of Agriculture.
The Department of Commerce.
The Department of Labor.
The Department of Health and Human Services.
The Department of Housing and Urban Development.
The Department of Transportation.
The Department of Energy.
The Department of Education.
The Department of Veterans Affairs.
The Department of Homeland Security.

5 U.S.C. § 102: The military departments are:

The Department of the Army.
The Department of the Navy.
The Department of the Air Force.

5 U.S.C. § 103: For the purpose of this title - (1) "Government corporation" means a corporation owned or controlled by the Government of the United States; and (2) "Government controlled corporation" does not include a corporation owned by the Government of the United States.

5 U.S.C. § 104: For the purpose of this title, "independent establishment" means - (1) an establishment in the executive branch (other than the United States Postal Service or the Postal Regulatory Commission) which is not an Executive department, military department, Government corporation, or part thereof, or part of an independent establishment; and (2) the Government Accountability Office.

5 U.S.C. § 105: Cited above.

DoD Recommendation: DoD requests the report be revised to reflect the definition of "agency" for VEOA as cited in 5 CFR 315.611(b).

(2) Pages 18 and 19, Chapter 2.

The report references the MSPB case, *Washburn v. Department of the Air Force*, which did not cite the "agency" definition in 5 CFR 315.611(b). The definition cited also conflicts with the U.S. Office of Personnel Management, *Vet Guide*, which, although not regulatory, states the following under VEOA:

"The Veterans Employment Opportunities Act (VEOA) of 1998 as amended by Section 511 of the Veterans Millennium Health Care Act (Pub. Law 106-117) of November 30, 1999, provides that agencies must allow preference eligibles or eligible veterans to apply for positions announced under merit promotion procedures when the agency is recruiting from outside its own workforce. ("Agency," in this context, means the parent agency, i.e., Treasury, not the Internal Revenue Service and the Department of Defense, not Department of the Army.) A VEOA eligible who competes under merit promotion procedures and is selected will be given a career or career conditional appointment. Veterans' preference is not a factor in these appointments."

DoD Recommendation: DoD requests the report delete references to the Washburn decision in deference to the "agency" definition in 5 CFR 315.611(b) to avoid confusion.

(3) Page 47, Chapter 4.

The report states "In a 1992 report on hiring veterans, the Government Accountability Office (GAO) reviewed 1,136 certificates, of which **324** had a veteran at the top of the list." However, after a review of the 1992 GAO report, the number of certificates where veterans were top-ranked appears to be **357**, not 324. In reading the 1992 GAO report, there are three areas of inconsistency of data.

- First, in the report's Executive Summary (page 3), it states "GAO reviewed 1,136 randomly selected certificates of eligible candidates....... The applications included **342** from veterans..."
- Second, in Principle Findings section (page 4), it states "Of the 1,136 certificates, a veteran was the top-ranked candidate on **357** certificates."
- Third, in the Many Veterans Were Not Hired Even Though They Headed Certificates section (page 26), the report states "Of 1,136 certificates we examined at OPM and executive agencies, veterans were the top-placed candidates on **357**."

DoD Recommendation: We suggest MSPB validate that the data in the draft report is accurate as referenced in the 1992 GAO report.

(4) Page 55, Chapter 5.

The report states "Unlike competitive examining, in which the candidate must be among the best qualified, a VEOA applicant can be referred after meeting only minimum qualifications and any other merit-based qualifications that the agency chooses to impose."

DoD Recommendation: We suggest MSPB review its comments on VEOA throughout the report in context with the regulatory guidance in 5 CFR 315.611. In this case, the report is inconsistent with 5 CFR 315.611(a) that indicates "An agency may appoint a preference eligible or veteran ...provided (1) The veteran was selected from among the best qualified following competition under a merit promotion announcement open to candidates outside of the agency's workforce...."

Appendix D: Department of Defense Restriction Memorandum and Law

Gilpatric Memorandum

JULY 5, 1961.

Memorandum for—
The Secretary of the Army.
The Secretary of the Navy.
The Secretary of the Air Force.
Subject: Employment of retired military personnel.

The basic objective in filling civil service positions is to assure the appointment of fully qualified individuals—generally the "best qualified" among those under consideration. In most instances this should be a candidate selected from eligible career employees, in accordance with inservice placement and promotion procedures.

There are, however, instances in which it is desirable and necessary to recruit from outside the Federal service. In such instances, the objective remains the same—to appoint the best qualified person available.

One source of outside recruitment is retired military personnel who, within statutory limitations, have every right to seek and to be considered for civil service positions on the same basis as other citizens. Furthermore, for some positions, there will be retired military personnel who possess qualifications which make them a particularly good recruitment source.

In the Department of Defense, however, we have a special obligation to assure that consideration of retired military personnel for civil service positions is extended on an equitable basis and that there is strict compliance in spirit and in procedure with the fundamental merit system principle of open public competition. Such an approach is essential not only in the interests of the public and of career civil service employees, but in order to protect retired military personnel from unwarranted allegations that they obtained their positions through influence based upon prior military service.

To establish safeguards which will reassure all concerned that selections for civilian positions in the Department of Defense are being made on an equitable basis it is requested that, to the extent not already incorporated in your respective personnel regulations, you include the following instructions and establish any controls needed to assure that they are complied with:

1. Full consideration, in accordance with inservice placement and promotion procedures, will be given to eligible career employees before selecting retired military personnel for a civil service position.

2. When selection is from an established civil service register, retired military personnel will be accorded treatment consistent with the provisions of the Veterans' Preference Act and civil service regulations.

3. Before selecting a retired military person for a civilian position, other than by certification from an established civil service register, recruitment for the position will be conducted in a way designed to assure that reasonable efforts are made to obtain applicants from all possible sources and in a manner that will avoid any suspicion of attempts to unduly limit competition. This requires that the vacancy be well publicized and recruitment conducted over a period of time long enough to give all interested candidates an opportunity to apply and that qualification requirements for a position not be written in a manner designed to give advantage to a particular individual. This will not be interpreted, however, to require any special recruitment efforts or delays in selections for shortage category positions for which advanced in-hiring rates have been approved.

4. Positions will not be held open pending the retirement of a person in the military service in order to provide that person with a preferential opportunity to be appointed to the position.

5. Action to employ a retired military person at an installation at which he was stationed for duty within the 6 months' period immediately preceding the proposed appointment will require prior approval by the Secretary of the military department concerned or his designee for the purpose. Requests for such approval will be accompanied by a statement of the actions taken to comply with numbered paragraphs 1 to 4 above, and of the procedures followed in determining that the retired person was the best qualified applicant. Exception to this requirement for prior clearance may be made for shortage category positions for which advanced in-hiring rates have been approved.

ROSWELL L. GILPATRIC,
Deputy Secretary of Defense.

5 U.S.C. § 3326—Appointments of Retired Members of the Armed Forces to Positions in the Department of Defense

(a) For the purpose of this section, "member" and "Secretary concerned" have the meanings given them by section 101 of title 37.
(b) A retired member of the armed forces may be appointed to a position in the civil service in or under the Department of Defense (including a nonappropriated fund instrumentality under the jurisdiction of the armed forces) during the period of 180 days immediately after his retirement only if—
  (1) the proposed appointment is authorized by the Secretary concerned or his designee for the purpose, and, if the position is in the competitive service, after approval by the Office of Personnel Management;
  (2) the minimum rate of basic pay for the position has been increased under section 5305 of this title; or
  (3) a state of national emergency exists.
(c) A request by appropriate authority for the authorization, or the authorization and approval, as the case may be, required by subsection (b)(1) of this section shall be accompanied by a statement which shows the actions taken to assure that—
  (1) full consideration, in accordance with placement and promotion procedures of the department concerned, was given to eligible career employees;
  (2) when selection is by other than certification from an established civil service register, the vacancy has been publicized to give interested candidates an opportunity to apply;
  (3) qualification requirements for the position have not been written in a manner designed to give advantage to the retired member; and
  (4) the position has not been held open pending the retirement of the retired member.

APPENDIX E: STRUCTURING CATEGORIES FOR CATEGORY RATING

Because category rating is a flexible system, there is no single way to determine the categories. This means that agencies have the responsibility to consider what structure for the categories is most likely to result in the referral of a suitable number of candidates with the highest probability to be the greatest assets to the Government in the positions.

An agency can place the entire definition of the category in one place. For example:

Highly Qualified	*Senior* Specialist in an agency *headquarters office* with experience *writing regulations or agency policy* on staffing, downsizing, realignments, classification, or compensation.
Qualified	Specialist with operations experience applying policies in staffing, downsizing, realignments, classification, or compensation.*

Or, the agency can identify a proficiency level for different aspects of the job criteria and then create a formula that combines the criteria ratings to create the category rating. For example, a single skill, knowledge, or ability (KSA) could be scored like this:

Proficiency Level	*Proficiency Level Definition*
5	Communicates complex ideas clearly.
3	Communicates moderately complex ideas clearly.
1	Communicates basic ideas clearly.**

* Modified from U.S. Office of Personnel Management, Delegated Examining Operations Handbook, at 103, available at www.opm.gov/deu.

** Modified from U.S. Office of Personnel Management, Delegated Examining Operations Handbook, at 104, available at www.opm.gov/deu.

The requirements to be placed in the highly qualified category then could be, for example, a score of 5 in at least half of the KSAs and no score below 3. If a particular KSA is more important than other KSAs, that can be reflected in the score required for that specific criterion to meet each category.[210]

If the top category does not have three or more candidates, agencies have the option to merge categories.[211] For this reason, it is acceptable for an agency to make the top category challenging. However, the second category should also be composed of criteria that would enable a person to do the job, because, as stated before, the criteria to enter a category cannot be modified around the candidate pool.[212] *Agencies must fully specify the category rating plan before announcing the position.*[213] The plan can have as many different levels as the agency deems appropriate for the recruitment strategy, and multiple levels can be merged as long as there are still positions to be filled and there are less than three candidates remaining in the categories above the one being merged. However, while categories can be merged, they cannot be divided if there are more candidates than the agency would like in the top category. For this reason, we recommend that agencies operate on the side of caution and create multiple categories before announcing a vacancy, as long as there are still meaningful differences between the quality levels.[214]

APPENDIX F: GLOSSARY

Definition of Veteran and Related Terms (5 U.S.C. § 2108)

For the purpose of this title—

(1) "veteran" means an individual who—

(A) served on active duty in the armed forces during a war, in a campaign or expedition for which a campaign badge has been authorized, or during the period beginning April 28, 1952, and ending July 1, 1955;

(B) served on active duty as defined by section 101 (21) of title 38 at any time in the armed forces for a period of more than 180 consecutive days any part of which occurred after January 31, 1955, and before October 15, 1976, not including service under section 12103 (d) of title 10 pursuant to an enlistment in the Army National Guard or the Air National Guard or as a Reserve for service in the Army Reserve, Navy Reserve, Air Force Reserve, Marine Corps Reserve, or Coast Guard Reserve;

(C) served on active duty as defined by section 101 (21) of title 38 in the armed forces during the period beginning on August 2, 1990, and ending on January 2, 1992; or

(D) served on active duty as defined by section 101 (21) of title 38 at any time in the armed forces for a period of more than 180 consecutive days any part of which occurred during the period beginning on September 11, 2001, and ending on the date prescribed by Presidential proclamation or by law as the last date of Operation Iraqi Freedom;

and, except as provided under section 2108a, who has been discharged or released from active duty in the armed forces under honorable conditions;

(2) "disabled veteran" means an individual who has served on active duty in the armed forces, (except as provided under section 2108a) has been separated therefrom under honorable conditions, and has established the present existence of a service-connected disability or is receiving compensation, disability retirement benefits, or pension because of a public statute administered by the Department of Veterans Affairs or a military department;

(3) "preference eligible" means, except as provided in paragraph (4) of this section or section 2108a (c)—

(A) a veteran as defined by paragraph (1)(A) of this section;

(B) a veteran as defined by paragraph (1)(B), (C), or (D) of this section;

(C) a disabled veteran;

(D) the unmarried widow or widower of a veteran as defined by paragraph (1)(A) of this section;

(E) the wife or husband of a service-connected disabled veteran if the veteran has been unable to qualify for any appointment in the civil service or in the government of the District of Columbia;

(F) the mother of an individual who lost his life under honorable conditions while serving in the armed forces during a period named by paragraph (1)(A) of this section, if—

(i) her husband is totally and permanently disabled;

(ii) she is widowed, divorced, or separated from the father and has not remarried; or

(iii) she has remarried but is widowed, divorced, or legally separated from her husband when preference is claimed;

(G) the mother of a service-connected permanently and totally disabled veteran, if—

(i) her husband is totally and permanently disabled;

(ii) she is widowed, divorced, or separated from the father and has not remarried; or

(iii) she has remarried but is widowed, divorced, or legally separated from her husband when preference is claimed; and

(H) a veteran who was discharged or released from a period of active duty by reason of a sole survivorship discharge (as that term is defined in section 1174 (i) of title 10);

but does not include applicants for, or members of, the Senior Executive Service, the Defense Intelligence Senior Executive Service, the Senior Cryptologic

Executive Service, or the Federal Bureau of Investigation and Drug Enforcement Administration Senior Executive Service;

(4) except for the purposes of Chapters 43 and 75 of this title, "preference eligible" does not include a retired member of the armed forces unless—

(A) the individual is a disabled veteran; or

(B) the individual retired below the rank of major or its equivalent; and

(5) "retired member of the armed forces" means a member or former member of the armed forces who is entitled, under statute, to retired, retirement, or retainer pay on account of service as a member.

Hiring Authorities

Competitive examining: A process for considering applicants to the competitive service under which all qualified U.S. citizens or nationals may apply, including current and former employees.[215]

Veterans Employment Opportunities Act of 1998 (VEOA): An authority that grants the right to compete to eligibles or veterans who have been separated from the armed forces under honorable conditions after 3 years or more of active service. It applies to positions in the competitive service for which candidates are being considered from outside the agency using merit promotion procedures.[216]

Veterans Recruitment Appointment (VRA): An excepted service hiring authority for disabled veterans; veterans who served on active duty in the Armed Forces during a war or in a campaign or expedition for which a campaign badge has been authorized; veterans who, while serving on active duty in the Armed Forces, participated in a United States military operation for which an Armed Forces service medal was awarded pursuant to Executive Order No. 12985; or recently separated veterans. It applies to positions that are in the competitive service prior to the appointment, provided that the grade of the position is no greater than GS–11 or its equivalent.[217]

Thirty Percent Disabled Veteran Authority (30% DVA): An excepted service hiring authority for disabled veterans, who have a compensable service-connected disability of 30 percent or more, into positions that are in the competitive service prior to the appointment.[218]

Training Program Certified: A hiring authority for disabled veterans who have satisfactorily completed an approved course of training prescribed by the Department of Veterans Affairs under Chapter 31 of Title 38 of the United States Code. Applies to positions in the competitive service that are in the class of positions for which the veteran was trained.[219]

Other Terms Used in the Report

The definitions below are modified from OPM's *Guide to Processing Personnel Actions* Glossary.

Applicant: A person who has asked to be considered for a job with an agency. An applicant may be a current employee of the agency, an employee of another agency, or a person who is not currently employed by any agency.

Certificate: A list of eligibles submitted to an appointing officer for employment consideration.

Competitive Service: All civilian positions in the Federal Government that are not specifically excepted from the civil service by law, executive order, or OPM regulation. Does not include positions in the Senior Executive Service.

Disabled Veteran: A person who was separated under honorable conditions from active duty in the Armed Forces performed at any time and who has established the present existence of a service-connected disability or is receiving compensation, disability retirement benefits, or pension because of a public statute administered by the Department of Veterans Affairs or a military department.

Excepted Service: Positions excepted from the requirements of the competitive service by law, Executive order, or OPM regulation. Does not include positions in the Senior Executive Service.

Merit Promotion Procedures (also known as Merit Promotion Program): The system under which agencies consider employees and others with status for vacant positions on the basis of personal merit.

Preference Eligible: Veterans, spouses, widows, or mothers who meet the definition of "preference eligible" in 5 U.S.C. 2108. Preference eligibles are entitled to have 5 or 10 points added to their earned score on a civil service examination (*see* 5 U.S.C. 3309). They are also accorded a higher retention standing in the event of a reduction in force (*see* 5 U.S.C. 3502). Preference does not apply, however, to in-service placement actions such as promotions.

Veterans' Preference: An employee's category of entitlement to preference in the Federal service based on active military service that was terminated honorably:

5-point preference is the preference granted to a preference eligible veteran who does not meet the criteria for one of the types of 10point preferences listed below.

10-point (disability) preference is the preference to which a disabled veteran is entitled.

10-point (compensable disability) preference is the preference to which a disabled veteran is entitled if he or she has a compensable service-connected disability rating of 10-percent or more.

10-point (30% compensable disability) preference is the preference to which a disabled veteran is entitled if he or she is entitled to a 10point preference due to a compensable service-connected disability of 30 percent or more.

10-point (other) preference is the preference granted to the widow/widower or mother of a deceased veteran or to the spouse or mother of a disabled veteran. It is called "derived preference" because it is derived from the military service of someone else—a veteran who is not using it for preference. When the disabled veteran does use the service for preference, then the spouse or mother is no longer entitled to preference.

End Notes

[1] George Washington to John Bannister, April 21, 1778, available at www.loc.gov/ teachers/ classroommaterials/ presentationsandactivities/presentations/timeline/amrev/turning/dissolve.html.

[2] *See Hilton v. Sullivan*, 334 U.S. 323, 336-37 (1948) (explaining the retention provisions for veterans in an 1876 statute).

[3] Pendleton Act of 1883, § 7.

[4] These rights are enforceable through administrative procedures. "A preference eligible who alleges that an agency has violated such individual's rights under any statute or regulation relating to veterans' preference may file a complaint with the Secretary of Labor." If the result of the Department of Labor's efforts is unsatisfactory to the individual, an appeal may be filed with MSPB. 5 U.S.C. § 3330a.

[5] Differential treatment between veterans and non-veterans does not offend the Equal Protection Clause of the Fourteenth Amendment to the U.S. Constitution. *See Hooper v. Bernalillo County Assessor*, 472 U.S. 612, 620 (1985).

[6] 5 U.S.C. §§ 2302(b)(11), 2301(b)(1).

[7] An example of the effect of preferences in non-Federal merit systems can be found in: Charles Chieppo, "The Civil Service Systems Governments Need for the Modern Era," *Governing Magazine*, Sep. 4, 2013, available at www.governing.com (discussing preferences in the city of Boston and how they prevented anyone who scored 100 percent on a particular exam from being in the top 200 on a specific referral list).

[8] *See, e.g.*, Exec. Ord. No. 13518 (stating that it is the administration's policy "to enhance recruitment of and promote employment opportunities for veterans within the executive branch, consistent with merit system principles and veterans' preferences prescribed by law").

[9] As discussed in greater depth in Section Four, data from our 2010 Merit Principles Survey (MPS) indicate that there are Federal employees who perceive that some veterans have been denied the preference to which they are entitled by law. There are also those who perceive that supervisors are providing "inappropriate" preferences to veterans.

[10] Agencies may have flexibility in their choice of hiring authorities, but also can have flexibility in the assessment criteria they use within each of those authorities such as the knowledge, skills, or abilities upon which an applicant may be rated. This report is limited to hiring authorities and does not address assessment criteria. Our upcoming report on fair and open competition will discuss flexibilities related to the entire hiring process including assessment criteria.

[11] www.m-w.com.

[12] *Black's Law Dictionary* 1700 (9th ed. 2009). An earlier edition of Black's defined a veteran as "any honorably discharged soldier, sailor, marine, nurse, or army field clerk, who has served in military service of the United States *in any war*." *Black's Law Dictionary* 1736 (4th ed. 1968) (emphasis added).

[13] 38 U.S.C. § 101(2).

[14] 5 U.S.C. § 2108.

[15] For example, "[p]reference eligibles or veterans who have been separated from the armed forces under honorable conditions after 3 years or more of active service may not be denied the opportunity to compete for vacant positions for which the agency making the announcement will accept applications from individuals outside its own workforce under merit promotion procedures." 5 U.S.C. § 3304(f)(1).

[16] For example, "an agency may make a noncompetitive appointment leading to conversion to career or career-conditional employment of a disabled veteran who has a compensable service-connected disability of 30 percent or more." 5 U.S.C. § 3112.

[17] 5 U.S.C. § 2108; 5 C.F.R. § 211.102 (preference eligible means veterans, spouses, widows, or mothers).

[18] *Compare* 5 U.S.C. § 2108(1)-(2) (defining "veteran" and "disabled veteran" to include only those who "served on active duty") *with* § 2108(3) (defining "preference eligible" as certain types of veterans and disabled veterans, but also relatives of certain veterans who meet extremely specific criteria).

[19] 5 U.S.C. § 2108(4).

[20] 5 U.S.C. § 3326. A copy of the section of the law and the memorandum upon which that law was based can be found in Appendix D.

[21] The 2010 MPS was administered to permanent, full-time Federal employees in 18 departments and 6 independent agencies, representing over 97 percent of the permanent, full-time Federal workforce as of September 2009. MSPB distributed 71,970 surveys and received 42,020 surveys—a response rate of 58 percent. The 2011 FMSS was administered between July and October of 2011. We received 17,339 usable survey responses out of 52,620 surveyed for a response rate of 33 percent. The 2011 FOCS was sent to approximately 34,000 Federal HR specialists and assistants Government-wide. It was administered from June-August of 2011 and had a response rate of 30 percent.

[22] The CPDF does not include data from the U.S. Postal Service or certain security and intelligence agencies, such as the Central Intelligence Agency or National Security Agency.

[23] Res. of Mar. 3, 1865, No. 27, 13 Stat. 571.

[24] *See* U.S. Office of Personnel Management, *Guide to Processing Personnel Actions*, Glossary, available at www.opm.gov/policy-data-oversight/data-analysis-documentation/personnel-documentation/processing-personnel-actions/gppa35.pdf.

[25] 5 U.S.C. § 2108(3).

[26] There are numerous hiring authorities for competitive service positions. This report focuses on those which are most common or deliberately designed to bring veterans into the civil service.

[27] U.S. Office of Personnel Management, Hiring Authorities, available at www.opm.gov/policy-data-oversight/hiring-authorities/.

[28] *Joseph v. Federal Trade Commission*, 505 F.3d 1380, 1384-85 (Fed. Cir. 2007) (explaining that an agency did not violate veterans' preference when it used parallel procedures and opted to select from the merit promotion list rather than appoint a veteran from the competitive examining certificate).

[29] *Sherwood v. Department of Veterans Affairs*, 88 M.S.P.R. 208, 10 (2001) (finding that an agency was permitted to hire a candidate using the reinstatement authority despite the presence of a veteran with preference on a competitive examining certificate because civil service rules gave the "agency the discretion to fill the…position by any authorized method, such as the reinstatement method"). *See Special Counsel v. Lee*, 114 M.S.P.R. 57, 21 (2010) (explaining that canceling a vacancy announcement and/or selecting one specific type of hiring authority over another are legally permissible absent any intent to afford preferential treatment to an individual), *rev' d in part on other grounds* in *Beatrez v. Merit Systems Protection Board*, 413 F. App'x 298 (Fed. Cir. 2011).

[30] *See* U.S. Merit Systems Protection Board, *Federal Appointment Authorities: Cutting through the Confusion*, at 4, available at www.mspb.gov (showing that in 2005, competitive examining accounted for less than one-third of new appointments).

[31] Current and former Federal employees may apply for competitive examining opportunities, but they will be assessed under the rules set forth for competitive examining and receive no advantage based on their status as current or former employees.

[32] *See* 5 U.S.C. §§ 3309; 2108. An extensive definition of veterans' preference may be found in the Glossary in Appendix F.

[33] From FY 2000 to FY 2012, Government-wide, 30 percent of external new hires were through competitive examining. In DoD, for this same period it was 24 percent, and for non-DoD agencies it was 34 percent. U.S. Office of Personnel Management, CPDF.

[34] *See* U.S. Merit Systems Protection Board, *Federal Appointment Authorities: Cutting through the Confusion*, at 28, available at www.mspb.gov/studies (explaining that the use of any particular hiring authority is often not well planned, but rather a result of which referral list contains the name of a desired candidate).

[35] U.S. Office of Personnel Management, Delegated Examining Operations Handbook, at 41, available at www.opm.gov/ deu.

[36] OPM still has the authority to conduct examinations, although the exercise of that authority is rare compared to the use of DEUs. U.S. Office of Personnel Management, CPDF, FY 2000-FY 2012.

[37] 5 U.S.C. §§ 3318(a), 3319.

[38] *Compare* 5 U.S.C. § 3318(a) *with* Presidential Memorandum, *Improving the Federal Recruitment and Hiring Process*, § 1(a)(3) (May 11, 2010), available at www.whitehouse.gov/ the-press-office/ presidential-memorandum- improving-federal-recruitment-and-hiring-process (directing agencies to stop the use of the rule of three and to instead only use category rating for competitive examining).

[39] *See* 5 U.S.C. § 3318 (explaining the process for the rule of three). The "rule of three" can be traced back as far as 1888, when a "rule of four" was reduced to three. *See* U.S. Merit Systems Protection Board, *The Rule of Three in Federal Hiring: Boon or Bane* (1995), Appendix 1, available at www.mspb.gov/studies.

[40] *See* 5 U.S.C. § 3309.

[41] Mothers are an example of how complex veterans' preference laws can be, because there are special requirements about a mother's private life that must be met for her to qualify for preference based on the service of her child. *See* 5 U.S.C. §§ 2108(3)(F), (G) (describing a husband, marriage, divorce, separation, or widowhood as a condition to qualify); Veterans' Preference Benefits—Extension to Widowed Mothers, H. Rep. No. 697 (1948 U.S.C.A.A.N. 995-97); U.S. Office of Personnel Management, *Vetguide*, available at www.opm.gov/staffingportal/vetguide.asp (explaining that it is a requirement that the mother "is or was married to the father of the veteran"). We asked OPM why it had concluded that the woman's spouse must be the father of the veteran and OPM indicated that the question required further study. U.S. Office of Personnel Management, Reply to MSPB's Veteran Questionnaire, Apr. 2, 2013. The Board has not had occasion to address the effect of a same-sex marriage on the requirement that a marriage has occurred. *See United States v. Windsor*, 133 S. Ct. 2675 (2013) (holding that it is unconstitutional to limit the Federal interpretation of marriage or spouse to apply only to heterosexual unions).

[42] For more on these categories, *see* U.S. Office of Personnel Management, *Vet Guide*, available at www.opm.gov/staffingportal/vetguide.asp. *See also* U.S. Office of Personnel Management, Delegated Examining Operations Handbook, at 99-100, available at www.opm.gov/deu.
The codes used to designate these categories on a referral list are as follows:

CPS 10-Point 30 Percent Compensable Disability Preference based on a service-connected disability of 30% or more;
CP 10-Point Compensable Disability Preference based on a service-connected disability of 10% or more, but less than 30%;
XP 10-Point Disability Preference; granted to recipients of the Purple Heart, persons with a non-compensable service-connected disability (less than 10%);
XP 10-Point Derived Preference; granted to widow/widower or mother of a deceased veteran, or spouse or mother of a disabled veteran;
TP 5-point preference; and
NV designates a non-veteran (this is an optional code that delegated Examining Offices may use; a blank space is also used to designate non-veterans).

[43] "Floating" does not occur for professional or scientific positions at grades GS-09 or higher. 5 U.S.C. §§ 3309, 3313.

[44] U.S. Office of Personnel Management, Delegated Examining Operations Handbook, at 150-54, available at www.opm.gov/deu. However, if "the top three eligible candidates are veterans, there is no distinction among the preferences. In this group, the veterans are equal and any one veteran can be selected regardless of preference." *Id.* at 153.

[45] *See* U.S. Merit Systems Protection Board, *The Rule of Three in Federal Hiring: Boon or Bane* (1995), available at www.mspb.gov/studies.

[46] U.S. Office of Personnel Management, Delegated Examining Operations Handbook, at 163, available at www.opm.gov/deu.

[47] U.S. Office of Personnel Management, Delegated Examining Operations Handbook, at 159-63, available at www.opm.gov/deu. *See also* U.S. Merit Systems Protection Board, *Clean Record Settlement Agreements and the Law* (explaining that, when asked about past employment, if an individual intentionally fails to disclose that he or she was removed or left a job by mutual agreement the individual's lack of candor can be a basis for removal and debarment from Federal service).

[48] U.S. Office of Personnel Management, Delegated Examining Operations Handbook, at 163, available at www.opm.gov/deu.

[49] U.S. Office of Personnel Management, Delegated Examining Operations Handbook, at 163, available at www.opm.gov/deu.

[50] *See* Homeland Security Act of 2002, Pub. L. No. 107-296, § 1312. Prior to this law, category rating was only permitted on a limited basis. *See* U.S. Merit Systems Protection Board, *The Rule of Three in Federal Hiring: Boon or Bane* (1995), available at www.mspb.gov/studies, in which MSPB described and compared the rule of three and category rating and concluded that category rating procedures "fit better with veterans' preference requirements and are arguably fairer to veterans, nonveterans, and managers than are the traditional register and case examining approaches."

[51] Presidential Memorandum, *Improving the Federal Recruitment and Hiring Process*, § 1(a)(3), available at www.whitehouse.gov/the-press-office/presidential-memorandum-improving-federal-recruitment-and-hiring-process.

[52] For a discussion of the formation of categories, please see Appendix E, *Structuring Categories for Category Rating*.

[53] U.S. Office of Personnel Management, Delegated Examining Operations Handbook, at 101, available at www.opm.gov/deu; *see* 5 C.F.R. § 337.303(c).

[54] *See* U.S. Department of Energy, Office of Inspector General Management Alert, *Allegations Regarding Prohibited Personnel Practices at the Bonneville Power Administration*, Jul. 2013, available at energy.gov/sites/prod/ files/2013/07/f2/IG-0891.pdf (alleging that the Bonneville Power Administration may have manipulated category rating by drawing the cut-off line after receiving applications in order to deny veterans their lawful preference). *But see* U.S. House of Representatives, Committee on Oversight and Government Reform, Aug. 1, 2013, at 1:02:50-1:03:15, available at oversight.house.gov/ hearing/ department-of-energys-bonneville-power-administration-discriminating-against-veterans-and-retaliating-against-whistleblowers/ (Inspector General Gregory Friedman testifying that he was "not there yet" on determining whether the denial of veterans' preference was intentional).

[55] *See* U.S. Office of Personnel Management, Delegated Examining Operations Handbook, at 106-07, available at www.opm.gov/deu.

[56] The ability of a preference eligible to block other candidates in the same category may not seem pertinent if the individuals in question do not qualify for the highest quality category. However, as explained in Appendix E, if there are fewer than three candidates in the highest quality category, an agency may merge the top two quality categories. Preference eligibles will be listed above non-preference eligibles in the newly merged category. *See* U.S. Office of Personnel Management, Delegated Examining Operations Handbook, at 107-10, available at www.opm.gov/deu.

[57] Within a category, "a selecting official may not pass over a preference eligible to select a non-preference eligible unless there are grounds for passing over the preference eligible and the agency has complied with the pass over procedures at 5 U.S.C. § 3318." U.S. Office of Personnel Management, Delegated Examining Operations

Handbook, at 106, available at www.opm.gov/deu; *see also* 5 U.S.C. § 3318(b) (explaining what is required when passing over a preference eligible for an individual without preference, and the additional steps necessary if the individual being passed over is a 30 percent compensable veteran). As stated earlier, OPM retains the authority to make pass over decisions for veterans with compensable disabilities of 30 percent or more. U.S. Office of Personnel Management, Delegated Examining Operations Handbook, at 106.

[58] U.S. Merit Systems Protection Board, *The Rule of Three in Federal Hiring: Boon or Bane* (1995), at 12.

[59] U.S. Merit Systems Protection Board, *The Rule of Three in Federal Hiring: Boon or Bane* (1995), at 16 (quoting U.S. Office of Personnel Management, "U.S. Department of Agriculture Personnel Management Demonstration Project Third Annual Evaluation Report" (prepared under contract by the Pennsylvania State University), Washington, DC, August 1994, p. 37).

[60] U.S. Merit Systems Protection Board, "Categorical Grouping Treats Veterans Better than Rule of Three," *Issues of Merit*, Nov. 2001, at 4, available at www.mspb.gov/studies.

[61] An agency is permitted to select from any properly constituted list, even if the effect of selecting from a different list is that a non-preference eligible individual is appointed. *See Joseph v. Federal Trade Commission*, 505 F.3d 1380, 1384-85 (Fed. Cir. 2007); *Abell v. Department of the Navy*, 343 F.3d 1378, 1384 (Fed. Cir. 2003).

[62] *See Isabella v. Department of State*, 106 M.S.P.R. 333, 29 (2007), *reconsideration denied*, 109 M.S.P.R. 453 (2008) (explaining that agencies may be required to waive age requirements in determining the qualifications of a preference eligible for appointment to a position in the competitive or excepted service unless the requirement is essential to the performance of the duties of the position). Outside of this exception, agencies are, generally, permitted to set age restrictions for certain positions, such as air traffic controller, firefighter, law enforcement officer, nuclear materials courier, customs and border protection officer, or foreign service special agent. *See* 5 U.S.C. § 3307; 22 U.S.C. § 4823.

[63] 5 U.S.C. § 3310 (applies to the position of guard, elevator operator, messenger, or custodian).

[64] If the applicant is informed of the law but disagrees with it, a perception of "inappropriate" favoritism may still occur, as "legal" and "appropriate" have different definitions.

[65] *See* U.S. Office of Personnel Management, *Vet Guide*, available at www.opm.gov/staffingportal/vetguide.asp.

[66] "Floating" does not occur for professional or scientific positions at grades GS-09 or higher. 5 U.S.C. §§ 3309, 3313. *See also* U.S. Office of Personnel Management, Delegated Examining Operations Handbook, at 107, available at www.opm.gov/deu.

[67] As discussed later, there are also rules that pose some challenges for explaining to employees what occurred, due to the privacy rights of the individuals to whom the rules were applied. *See* 5 U.S.C. §§ 552a(b); 552.

[68] Canceling a vacancy announcement or selecting one specific type of hiring authority over another are legally permissible absent any intent to afford preferential treatment to an individual. *Special Counsel v. Lee*, 114 M.S.P.R. 57, 21 (2010), *rev' d in part on other grounds* in *Beatrez v. Merit Systems Protection Board*, 413 F. App'x 298 (Fed. Cir. 2011); *Joseph v. Federal Trade Commission*, 103 M.S.P.R. 684, 11 (2006).

[69] This is also referred to as a "merit promotion program" or "merit staffing program." *Compare* 5 U.S.C. § 3304(f)(1) (merit promotion procedures) *with* U.S. Office of Personnel Management, *Guide to Processing Personnel Actions*, Glossary, available at www.opm.gov/ policy-data-oversight/ data-analysis-documentation/personnel-documentation/processing-personnel-actions/gppa35.pdf (merit promotion program and merit staffing program).

[70] As indicated in the introduction when discussing the definition of a veteran, under certain conditions, it is possible to be a preference eligible without being a veteran—such as widows, widowers, and mothers.

[71] In addition to granting the right to be considered for certain positions, VEOA created an additional PPP, codified at 5 U.S.C. § 2302(b)(11) (prohibiting a knowing violation of a preference right). VEOA also created a procedure for veterans and preference eligibles to seek redress for a violation of a preference right. *See* 5 U.S.C. § 3330a. VEOA is distinct from the Uniformed Services Employment and Reemployment Rights Act of 1994 (codified at 38 U.S.C. §§ 4301-4333) (USERR A), which protects reemployment rights for individuals returning from a period of service in the uniformed services (including the reserves or National Guard) and prohibits employer discrimination based on military service or obligations.

[72] 5 U.S.C. § 3304(f). In FY 2010, 15 percent of external new hires were brought into the civil service using the VEOA authority. For DoD, VEOA was used to appoint 22 percent of external new hires, while in non-DoD agencies it was 8 percent. U.S. Office of Personnel Management, CPDF, FY 2010.

[73] The military departments are considered separate agencies because of the law that created DoD in 1949. *See Washburn v. Department of the Air Force*, 119 M.S.P.R. 265, 7-8 (2013); *Francis v. Department of the Navy*, 53 M.S.P.R. 545, 550-51 (1992). In *Vassallo v. Department of Defense*, the Board noted that OPM's *VetGuide* states that DoD is an agency and that its components are not to be considered separate agencies for purposes of the VEOA hiring authority. However, the Board expressly rejected that interpretation, holding that the Defense Contract Management Agency (DCMA) was a distinct agency within DoD and that because DCMA accepted applications from outside DCMA for a particular vacancy, DCMA was obligated to also accept VEOA applications. *Vassallo v. Department of Defense*, 121 M.S.P.R. 70, 5, 7, 8, 11 (2014). OPM has filed a request that the Board reconsider its decision in *Vassallo.*

[74] *See, e.g., Scull v. Department of Homeland Security*, 113 M.S.P.R. 287, 18 (2010) (explaining that ICE and CBP are part of one agency—the Department of Homeland Security).

[75] In its reply to a draft copy of this report, DoD asserted that the decision in *Washburn* (and thus presumably in *Vassallo*) conflicts with OPM's regulation at 5 C.F.R. § 315.611(b), which states that "agency" in this context has the same meaning as "executive agency" as defined in 5 U.S.C. § 105. While we cannot resolve such an issue in a report, we note that in *Willingham v. Department of the Navy*, 118 M.S.P.R. 21, 10 (2012), the Board held that it is not at all clear that Congress intended that the unqualified and seemingly broader use of "agency" in section 3330a be constricted by the definition of "executive agency" in 5 U.S.C. § 105. Depending upon the arguments advanced in the *Vassallo* reconsideration case, this issue may be discussed at that time.

[76] Another complicating factor can be that DoD components each have non-appropriated fund instrumentalities (NAFIs), and the Board has held that, under certain circumstances, a NAFI is part of an agency for purposes of VEOA. *Willingham v. Department of the Navy*, 118 M.S.P.R. 21, 18 (2012) (addressing the applicability of VEOA redress procedures). Thus, if an agency opens recruitment to only competitive service and NAFI employees of the agency eligible for the interchange agreement, a veteran excluded from these categories may perceive a denial of the opportunity to compete.

[77] For example, in *Washburn v. Department of the Air Force*, the area of consideration was limited to employees of a single command within DoD that employed civilians from multiple DoD agencies. Because the command was composed of employees from more than one DoD agency, the area of consideration went beyond the hiring agency, and thus the hiring agency was required to consider VEOA applicants. *Washburn v. Department of the Air Force*, 119 M.S.P.R. 265, 9, 11 (2013).

[78] *See Scull v. Department of Homeland Security*, 113 M.S.P.R. 287, 18 (2010) (explaining that ICE and CBP are part of one agency—DHS). Congress's stated purpose for establishing DHS was to provide "for the common defense by uniting under a single department those elements within the government whose primary responsibility is to secure the United States homeland." H.R. Rep. 107-609, at 63 (2002 U.S.C.C.A.N. 1352, at 1352) (punctuation modified).

[79] *See* U.S. Office of Personnel Management, *Vet Guide* (explaining that "VEOA eligibles are rated and ranked with other merit promotion candidates under the same assessment criteria such as a crediting plan; however, veterans' preference is not applied").

[80] *See Brown v. Department of Veterans Affairs,* 247 F.3d 1222, 1225 (Fed. Cir. 2001); *Haasz v. Department of Veterans Affairs*, 108 M.S.P.R. 349, 10 (2008).

[81] An individual with preference who is within the area of consideration for the MPP announcement based on his or her civilian service could be referred on the MPP list as well, but would not receive preference on the MPP list.

[82] U.S. Office of Personnel Management, CPDF, FY 2005-2010.

[83] 38 U.S.C. § 4214.

[84] The term "excepted service" has been used to refer to: (1) the status of a person based on the nature of his or her appointment authority or position (*e.g.* VR A or attorney); (2) a position based on the nature of the work (*e.g.* attorney or chaplain); or (3) an agency based on its mission (*e.g.* Federal Bureau of Investigation, Central Intelligence Agency).

[85] The probationary period in the excepted service is typically referred to as a "trial period," however, the law authorizing VR A appointments and conversions refers to this period as a probationary period, despite the fact that it occurs during an excepted service appointment. 38 U.S.C. § 4214(b)(1)(D)(ii). For information on the use of the probationary period as the final assessment opportunity before an appointment is finalized, *see* U.S. Merit Systems Protection Board, *The Probationary Period: A Critical Assessment Opportunity*, available at www.mspb.gov/studies.

[86] *See, e.g., Williams v. Department of Air Force*, 97 M.S.P.R. 252, 8 (2004) (explaining veterans' preference ranking order for a VR A appointment); 38 U.S.C. § 4214(b)(1)(C) (granting a preference in VR A appointments to veterans entitled to disability compensation); 5 C.F.R. § 302.201 (explaining the application of preference in the excepted service).

[87] From FY 2000 to FY 2012, the average percent of external hires in DoD brought in under this authority was 9 percent, while for non-DoD agencies it was 3 percent. U.S. Office of Personnel Management, CPDF.

[88] *See* 38 U.S.C. § 4214(b)(1)(C).

[89] *See* U.S. Office of Personnel Management, *Vet Guide*, available at www.opm.gov/staffingportal/vetguide.asp.

[90] The categories of qualified individuals are:

(i) Disabled veterans.

(ii) Veterans who served on active duty in the Armed Forces during a war or in a campaign or expedition for which a campaign badge has been authorized.

(iii) Veterans who, while serving on active duty in the Armed Forces, participated in a United States military operation for which an Armed Forces service medal was awarded pursuant to Executive Order No. 12985.

(iv) Recently separated veterans.

38 U.S.C. §§ 4215(a)(2)(B), 4212(a)(3).

[91] *See* U.S. Office of Personnel Management, *Vet Guide*, available at www.opm.gov/staffingportal/vetguide.asp.
[92] *Compare* 38 U.S.C. § 4214(a)(2)(B) and 5 C.F.R. § 307.104(d) *with* 5 U.S.C. § 3304(f).
[93] 38 U.S.C. § 4214(b)(1)(D)(i).
[94] Expending resources on unnecessary training may also be seen as highly problematic by individuals who feel they need training to improve their knowledge or skills but are told that training funds are limited. *See* U.S. Merit Systems Protection Board, *Managing Public Employees in the Public Interest: Employee Perspectives on Merit Principles in Federal Workplaces*, at 21-23, available at www.mspb.gov/studies.
[95] 5 U.S.C. § 2302(a)(2)(B).
[96] 5 U.S.C. § 2302(b)(11).
[97] 5 U.S.C. §§ 2302(b)(6), (11) (internal punctuation modified); *see Special Counsel v. Lee*, 114 M.S.P.R. 57, 21 (2010) (explaining that it is not legally permissible to select one specific type of hiring authority over another if the intent is to afford preferential treatment to an individual), *rev' d in part on other grounds* in *Beatrez v. Merit Systems Protection Board*, 413 F. App'x 298 (Fed. Cir. 2011). For more information on the prohibited personnel practices, see our report, *Prohibited Personnel Practices: Employee Perceptions*, available at www.mspb.gov/studies.
[98] In the narrative responses on the Fair and Open Competition Survey, some respondents indicated that they had observed agency officials using non-competitive hiring authorities in order to be able to hire friends instead of more qualified candidates, with misuse of the VR A listed as one example of this activity.
[99] U.S. Merit Systems Protection Board, *Federal Appointment Authorities: Cutting through the Confusion*, at 22, available at www.mspb.gov/studies. It is possible, and perhaps probable, that there were other authorities used in addition to the VR A that may have brought in more candidates. However, because many supervisors did not even know they had used VR A at all, we could not reliably use the survey data to determine what other authorities may have been used.
[100] 5 U.S.C. § 3112.
[101] U.S. Office of Personnel Management, *Vet Guide*, available at www.opm.gov/staffingportal/vetguide. asp; *see* 5 C.F.R. § 315.707 (competitive service status is "automatically" acquired by such an individual upon completion of the probationary period).
[102] *See* 44 Fed. Reg. 10041, 10044 (Feb. 16, 1979).
[103] 5 U.S.C. §§ 3302, 1104(a)(1).
[104] U.S. Office of Personnel Management, Reply to MSPB's Veteran Questionnaire, Apr. 2, 2013 at 1-2.
[105] Government Accountability Office (GAO) (then called the General Accounting Office), *The Excepted Service: A Research Profile*, GGD-97-72 (May 1, 1997), at 1.
[106] In a 1997 report, GAO reported that 48 percent of Federal civilian workers were employed outside of the appointment provisions of Title 5. GAO, *The Excepted Service: A Research Profile*, GGD-97-72 (May 1, 1997), at 1.
[107] If a position is in the excepted service under 5 C.F.R. Part 302, OPM regulations explain how veterans' preference is to be applied. 5 C.F.R. § 302.201.
[108] *See* Central Intelligence Agency, https://www.cia.gov/careers/faq/ (explaining "that the CIA is not a veteran preference agency"); www.fedshirevets.gov/job/filled/index.aspx (explaining that some agencies, such as the CIA, "have only excepted service positions.") *See also* 5 U.S.C. § 2108 ("preference eligible. . . does not include applicants for, or members of, the Senior Executive Service, the Defense Intelligence Senior Executive Service, the Senior Cryptologic Executive Service, or the Federal Bureau of Investigation and Drug Enforcement Administration Senior Executive Service").
[109] 5 C.F.R. § 213.3102.
[110] *See* 38 U.S.C. § 4214 (VR A) (discussed in the last Section). *But see Dean v. Office of Personnel Management*, 115 M.S.P.R. 157, 25 (2010) (holding that the Federal Career Intern Program was invalid because the authority it used to hire individuals into the excepted service could only be used for positions where competitive examining was not practicable, yet competitive examining was also being used).
[111] U.S. Office of Personnel Management, CPDF, full-time, permanent workforce.
[112] The Department of State adds "0.175 for a five point standing and 0.35 for a 10 point standing." *See* http://careers.state.gov/officer/selection-process-printable#vetpref.
[113] *Scarnati v. Department of Veterans Affairs*, 344 F.3d 1246, 1248-49 (Fed. Cir. 2003) (emphasis added).
[114] *Scarnati v. Department of Veterans Affairs*, 344 F.3d 1246, 1249 (Fed. Cir. 2003) (internal punctuation and citations omitted).
[115] *Belhumeur v. Department of Transportation,* 104 M.S.P.R. 408, 6 (2007); *see* 49 U.S.C. § 40122(g)(2)(B) (explaining that the exceptions from Title 5 do not include sections 3308–3320, relating to veterans' preference). FA A's system also applies to the Transportation Safety Administration. *See* Aviation and Transportation Security Act, Pub. L. No. 107-71 ("The personnel management system established by the Administrator of the Federal Aviation Administration under section 40122 shall apply to employees of the Transportation Security Administration").
[116] *Belhumeur v. Department of Transportation,* 104 M.S.P.R. 408, 7 (2007) (explaining that "[w]hile sections 3308-3320 relating to veterans' preference apply to the FA A, section 3330a, which grants the Board

jurisdiction over violations of veterans' preference rights, is not among the sections of Title 5 applicable to the FA A.") *See* 49 U.S.C. § 40122(g)(2)(B) (explaining that the exceptions from Title 5 for the FA A do not include sections 3308–3320, relating to veterans' preference).

[117] 5 C.F.R. § 213.3102.

[118] *Jarrard v. Department of Justice*, 669 F.3d 1320, 1323 (Fed. Cir. 2012); *see* 5 C.F.R. § 302.101(c) (when a position is in the excepted service, "each agency shall follow the principle of veteran preference as far as administratively feasible"); *see also* 5 U.S.C. § 3320 (selection "for appointment to each vacancy in the excepted service in the executive branch" shall be "from the qualified applicants in the same manner and under the same conditions required for the competitive service by sections 3308-3318 of this title.")

[119] *Jarrard v. Department of Justice*, 669 F.3d 1320, 1323 (Fed. Cir. 2012). For such positions, veterans' preference may be used as a "positive factor." *See Patterson v. Department of the Interior*, 424 F.3d 1151, 1159 (Fed. Cir. 2005) (holding that "this approach represents a reasonable balance between" veterans' preference and the flexibilities of the excepted service).

[120] *Jarrard v. Department of Justice*, 669 F.3d 1320, 1324-26 (Fed. Cir. 2012).

[121] *See* 5 U.S.C. § 3320 ("The nominating or appointing authority shall select for appointment to each vacancy in the excepted service in the executive branch and in the government of the District of Columbia from the qualified applicants in the same manner and under the same conditions required for the competitive service by sections 3308–3318 of this title.") *See also* 5 C.F.R. Part 302 (containing rules for veterans' preference in the excepted service).

[122] 5 C.F.R. § 302.201.

[123] 5 C.F.R. § 302.304.

[124] In its 2003 report on hiring processes, GAO stated, "There is widespread recognition that the current federal hiring process all too often does not meet the needs of agencies in achieving their missions, managers in filling positions with the right talent, and applicants for a timely, efficient, transparent, and merit-based process. Numerous studies over the past decade have noted problems with the federal hiring process." GAO noted MSPB's own findings that "overly complex and ineffective hiring authorities" was a key problem with Federal hiring. Government Accountability Office, *Human Capital, Opportunities to Improve Executive Agencies' Hiring Processes*, GAO-03-450, May 2003, Highlight Sheet, 12 (citing U.S. Merit Systems Protection Board, *Making the Public Service Work: Recommendations for Change,* Washington, D.C.: September 2002).

[125] *Personnel Administrator of Massachusetts v. Feeney*, 442 U.S. 256, 280-81 (1979).

[126] James Surowiecki, *The Wisdom of Crowds: Why the Many Are Smarter than the Few and How Collective Wisdom Shapes Business, Economies, Societies and Nations*, New York: Doubleday (2003) at 4-5 (describing experiments in which responses from large groups led to more accurate answers than responses from single individuals).

[127] Please see the Methodology section in Section One for information about the sampling and response rates for the MPS and other surveys discussed in this report.

[128] The question was phrased to require that the violation be knowing because the 11th prohibited personnel practice involves the *knowing* violation of veterans' preference or a veterans' protection law. *See* 5 U.S.C. § 2302(b)(11). For more on the prohibited personnel practices, see our recent report, *Prohibited Personnel Practices: Employee Perceptions*, available at www.mspb.gov/studies.

[129] The margin for error for both of these items was +/-0.47 percent with a 95 percent confidence interval, meaning we can be 95 percent confident that the larger population represented by the survey population would give responses that are no more than 47/100ths of a percent distant from the data we report.

[130] Data is from the MPS 2010.

[131] The comparatively small number of employees reporting concerns about veteran hiring does not mean that efforts should not be made to improve the system. In a survey designed to elicit responses representative of a workforce of approximately 1.7 million employees, 6.5 percent of respondents represents more than 100,000 employees and 4.5 percent represents over 75,000. Additionally, as noted in a GAO report, the hiring system as a whole has problems beyond perceptions related to veterans' preference. *See* Government Accountability Office, *Status of Efforts to Improve Federal Hiring*, GAO-04-796T, Jun. 7, 2004, at 2 (explaining that "Congress, OPM, and agencies have recognized that federal hiring has needed reform" and that "additional attention is needed"); *see also* Government Accountability Office, *Human Capital, Opportunities to Improve Executive Agencies' HiringProcesses*, GAO-03-450, May 2003.

[132] Of the 18 questions on the MPS 2010 that would directly implicate a prohibited personnel practice, the following were the only ones perceived less often than a knowing violation of veterans' preference rights: (1) discrimination in favor or against someone in a personnel action based upon marital status (95.8% not observed); (2) discrimination in favor or against someone in a personnel action based upon religion (96.7%); (3) discrimination in favor or against someone in a personnel action based upon political affiliation (96.8%); and (4) trying to pressure someone to support or oppose a particular candidate or party for elected office (97.7%). U.S. Merit Systems Protection Board, *Prohibited Personnel Practices: Employee Perceptions*, at 35-36, available at www. mspb.gov/studies.

[133] Data is from the MPS 2010. The numbers on this chart correspond to their numbering in 5 U.S.C. § 2302(b). This chart does not show perceptions for 5 U.S.C. § 2302(b)(1) because our survey divided that PPP into seven different questions. For results for 5 U.S.C. § 2302(b)(1)-(b)11, *see* U.S. Merit Systems Protection Board, *Prohibited Personnel Practices: Employee Perceptions*, at 35-36, available at www.mspb.gov/ studies. Section 2302(b)(13) was not addressed by the survey because it had not yet been enacted. *See* Whistleblower Protection Enhancement Act of 2012, Pub. L. No. 112-199, 126 Stat. 1465, § 104 (WPEA) (adding a thirteenth PPP that prohibits non-disclosure policies or forms that conflict with whistleblower protection laws).

[134] As explained in our recent report, *Preserving the Integrity of the Federal Merit Systems: Understanding and Addressing Perceptions of Favoritism*, the origins of perceptions of favoritism may vary and rely upon a number of factors. *See Preserving the Integrity of the Federal Merit Systems: Understanding and Addressing Perceptions of Favoritism*, at 8, available at www.mspb.gov/studies.

[135] For more on the advantages of having an engaged workforce, please see our 2008 report, *The Power of Federal Employee Engagement*, available at www.mpsb.gov/studies.

[136] U.S. Merit Systems Protection Board, *Prohibited Personnel Practices: Employee Perceptions*, at 37, available at www.mspb.gov/studies.

[137] We recommend caution before concluding that the relationship between a particular PPP and an employee's engagement level depends *solely* upon that PPP, because the observance of additional PPPs and other workplace factors can influence engagement levels. *See* U.S. Merit Systems Protection Board, *Prohibited Personnel Practices: Employee Perceptions*, at 39, available at www.mspb.gov/studies. These engagement scores are based on an employee engagement scale that consists of 16 questions about the employee's attitude on a variety of issues. For more information on the reliability and validity of the engagement scale, *see The Power of Federal Employee Engagement*, Appendix A, available at www.mpsb.gov/studies.

[138] Data is from the MPS 2010.

[139] For more on motivation and its relationship to engagement, see our 2012 report, *Federal Employee Engagement: The Motivating Potential of Job Characteristics and Rewards*, available at www.mspb.gov/ studies.

[140] For perceived violations of veterans' preference, 46% of observers indicated it was likely they would leave the agency compared to 36% of observers of alleged preference towards veterans. The average for MPS respondents on the whole was 22% reporting that it was likely they would leave their agency.

[141] U.S. Merit Systems Protection Board, *Prohibited Personnel Practices: Employee Perceptions*, at 39, available at www.mspb.gov/studies.

[142] When explaining what the agency has done and why, it may be necessary to limit the information released in order to protect the crediting plan for future use.

[143] Use of the appeals or grievance processes are not adequate substitutes for resolving concerns as a part of the management-employee relationship for a multitude of reasons, including but not limited to: (1) adversarial processes can damage relationships; (2) in many situations, non-selection is not an appealable or grieveable event (particularly for non-veterans); and (3) even when an avenue for redress is available, not every employee will opt to exercise it.

[144] 5 U.S.C. § 552a(b); *see* 5 U.S.C. § 552.

[145] *See Tripp v. Department of Defense*, 193 F. Supp. 2d 229, 236 (D.C. Dist. 2002) (holding that the names, titles, and salaries of public employees are information generally in the public domain). *But see Long v. Office of Personnel Management*, 692 F.3d 185, 192 (2nd Cir. 2012) (holding that when the work of an agency or position is sensitive in nature, there is a "cognizable privacy interest" that can warrant withholding employee names in the FOIA context).

[146] MPS 2010 data for DoD consists of a combination of survey responses from civilian employees of the Army, Navy, Air Force, and other elements within DoD. The "DoD other" category includes the following organizations: Office of the Secretary of Defense; Organization of the Joint Chiefs of Staff; Defense Information Systems Agency; Defense Security Cooperation Agency; Defense Logistics Agency; Defense Contract Audit Agency; Defense Security Service; Defense Advanced Research Projects Agency; Department of Defense Education Activity; Washington Headquarters Services; Defense Legal Services Agency; Office of Inspector General; Missile Defense Agency; Defense Technology Security Administration; Defense Commissary Agency; Defense Finance and Accounting Service; Defense Human Resources Activity; Defense Prisoner of War/Missing Personnel Office; Defense Health Agency; Defense Threat Reduction Agency; Defense Contract Management Agency; Pentagon Force Protection Agency; Department of Defense Test Resource Management Center; National Defense University; Defense Technical Information Center; Business Transformation Agency; and Defense Media Activity.

[147] In FY 2012, veterans comprised 60 percent of the DoD workforce, but only 34 percent of the non-DoD Federal workforce. Source: U.S. Office of Personnel Management, CPDF, full-time, permanent employees with a known veteran status.

[148] Data is from the MPS 2010.

[149] We did not specifically ask about the 180-day rule on any of our surveys and thus cannot measure the extent of its influence on perceptions. However, there were respondents on both the FOCS and MSS who mentioned this concern. Their unprompted mention of such a specific policy drew our attention.

[150] After we provided our 2010 MPS data to the Department of the Army, we were contacted by Army researchers who were assigned to look at this issue. We commend the Army for its commitment to exploring this matter.

[151] Data is from the FOCS.

[152] The other types of guidance that were reported as being given either always or most of the time were: areas of consideration (68%); methods of recruitment (68%); sources of recruitment (66%); fair and open competition (65%); prohibited personnel practices (54%); and favoritism (41%).

[153] As explained in Section Two, the presence of a veteran on a list can prevent the selection of a non-veteran.

[154] Government Accountability Office, *Federal Hiring: Does Veteran's Preference Need Updating*? GAO/GGD-92-53, Mar. 1992, at 4, 27, available at www.gao.gov/assets/160/151726.pdf. (At the time, GAO was known as the General Accounting Office.)

[155] A selective factor is a specific qualification, beyond the minimum requirements established by OPM, which is absolutely required for a job because a person cannot perform successfully in the position without such qualification. A particular knowledge, skill, or ability can be used as a selective factor. *See* U.S. Office of Personnel Management, General Schedule Qualification Policies, available at www.opm.gov/policy-data-oversight/classification-qualifications/general-schedule-qualification-policies.

[156] *See* U.S. Office of Personnel Management, Delegated Examining Operations Handbook, at 159-63, available at www.opm.gov/deu.

[157] The Partnership for Public Service interviewed 55 Chief Human Capital Officers and reported that "nearly half expressed misgivings about the process for providing [veterans'] preference and were concerned about conflicts with other public policy objectives and the original intent of the law." Partnership for Public Service, *Bracing for Change: Chief human capital officers rethink business as usual*, at 4, available at http://ourpublicservice.org/OPS/ publications/download.php?id=209.

[158] Roswell L. Gilpatric, Memorandum: Employment of Retired Military Personnel, Jul. 5, 1961, available in Hearings Before the Committee on Post Office and Civil Service, H.R. 7381, Jul.-Aug. 1963 at 149.

[159] *See* Pub. L. No. 88-448 (1964); 5 U.S.C. § 3326(b) (2014).

[160] 5 U.S.C. § 3326(b).

[161] Roswell L. Gilpatric, Memorandum: Employment of Retired Military Personnel, Jul. 5, 1961, available in Hearings Before the Committee on Post Office and Civil Service, H.R. 7381, Jul.-Aug. 1963 at 149. A copy of this memorandum and the current statute that was developed from it is in Appendix D.

[162] Roswell L. Gilpatric, Memorandum: Employment of Retired Military Personnel, Jul. 5, 1961, available in Hearings Before the Committee on Post Office and Civil Service, H.R. 7381, Jul.-Aug. 1963 at 149.

[163] Hearings Before the Committee on Post Office and Civil Service, H.R. 7381, Jul.-Aug. 1963 at 29, 145, 157-59. (The Chairman of the Civil Service Commission, in testimony, assured the Congressman that the Gilpatric memorandum should have prevented military members after 1961 from writing the position descriptions of their future jobs by limiting the placement of an individual at the same installation immediately following his or her retirement. *Id.* at 29.)

[164] Testimony of John W. Macy, Jr., Chairman of the U.S. Civil Service Commission, Hearings Before the Committee on Post Office and Civil Service, H.R. 7381, Jul.-Aug. 1963 at 35-36.

[165] *See* Pub. L. No. 88-448; S. Rep 88-935, Mar. 4, 1964.

[166] *See* Pub. L. No. 88-448; S. Rep 88-935, Mar. 4, 1964.

[167] S. Rep. 88-935, 1964 U.S.C.A.A.N. Vol. 2 at 2840 (verb tenses modified). Section 204(b) referred to the waiver criteria.

[168] At the time of the CSR A, to hire a retired service member with no prior civilian service into the competitive service required the use of competitive examining and the rule of three. This meant that an HR official certified to conduct competitive examinations (under either OPM's direct authority or DEU) had to find that the individual was one of the three top candidates, after preference was applied.

[169] U.S. Office of Personnel Management, CPDF, FY 2005-2010.

[170] 5 C.F.R. § 315.611 (the VEOA selectee must be among the best qualified under merit promotion procedures); U.S. Office of Personnel Management, Delegated Examining Operations Handbook, at 90, available at www.opm.gov/deu (selection should be from among the best qualified candidates). *See Ramsey v. Office of Personnel Management*, 87 M.S.P.R. 98, 9 (2000) (holding that a VEOA candidate must meet OPM's minimum qualifications); 5 C.F.R. § 335.103(b)(3) (explaining that candidates under a merit promotion plan must meet OPM's minimum qualification standards); U.S. Office of Personnel Management, *Vet Guide* (explaining that VEOA eligibles are rated and ranked with other merit promotion candidates under the same assessment criteria such as a crediting plan).

[171] A lower bar may also be set with good intentions. Seventy-one percent of respondents to the FOCS indicated that in their work unit it was important that they submit as many candidates as possible to selecting officials. Without further study, we cannot state the extent to which VEOA (and MPP) crediting plans set a lower bar for "best qualified" than is set for competitive examining, or management's motives for wherever the bar is being set.

[172] According to one HR staffer who responded to the FOCS: "When using the VEOA authority, selecting officials will always hire individuals who are or have just separated from military service in their organizations and

assist them in gaining the highest salary via negotiation as possible, regardless as to how many qualified applicants were referred."

[173] The FPM Bulletin stated, "Prior OPM approval on competitive jobs is removed." U.S. Office of Personnel Management, FPM Bulletin 300-48.

[174] *See* Delegation of Authority at 44 Fed. Reg. 10042, 10046 (no expiration date mentioned); U.S. Office of Personnel Management, FPM Bulletin 300-48 (no expiration date mentioned). Most of the FPM was made obsolete by December 31, 1993, with the remainder rendered inoperable by December 31, 1994. *See* 59 Fed. Reg. 66629 (explaining that the majority of the FPM was subject to "sunset" in 1993, with some portions remaining in effect for another year to permit time to establish regulations and manuals necessary in the absence of the FPM).

[175] OPM Response to MSPB Second Questionnaire, June 4, 2013.

[176] Department of Defense Instruction, Employment of Retired Members of the Armed Forces, No. 1402-01, Sept. 9, 2007, § 5.1.

[177] All SES candidates must have their qualifications certified by a Qualifications Review Board (QRB) before being appointed as career members of the SES. www.opm.gov/policy-data-oversight/senior-executive-service/selection-process/#url=Qualifications-Review-Board.

[178] *See* U.S. Office of Personnel Management, *Guide to Senior Executive Service Qualifications*, at 6, available at http://www.opm.gov/policy-data-oversight/senior-executive-service/reference-materials/guidetosesquals_2012.pdf (explaining that the hiring agency chooses the selection method, advertises the position, evaluates each candidate's qualification, and selects a candidate. The agency then "forwards the candidate's application" to OPM for consideration by an OPM-administered QRB).

[179] Department of Defense Instruction, Employment of Retired Members of the Armed Forces, No. 1402-01, Sept. 9, 2007, § 5.2.

[180] Department of Defense Instruction, Employment of Retired Members of the Armed Forces, No. 1402-01, Sept. 9, 2007, § 5.3.

[181] A copy of OPM's full reply is in Appendix B.

[182] We asked OPM if it had an opinion on whether the statute mandates or merely confers discretion to bypass the waiver process, and OPM stated that it was "an interesting question" that it declined to answer. OPM Response to MSPB Second Questionnaire, June 4, 2013. The language in the statute also does not state if the special pay tables provision permits or mandates that the 180-day rule not apply. *See* 5 U.S.C. § 3326.

[183] *See* 5 U.S.C. § 1204(h) (prohibiting the Board from expressing an advisory opinion).

[184] Suspension of the need for a waiver based upon a state of national emergency is available at http://cpol.army.mil/library/nonarmy/dod_092401.html.

[185] President Barack Obama, *Continuation of the National Emergency With Respect to Certain Terrorist Attacks*, September 10, 2013, available at 78 Fed. Reg. 56581 (Sept. 12, 2013).

[186] DoD has informed Congress that it estimates the Global War on Terror will last at least another 10-20 years. Charlie Savage, "Debating the Legal Basis for the War on Terror," *New York Times*, May 16, 2013.

[187] Hearings Before the Committee on Post Office and Civil Service, H.R. 7381, Jul.-Aug. 1963.

[188] A non-veteran is less likely to be a supervisor or manager in a DoD agency compared to a non-DoD agency. While 11 percent of non-veterans in DoD are in civilian supervisory and managerial positions, 17 percent of veterans are in such positions. In the non-DoD Federal agencies, an average of 13 percent of non-veterans are in such positions, and 14 percent of veterans are in such positions. U.S. Office of Personnel Management, CPDF, FY 2012.

[189] The DoD individuals who were appointed within 180-days or less from their retirement dates were, in comparison to their representation in the larger military, disproportionately retired officers. Overall, in 2011, 15 percent of the active military were in the officer corps, 1 percent were warrant officers, and 83 percent were enlisted. (Total does not equal 100 due to rounding). However, in the 180-day appointee population for FY 2002-2012, 23 percent were officers, 4 percent were warrant officers, and 73 percent were enlisted. With respect to "no Colonel left behind," in 2011, 3 percent of the military were at a rank of O5 or O6 (Lieutenant Colonel and Colonel, respectively), while 15 percent of the 180-day appointees retired from such ranks (10 percent LTC, 5 percent COL). Military composition data source: Office of the Undersecretary of Defense, Personnel and Readiness, *Population Representation in the Military Services, 2011*, Appendix B at 69, 72, 76, available at http:// prhome.defense.gov/ portals/ 52/ Documents/ POPREP/ poprep2011/).

[190] Terminal leave occurs when a service member takes the leave that he or she has earned from the military before the effective date of the retirement. *See* 5 U.S.C. § 5534a. If the individual is working in the same office from which he retired, this use of leave may be a particular sore point for some respondents, as the individual is collecting pay for working and pay for being on leave at the same time from the same employer.

[191] OPM Response to MSPB Second Questionnaire, June 4, 2013.

[192] "External" employees do not include transfers or reinstatements of individuals who have already earned career or career-conditional status in the civil service. MSPB uses the full-time permanent workforce for its usual measurements of the Federal workforce. However, we did not ask DoD to limit its database in this manner.

[193] The percentage of external new hires into GS-11 through GS-15 positions in DoD was 32.7% overall and 52.3% for the 180-day veterans from FY 2002 to FY 2012. Seventy percent of the 180-day veterans were hired into the General Schedule.

[194] U.S. Secretary of Defense, Personnel & Readiness, at http://militarypay.defense.gov/retirement/ (explaining that in the absence of a disability, 20 years or more of service is typically required to qualify for retirement).

[195] *See* U.S. Merit Systems Protection Board, *Preserving the Integrity of the Federal Merit Systems: Understanding and Addressing Perceptions of Favoritism*, at 52 (explaining that survey data show favoritism can have a negative effect on recruitment and retention).

[196] The appointment prior to retirement is likely an effect of the use of terminal leave, in which a service member takes the leave that he or she has earned from the military immediately before the effective date of the retirement. The extent to which the appointments occurred prior to retirement varied by component: Air Force (43.5%), Army (36.5%), Navy (35.0%), and DoD Other (29.8%).

[197] Data supplied by the Department of Defense. Total does not equal 100% due to rounding.

[198] 5 U.S.C. § 2302(b)(6).

[199] The random samples for the MPS, FMSS, and the FOCS were drawn separately. This means that a few individuals may have been invited to respond to more than one survey. We estimate that the overlap caused by a random sampling should be relatively small—approximately 1 percent. Such overlap is common and acceptable when scientists study multiple surveys, and does not affect the ability of a sample to accurately reflect the views of the larger population it represents.

[200] The 2010 MPS did not ask about retiring members of the armed forces and provided no open-ended questions in which respondents could discuss such a topic.

[201] The law addresses appointments in "the period of 180 days immediately after [the veteran's] retirement" and does not expressly state what should occur for appointments prior to retirement. 5 U.S.C. § 3326. Given that more than a third of such appointments are beginning prior to retirement from military service, we recommend the language of the statute be amended to address the periods immediately before and following the veteran's retirement.

[202] President Barack Obama, *Continuation of the National Emergency With Respect to Certain Terrorist Attacks*, September 10, 2013, available at 78 Fed. Reg. 56581 (Sept. 12, 2013) (explaining that the national emergency declaration will remain in effect for at least another year).

[203] A copy of DoD's full reply is in Appendix C.

[204] While we have not reached a conclusion about the validity of OPM's delegation of the waiver authority, we note that the validity of the delegation is an open question. Under the CSR A, OPM's director has the authority to "delegate, in whole or in part, any function vested in or delegated to the Director." 5 U.S.C. § 1104. However, "[i]t is a basic principle of statutory construction that . . . where there is no clear intention otherwise, a specific statute will not be controlled or nullified by a general one, regardless of the priority of enactment." *Radzanower v. Touche Ross & Co.*, 426 U.S. 148, 153 (1976) (internal punctuation omitted); *see Carney v. Board of Governors of Federal Reserve System*, 64 M.S.P.R. 394, 396 (1994).

[205] Congress may grant a power to an agency head while restricting its redelegation. The maxim is "*delegata potestas non potest delegari*—a delegated authority cannot be redelegated." This principle of law applies to situations in which "Congress delegated to a high executive officer the responsible duties. . . in reference to a very important [ ] matter, and for him in turn to redelegate the same is a failure to comply with the mandate of the legislature." *United States v. Gilson Bros.*, 20 C.C.P.A. 117, 123 (Court of Custom and Patent Appeals 1932). *See United States v. Tower & Sons*, 14 Ct. Cust. 421 (Ct. Cust. App. 1927) (holding that the Secretary of the Treasury did not have the power to delegate a particular power to a special agent); *Whaley v. State*, 168 Ala. 152 (Ala. 1909) (explaining that "[a]mong the principal axioms of jurisprudence, political and municipal, is to be found the principle that an agent unless expressly empowered, cannot transfer his delegated authority to another, more especially when it rests in a confidence, partaking the nature of a trust, and requiring for its due discharge understanding, knowledge, and rectitude").

[206] "A Speech by the President, New York Times, Mar. 22, 1864, available at http://www.nytimes.com/1864/03/22/news/a-speech-by-the-president.html.

[207] We sent inquiries to OPM and DOL regarding the extent to which the laws may also confuse veterans about their rights. DOL did not respond and OPM's response indicated that it had no data to provide in this area. OPM Response to MSPB First Questionnaire, Apr. 2, 2013.

[208] The extent to which reinstatement of the Gilpatric memorandum would comport with section 3326 is a decision that must be made by DoD and its legal advisors, as the Board is prohibited from issuing an advisory opinion. *See* 5 U.S.C. § 1204(h). The outcome of such an analysis would likely be heavily dependent on whether the law is read as permitting or mandating that DoD disregard the 180-day rule during the national emergency.

[209] The Board is also required, by 5 U.S.C. § 1206, to annually review and analyze OPM's significant actions and report its findings to Congress and the President.

[210] *See* U.S. Office of Personnel Management, Delegated Examining Operations Handbook, at 105, available at www.opm.gov/deu.

[211] U.S. Office of Personnel Management, Delegated Examining Operations Handbook, at 107, available at www.opm.gov/deu.

[212] U.S. Office of Personnel Management, Delegated Examining Operations Handbook, at 101, available at www.opm.gov/deu; *see* 5 C.F.R. § 337.303(c).

[213] U.S. Office of Personnel Management, Delegated Examining Operations Handbook, at 101, available at www.opm.gov/deu ("Quality categories must be established and defined by the employing agency prior to announcing the job.")

[214] U.S. Office of Personnel Management, Delegated Examining Operations Handbook, at 107, available at www.opm.gov/deu (explaining that: "There is no limit to the number of times you can merge categories. The number of times you can merge categories is restricted only by the number of categories you establish.")

[215] "No person shall be given any appointment in the competitive service unless such person is a citizen or national of the United States." 5 C.F.R. § 7.3 (b). OPM may authorize the appointment of aliens to positions in the competitive service in "specific cases" when necessary. 5 C.F.R. § 7.3(c).

[216] 5 U.S.C. § 3304(f)(1).

[217] 38 U.S.C. §§ 4214(a)(2)(B), 4214(b)(1)(A), 4212(a)(3).

[218] 5 U.S.C. § 3112.

[219] 5 C.F.R. § 315.604.

In: Hiring Veterans into Civil Service Positions
Editor: Sergio Ruiz

ISBN: 978-1-63484-436-9

Chapter 2

VETERANS' EMPLOYMENT REDRESS LAWS IN THE FEDERAL CIVIL SERVICE*

U.S. Merit Systems Protection Board

EXECUTIVE SUMMARY

This report describes the statutes and pertinent case decisions for two laws designed to protect the employment rights of veterans in the civil service: (1) the Veterans Employment Opportunities Act of 1998 (VEOA) (codified at 5 U.S.C. § 3330a); and (2) the Uniformed Services Employment and Reemployment Rights Act of 1994 (USERRA) (codified as amended at 38 U.S.C. §§ 4301-4335).

VEOA provides a redress procedure for preference eligibles and certain veterans who believe that an agency has not treated them in accord with Federal employment laws and regulations designed to reward particular types of military service. USERRA provides procedures to address claims of discrimination based on military service and to ensure that service members can resume their civilian careers when their military service is completed. USERRA applies to the private sector as well as the public sector. However, this report only discusses the USERRA redress procedures used when the employer in question is the Federal government.

USERRA and VEOA share some common elements but differ in several important respects. In particular, VEOA requires that, before filing an appeal with the U.S. Merit Systems Protection Board ("MSPB" or "the Board"), an appellant exhaust his or her administrative remedies with the Department of Labor (DOL) and adhere to strict deadlines in the absence of an exception known as equitable tolling. In contrast, USERRA does not require the exhaustion of administrative remedies and does not have strict deadlines for filing, although there are certain requirements if the appellant seeks the assistance of DOL. VEOA does not guarantee a right to a hearing; however, USERRA does once jurisdiction is established. Under VEOA, an appellant has the burden of proof on the merits. Under USERRA, placement of the burden of proof depends on whether the appellant alleges

---

* This is an edited, reformatted and augmented version of a report to the President and Congress, issued November 2014.

discrimination or a failure to reemploy. VEOA is particularly challenging for parties and adjudicators because it uses more undefined terms and intersects with more laws and regulations than USERRA. For that reason, this report contains more discussion of VEOA than it does of USERRA.

While the information in this report should be of use to Congress, the President, appellants, and agencies, the lessons that each may draw from the facts may differ. Our major findings and recommendations are as follows:

For Congress and the President: The laws for veterans' redress are complicated, especially VEOA because of the way in which it interacts with so many other parts of the civil service. Vague and undefined terms in 5 U.S.C. § 3330a and the statute's applicability to "any statute or regulation relating to veterans' preference" have resulted in an extensive body of case law that may be confusing for the average veteran or preference eligible. It is for Congress and the President to decide what rights a veteran, preference eligible, or service member should have. But, individuals and the Federal Government as an employer would be well served by clarity in the laws and regulations, particularly in the VEOA statute and in any statute or regulation that intersects with it. Whenever Congress amends a section of title 5 in which veterans' preference can play a role, such as Chapter 33 (which pertains to hiring), we encourage the members to consider how such changes may interact with VEOA and ensure the statutory effect is one that Congress intends.

For the Office of Personnel Management (OPM): OPM has been given a complex system of civil service laws under which to operate, extensive responsibilities in that system, and limited resources to accomplish those responsibilities. Competing priorities have made it challenging for O PM to update policies and guidance to comport with changes in the law. We recommend that OPM make a greater effort to ensure that its regulations, policies, and guidance, including the *Delegated Examining Operations Handbook* and the *Vet Guide*, are regularly checked against new Acts of Congress as well as developments i n Federal Circuit and Board law and are amended as needed. To the extent that the complexities of the system permit it, OPM's guidance should be clear, unambiguous, and accurate.

For Veterans, Preference Eligibles, and Service Members: Appellants are responsible for meeting the requirements of the statutes, even if the statutes are complex or confusing. Appellants should pay close attention to the requirements of any redress procedures, particularly VEOA's provisions for exhausting administrative remedies and strict deadlines for filing complaints with DOL and appeals with MSPB. An understanding of managerial discretion, and when it applies, also would be helpful to individuals seeking to understand whether their rights have been violated.

For Agencies: It is crucial that agencies promptly give veterans, preference eligibles, and service members all of their entitlements. Not only is it the right thing to do, but, if an agency fails to do this, it will be required to reconstruct what would have occurred if the laws had been followed properly. Such reconstructions can be expensive for agencies and harmful to innocent bystanders who may need to be removed from positions through no fault of their own.

SECTION ONE: INTRODUCTION

"I believe that the Federal Government, functioning in its capacity as an employer, should take the lead in assuring those who are in the armed services that when they return special consideration will be given to them in their efforts to obtain employment. It is absolutely impossible to take millions of our young men out of their normal pursuits for the purpose of fighting to preserve the Nation, and then expect them to resume their normal activities without having any special consideration shown them. "

—President Franklin Delano Roosevelt [1]

The Board recently released a report, *Veteran Hiring in the Civil Service: Practices and Perceptions*, which discussed the complexity of the laws and regulations pertaining to the hiring of veterans in the Federal Government.[2] The rules for seeking redress for the violation of such laws and regulations are also complex. This report discusses the two main types of claims an individual may assert before MSPB when seeking such redress. The first is the Veterans Employment Opportunities Act of 1998 (VEOA) (codified at 5 U.S.C. § 3330a), which provides a remedy if a Federal agency has improperly denied a veterans' right to preference or consideration for a vacancy under a law granting such consideration.[3] The second is the Uniformed Services Employment and Reemployment Rights Act of 1994 (USERRA) (codified as amended at 38 U.S.C. §§ 4301-4335), which provides a remedy when an agency has discriminated on the basis of military service or refused to allow an individual to return to his or her position following such service.

Background

The history of veterans' preference in Federal hiring and retention predates the founding of the civil service in the Pendleton Act of 1883.[4] However, there is a difference between a right and an opportunity to seek redress of that right. In the Veterans' Preference Act of 1944 (VPA), Congress recognized that millions of Americans had delayed or put on hold their civilian careers so that they could serve the Nation in uniform. The VPA was intended to help with their readjustment, rehabilitation, and re - employment by providing a preference in Federal hiring and an avenue for redress if that preference was denied.[5] The primary avenues for redress today—VEOA and USERRA—have their roots in the VPA.[6]

The last major reorganization of Federal civil service laws was the Civil Service Reform Act of 1978 (CSRA), Pub. L. No. 95-454, 92 Stat. 1111. The CSRA requires that the Federal Government give veterans and preference eligibles certain preferences in hiring as well as other aspects of employment such as retention in a reduction in force (RIF). As explained in our report, *Veteran Hiring in the Civil Service: Practices and Perceptions*, defining veterans and other preference eligible s is complicated. Depending on the law or regulation at issue, whether a particular individual is a "veteran" can vary. A preference eligible can include the spouse, widow, or mother of a person who served in the military, even if the person seeking to use the preference has never served. Appendix A contains the statutory definitions for veteran, disabled veteran, and preference eligible.

In 1998, the Senate Committee on Veterans' Affairs held hearings in which it found that veterans were represented in the Federal workforce at twice the rate as the private sector and that a veteran was four times as likely as a non - veteran to be retained in a RIF.[7] However, the committee also determined "that while veterans as a group appear to be faring well in Federal employment, individual cases reveal that there is a pressing need for a uniform redress mechanism for the enforcement of veterans ' preference laws in both hiring and reductions -in-force decisions."[8] To achieve this purpose, Congress enacted VEOA.

VEOA enables those entitled to preference to seek redress through DOL and if unsatisfied with that result, to file an appeal with MSPB.[9] VEOA also added a new right for veterans —with three years of service —to be considered for positions if the hiring agency accepts applicants from outside its own workforce. A violation of this right can also be redressed through a complaint to DOL and, if the appellant remains unsatisfied, a subsequent appeal to MSPB.[10] Sections Two through Six will discuss VEOA redress in greater depth.[11]

The other avenue for redress discussed in this report is USERRA, enacted in 1994 to prevent discrimination based on military service. USERRA is different from VEOA in several ways. Most importantly, USERRA is not unique to the Federal Government; it applies to all U.S. employers. It also covers a different but overlapping population—service members—which can include those who meet the VEOA definition of "veteran," but also covers additional individuals who have served the Nation. Unlike VEOA, USERRA does not require that an individual first seek assistance from DOL.[12] Appendix B contains a chart showing the major differences and similarities between USERRA and VEOA.

There are two main aspects to USERRA. The first is employment: An employer is prohibited from discriminating against an applicant or employee on the basis of past, current, or future military obligations.[13] The second is reemployment: A person who has temporarily departed employment to serve in the uniformed services has a right to return to the posit ion he or she would have held if not for that service.[14] Sections Seven and Eight will discuss USERRA in greater depth.

Subject Matter Jurisdiction

The Board's power to adjudicate an action is restricted to matters where its jurisdiction is specifically provided by law, rule, or regulation. [15] This means that Congress must have granted to MSPB the authority to adjudicate the subject being placed before MSPB, or authorized an agency to create a regulation or rule that grants MSPB jurisdiction over the subject. This is known as "subject matter jurisdiction."[16] Without subject matter jurisdiction, there cannot be a recognizable decision on the merits of a case.[17] As our reviewing court has noted, "Although often effecting a seemingly harsh result, courts cannot disregard jurisdictional requirements established by Congress out of sympathy for particular litigants. . . When jurisdiction is lacking, the only function remaining to the court is that of announcing the fact and dismissing the cause."[18]

The issue of Board jurisdiction is always before the Board and may be raised by either party or by the Board on its own motion at any time during a Board proceeding. [19]

The Board has authority over a wide variety of subject matters, including but not limited to appeals of adverse actions for cause (i.e. removals, suspensions, demotions), RIFs, and retirement benefit decisions reached by OPM. The Board also has jurisdiction over individual right of action (IRA) appeals alleging retaliation for whistleblowing and appeals brought under VEOA and USERRA. Additionally, the Board has jurisdiction over complaints alleging

the commission of prohibited personnel practices (PPPs) when such complaints are filed by the Office of Special Counsel (OSC).[20] *Each subject matter can have a different set of criteria to establish jurisdiction*, including who may file the appeal, the time limits in which to act, and any administrative remedies that must be exhausted before seeking a judgment from MSPB.

When Congress explicitly establishes a requirement—such as filing a complaint within a certain time period —the Board generally cannot waive it.[21] However, where Congress is silent and the Board has the power to establish a requirement, that requirement can be waived.[22] For this reason, it is important to recognize that MSPB's rules for filing one type of case (such as a VEOA appeal) can be different than the rules for another type of case (such as an appeal of a removal).[23] Parties must look to the rules established for their specific subject matte r or risk having their case be dismissed.

Jurisdiction in VEOA and USERRA cases can be confusing because of the way in which it may be intertwined with the merits of the case. Parties may find it helpful to focus on the legal terms "nonfrivolous" and "preponderance of the evidence." To establish MSPB's *jurisdiction* over a VEOA or USERRA claim, the appellant's allegations must be nonfrivolous.[24] An allegation is enough to show jurisdiction.[25] However, to prove the *merits* of the case the party must use evidence to prove that it is more likely than not that his or her allegations are true.[26] The party bearing the obligation to prove an element of the case can vary.[27] In a VEOA or USERRA case, the term for "winning" the case is that "relief" is granted to the appellant. Jurisdiction means the Board will be able to look at the merits to decide whether or not to grant relief —but jurisdiction alone is not a guarantee that the merits will be proven and relief granted.

When the jurisdictional elements of a claim ar e intertwined with the merits of the claim and the appellant makes the requisite jurisdictional allegations, the preferred approach is for the Board to take jurisdiction and then resolve the merits.[28] Thus, the Board may accept a claim as nonfrivolous for purposes of jurisdiction, but then find that the merits were not proven by a preponderance of the evidence.[29]

A VEOA or USERRA claim may occur in a matter over which the Board has jurisdiction under a different statute. For example, the removal of an employee under 5 U.S.C. chapter 75 may be appealed to the Board. Such an action is known as an "otherwise appealable action." If an appellant files a timely appeal of an otherwise appealable action and also raises a VEOA or USERRA claim for that appeal, the VEOA or USERRA claim will be adjudicated as an affirmative defense.[30]

However, if an appellant raises VEOA or USERRA as an affirmative defense in an appeal of an adverse action that is either untimely or not within the Board's jurisdiction, the Board will consider the appellant's allegations that an adverse action was taken in violation of USERRA or VEOA as separate claims. Thus, if a VEOA or USERRA appeal is timely but an adverse action appeal of the same personnel action is untimely, the VEOA or USERRA appeal can be adjudicated while the untimely action will be dismissed.[31]

Purpose

Under its statutory authority to conduct studies of the civil service, MSPB is authorized to conduct research and report upon laws, regulations, and Government actions that affect the health of the merit systems, and in particular upon actions that affect the extent to which the civil service is free from the commission of prohibited personnel practices.[32] Veterans' preference is an important part of the civil service and a knowing violation of veterans' preference is a PPP. Enabling preference eligibles to obtain redress for violations of their rights is an important mechanism to ensure lawful preference is not denied.[33]

We have determined that it would be helpful to Congress, agencies, stakeholders, service members, veterans, and preference eligibles if we provided a report that explained how VEOA and USERRA currently operate. Our purpose is to help those who create and amend laws understand the current state of the law; help those responsible for complying to understand their obligations; and help those who seek its protections to understand their specific rights.

In addition to its studies authority, MSPB has jurisdiction over appeals brought under both VEOA and USERRA. The Board is prohibited from issuing advisory opinions on adjudicatory matters.[34] For this reason, this report differs from many products issued under our studies function. We can inform readers about prior holdings by the Board and its reviewing court, the Federal Circuit. We are also permitted to discuss holdings by other courts of mandatory or persuasive jurisdiction. [35] However, we will not fill in any gaps where the Board or a court has not yet interpreted the law. While we hope this report will be useful in clarifying how veterans' redress laws function, it is not a holding of the Board and we recommend that parties refer directly to the statutes, regulations, and cases applicable to their particular situations.

Unlike VEOA, which is unique to the Federal Government, USERRA applies to employers in the private sector and state governments as well as in the Federal Government.[36] However, the enforcement proceedings are different if the employer in question is a Federal agency. [37] *This report only addresses the Federal process and cases pertinent to adjudication of USERRA claims against the Federal Government as an employer.* Individuals interested in USERRA for the private sector should consult the Department of Labor's Veterans' Employment and Training Service (VETS) website at http://www.dol.gov/vets/ or contact DOL directly.

Methodology

This report relies primarily upon statutes, regulations, and decision s issued by the Board and the courts. Our research for this report included a request for information sent to DOL and questionnaires sent to two veterans groups. Neither DOL nor the veterans groups submitted replies. We also submitted questions to the U.S. Office of Personnel Management (OPM), which did respond. OPM reported that it did not have data indicating the most common misunderstandings that veterans or others with preference eligibility have about their rights and opted not to express an opinion on how the redress procedure laws or regulations could be improved.

SECTION TWO: ESTABLISHING A VEOA CASE—OVERVIEW

VEOA provides a system of redress for two sets of situations:

1. A preference eligible (veteran or not) alleges that his or her preference under any statute or regulation relating to veterans' preference has been violated.[38]
2. A veteran who has been separated from the armed forces under honorable conditions after 3 years or more of active service alleges that he or she has been denied the opportunity to compete for vacant positions for which the agency making the announcement will accept applications from individuals outside its own workforce under merit promotion procedures (MPP).[39]

The criteria to establish that MSPB has jurisdiction over one of these two types of cases are similar, but slightly different. Parties need to identify the correct jurisdictional rule for their particular set of facts. Once jurisdiction is established, an appellant will need to prove the exact same criteria, but to a different standard. Remember, jurisdiction requires the appellant make a nonfrivolous assertion ; obtaining relief ("winning" the case) requires that the appellant use evidence to prove that it is more likely than not that his or her allegations are true.[40] The term "dismissal for failure to state a claim" refers to a situation in which, if every fact asserted by the appellant were true, and all reasonable inferences applied in the appellant's favor, the appellant still could not prevail as a matter of law. In other words, if the appellant could prove everything he or she asserts, but those facts could not reasonably be interpreted in a way that would constitute a violation of his or her rights as a veteran or preference eligible, then the MSPB administrative judge (AJ) can dismiss the case for a failure to state a claim for which relief could be granted.[41] Whether an appellant has stated a claim upon which relief may be granted goes to the sufficiency of the pleading and is a separate question from jurisdiction.[42]

A VEOA appellant is not automatically entitled t o a hearing regarding either jurisdiction or the merits of a VEOA appeal.[43] The AJ may order a hearing for a VEOA case if he or she determines it is necessary to resolve issues of jurisdiction or timeliness. [44] However, the Board has the authority to decide the merits of a VEOA appeal without a hearing if there is no genuine dispute of material fact and one party must prevail as a matter of law. [45]

The jurisdictional standards for the two types of VEOA cases are as follows:

A preference rights appeal: To establish Board jurisdiction over a preference rights appeal brought under VEOA, an appellant must: (1) show that the appellant exhausted his or her remedies with DOL, and (2) make nonfrivolous allegations that: (i) the appellant is a preference eligible within the meaning of the VEOA; (ii) the action(s) at issue took place on or after the October 30, 1998 enactment date of the VEOA ; and (iii) the agency violated the appellant's rights under a statute or regulation relating to veterans' preference.[46]

A right to compete appeal: To establish Board jurisdiction over a right to compete appeal brought under VEOA, an appellant must: (1) show that he or she exhausted his or her remedy with DOL, and (2) make nonfrivolous allegations that: (i) the appellant is a veteran within the meaning of 5 U.S.C. § 3304(f)(1);[47] (ii) the actions at issue took place on or after the December 10, 2004 enactment date of the Veterans' Benefits Improvement Act of 2004 (VBIA); and (iii) the agency denied him or her the opportunity to compete under merit promotion procedures for a vacant position for which the agency accepted applications from individuals outside its own workforce in violation of 5 U.S.C. § 3304(f)(1). [48]

For both types of VEOA cases, once jurisdiction is established through a nonfrivolous claim, the appellant will be required to prove by preponderant evidence that the agency violated one or more of the appellant 's statutory or regulatory veterans ' preference rights.[49]

Because the administrative exhaustion requirement is the same for both sets of appeals, we will address it before discussing the other criteria.

SECTION THREE: FILING VEOA COMPLAINTS AND APPEALS

The discussion in this section is limited to actions filed directly under the VEOA redress authority. As noted earlier, if an appellant files a timely appeal with MSPB for an otherwise appealable action (such as the removal of an employee) and also raises a VEOA claim for that appeal, the VEOA claim will be adjudicated as an affirmative defense. Appellants filing under a statutory authority other than VEOA should consult the rules and regulations that pertain to that authority. [50]

When filing a complaint under VEOA, an appellant must exhaust his or her administrative remedies with DOL prior to seeking redress before MSP B. "The doctrine of exhaustion of administrative remedies is well established in the jurisprudence of administrative law. The doctrine provides that no one is entitled to judicial relief for a supposed or threatened injury until the prescribed administrative remedy has been exhausted."[51] There are several reasons why the law supports this doctrine:

1. It provides an agency with "an opportunity to correct its own mistakes with respect to the programs it administers before it is haled into federal court[.]"[52]
2. It promotes efficiency because "[c]laims generally can be resolved much more quickly and economically in proceedings before an agency than in litigation in federal court. In some cases, claims are settled at the administrative level, and in others, the proceedings before the agency convince the losing party not to pursue the matter in federal court. "[53]
3. If the claim is brought before MPSB or another adjudicator y body, the record created by the administrative process may be useful in those proceedings.[54]

Filing a Complaint to Exhaust Remedies before Department of Labor

The first step of the exhaustion process is for the appellant to file a written complaint with DOL containing "a summary of the allegations that form the basis for the complaint."[55] Unlike some aspects of VEOA, which will be liberally construed in favor of the veteran, exhaustion has very strict rules.[56] A VEOA complaint must be filed with DOL within 60 days after the date of the alleged violation, unless a concept called "equitable tolling" applies.[57]

Equitable tolling may permit a rare exception to this deadline if: (1) the complainant has actively pursued his claim by filing a defective pleading during the statutory period; or (2) the complainant was "induced or tricked by his adversary's misconduct into allowing the filing deadline to pass."[58] The Federal Circuit has held that the principles of equitable tolling apply to the deadline for filing a complaint with DOL and filing an appeal with MSPB.[59] For more on equitable tolling, please see Appendix C. Absent equitable tolling, a failure to timely file a complaint with DOL will deprive MSPB of jurisdiction.[60]

Once the complaint is filed, DOL will investigate it.[61] However, the complaint must be adequately specific as to what issues are being raised. For example, in *Burroughs v. Department of the Army*, 115 M.S.P.R. 656 (2011), the appellant informed DOL that he objected to a particular vacancy announcement. However, his complaint did not make allegations that the agency had passed over him, failed to apply veterans' preference points, or denied his right to compete for the position. [62] When the appellant attempted to raise these three issues on appeal to MSPB, the Board held that because the appellant's complaint was not sufficient to inform DOL of his allegations, he had not exhausted the administrative remedies. Therefore, the Board lacked jurisdiction over those allegations.[63]

After investigation, if DOL finds that it is more likely than not that the alleged violation occurred, DOL will make "reasonable efforts" to ensure that the agency involved complies with the statute or regulation that has been violated. [64] If the complaint is not resolved, DOL will provide a written notice to the complainant of the results of the investigation. [65]

Cases have arisen in which DOL has issued a notice that it considers the complaint satisfactorily resolved, yet the complainant is not satisfied and wishes to file an appeal with MSPB. For example, in *Gingery v. Department of the Treasury*, during DOL's investigation, the Treasury Department admitted that it had violated the appellant's veterans' preference rights by failing to grant him veterans' preference status when processing his application. The agency had not allowed the appellant to take a test that assessed skills necessary for the position to which he had applied. The Treasury Department offered to allow him to take the test, and promised that he would receive a tentative job offer if he passed. DOL considered this a satisfactory resolution —the appellant did not. The appellant filed a VEOA appeal with MSPB, and the Board held that DOL's resolution of the appellant's VEOA complaint did not divest the Board of jurisdiction over his VEOA appeal. DOL's action in closing the case served as exhaustion of the appellant's administrative remedies, but the nature of the disposition did not alter the appellant's entitlement to appeal to the Board.[66]

Cases have also arisen in which DOL has concluded that a complaint does not fall under its VEOA jurisdiction. The Board has held that it can find that a pre -appeal complaint process has been exhausted when an appellant has attempted to obtain a necessary determination and the agency responsible for making that determination has refused to do so. Therefore, a refusal by DOL to address an appellant's complaint allows the Board to find that the appellant has exhausted his DOL remedy.[67]

Closing Out the Department of Labor Complaint

Before filing an appeal with MSPB, the matter must be closed at DOL through one of two means: (1) DOL issues a notice informing the appellant that the matter is closed; or (2) the appellant notifies DOL that he or she has decided to file an appeal with MSPB (after which, DOL "shall not continue to investigate or further attempt to resolve the complaint to which the notification relates").[68] Until one of these two things has happened, MPSB will not have jurisdiction over the case. [69]

For example, in *Burroughs v. Department of the Army*, 116 M.S.P.R. 292 (2011), the appellant filed a VEOA appeal but did not submit evidence that he had received a letter from DOL or informed DOL of his intent to file an appeal with the Board. The Clerk of the Board issued a show cause order providing the appellant with notice regarding the exhaustion issue and ordering him to file evidence and argument to show that he either received written notification of the results of DOL's investigation or notified DOL in writing of his intention to file a Board appeal. When the appellant failed to provide this evidence and argument, the Board dismissed the appeal for a lack of jurisdiction because exhaustion of remedies at DOL is a requirement for VEOA jurisdiction to attach.[70]

The VEOA statute includes strict time requirements for both of these options (unless equitable tolling applies).[71] If DOL issues a letter, the appeal cannot be filed more than 15 days after receipt of the letter. If the appellant opts to file without the letter, the appellant cannot file "before the 61st day" after the complaint was filed.[72] As noted before, it is very important that veterans and preference eligibles pay close attention to these requirements. The Board does not have the authority to waive a statutory deadline for "excusable neglect."[73]

Filing a Complaint with a District Court

A rarely used provision of the VEOA statute permits an individual to seek redress in a United States district court.[74] The individual still must exhaust the administrative remedies before DOL and must file an initial appeal with MSPB.[75] Once that is done, a VEOA claim may be filed in district court, **provided that all of the following criteria are met:**

1. The claim cannot be filed before the 121st day after the appeal was filed with MSPB.[76]
2. The individual has filed a document with MSPB informing MSPB that the individual has elected to pursue relief in the district court in lieu of continuing the appeal before MSPB.[77]
3. MSPB has not yet issued a "judicially reviewable decision on the merits of the appeal."[78]

A decision by MSPB is not judicially reviewable until it is a "final decision."[79] A decision by an administrative judge typically becomes a final decision 35 days after it is issued unless a timely petition for review is filed with the Board.[80] If a petition for review is filed and denied or dismissed, the administrative judge's decision becomes the final decision of the Board. If the petition is granted, the Board's decision fully disposing of the matter becomes the final decision.[81]

Section Four: VEOA Allegations of a Violation of Preference Rights

As noted before, in addition to the exhaustion of remedies before DOL, if an appellant is claiming a violation of his or her preference rights, the appellant must assert that: (1) the appellant is preference eligible within the meaning of the VEOA; (2) the action(s) at issue took place on or after the October 30, 1998 enactment date of the VEOA; and (3) the agency violated the appellant's rights under a statute or regulation relating to veterans' preference.[82] Because allegations involving actions that took place prior to 1998 are unlikely to be decided in the future due to the statutory deadlines to file, we will not discuss that portion of the jurisdictional requirement in this report. However, Appendix C discusses the rare situations in which an exception to the deadlines to file may apply due to equitable tolling.

Preference Eligible within the Meaning of VEOA

When examining whether a person is a preference eligible, the Board looks at the *person*, not the *position* at issue in the case. The issue is one of "standing"—whether this is a person the law intended should be able to bring the case.[83] In *Wilks v. Department of the Army*, the Board held that the term "preference eligible " is defined based upon 5 U.S.C. § 2108 and that VEOA redress procedures could therefore apply to a person applying for positions in title 10 as well as title 5.[84] In *Willingham v. Department of the Navy*, the Board noted the possibility that an agency's regulations could potentially provide a preference that might meet the requirement that the appellant be a "preference eligible."[85] The Board raised the issue, but held that it did not need to resolve the question of regulation -based preference because the appellant met the definition provided in 5 U.S.C. § 2108.[86] A copy of section 2108 is in Appendix A.

Agency Violation of Rights Under a Statute or Regulation Relating to Veterans' Preference

Defining an "Agency" for Veterans' Preference Rights Cases

The VEOA statute does not define "agency" and there is nothing in that Act's legislative history to illuminate the meaning of that word in the context of 5 U.S.C. § 3330a.[87] Unlike "preference eligible"—which focuses on the person—"agency" focuses on the employer. Therefore, whether a potential employer is an "agency" is a question that must be decided on a case-by-case basis. Below we provide examples of a few such cases.

In *Willingham*, the issue was whether a preference eligible could seek redress under VEOA for non-selection by a Non-Appropriated Fund Instrumentality (NAFI) operating under the authority of the Department of the Navy. A NAFI is an organization "under the jurisdiction of the armed forces which is conducted for the comfort, pleasure, contentment, or physical or mental improvement of members of the armed forces."[88] For most personnel issues, a NAFI is not managed under civil service rules. For example, NAFIs have their own set of laws for whistleblowing and for compensation for workplace injuries.[89] Most NAFI employees are also "deemed" not to be employees for the purpose of laws administered by OPM, which comprise a majority of the laws that apply to the civil service.[90]

However, the Board has long and consistently applied the well -established maxim that a remedial statute should be broadly construed in favor of those whom it was meant to protect, and that this principle particularly applies to statutes involving veterans ' rights and benefits. Because of the extent to which the particular NAFI in question in *Willingham* was "integrated" into the civilian personnel system, the Board held that it was an agency for the purposes of VEOA jurisdiction.[91]

In *Sedgwick v. World Bank*, an appellant similarly asserted that he had been denied preference rights when the employer did not apply veterans ' preference to his situation. The Board noted that neither World Bank employees nor recipients of World Bank funding are employed in the Federal civil service system. This case differed from *Willingham* because the Board held that the Bank is not a part of the United States Government, but is instead an international organization in which the United States and many other nations participate. Accordingly, it is not an "agency" under VEOA, and therefore VEOA redress procedures do not apply to its decisions.[92]

It is possible for an employer to be an "agency" and yet have a section of the agency not be an *employer to which VEOA applies*. For example, VEOA redress procedures apply to the Department of Homeland Security (DHS) in general.[93] However, as explained below, they do not apply to every segment of DHS.

In *Morse v. Merit Systems Protection Board*, an individual claimed that the Transportation Security Administration (TSA) within DHS violated his veterans' preference rights when it declined to waive an age restriction for an air marshal position. TSA is a unique organization in many ways, including the fact that the rules for appointments to the Federal Aviation Administration (FAA) (a part of the Department of Transportation) apply to TSA hiring.[94]

The court noted that 5 U.S.C. § 3312, which requires a waiver of age restrictions for preference eligibles who are able to perform the duties of a position, applies to FAA employees, and thus to TSA employees. However, it also found that "section 3300a of title 5, which provides preference eligible veterans with rights to appeal to the Board " (VEOA redress) does not apply to the FAA and therefore does not apply to TSA hiring.[95]

The court recognized that its holding create s a situation in which preference eligibles have a right, and yet at the same time are not provided the means to seek redress for violations of that right. The court explained that its "role is merely to interpret the language of the statute enacted by Congress " and not to judge the wisdom of the result. [96] This case highlights the important point that every element of jurisdiction is distinct. A situation can exist where the employer is a Federal agency for purposes of owing a preference right, yet not an agency for purposes of seeking redress of that right.

The word "agency" can be pertinent to a series of different inquiries, including whether the potential employer is one to which: (1) the *rules* for veterans' preference applies; and /or (2) the *redress procedures* for veterans' preference applies. However, for cases involving the right to compete, discussed in Section Five, the question of what constitutes an "agency" is an even more complicated issue because in addition to the questions of whether VEOA rights and redress procedures apply to the potential employer, how the agency's "own workforce" is defined can determine whether there is a right to be considered for a specific vacancy. Section Five will discuss what it means to be an agency in that context.

Violation of Rights under a Statute or Regulation Relating to Veterans' Preference and Hiring

When examining allegations of a veterans' preference violation, it is necessary to determine whether preference applies to the particular situation in question and if so, what type of preference is due. It is possible for an employer to be covered by VEOA redress procedures, but for the *position* in question to not carry a veterans' preference requirement.

Earlier, we explained that the type of appointment authority was not pertinent to the question of whether the individual was a preference eligible.[97] Similarly, whether the *person* has preference is a separate question from whether the *position* is one to which preference applies.[98] Parties must look to the section of the jurisdictional test they are seeking to establish when applying case law.

As we discussed in our recent report, *Veteran Hiring in the Civil Service: Practices and Perceptions*, there can be large sections of Federal agencies or specific positions that are exempt from the rules for veterans ' preference.[99] Below we offer examples of each.

There is no question that the Department of Veterans Affairs (DVA) is an agency for purposes of VEOA redress.[100] However, that does not mean that all veterans' preference statutes and regulations apply to all of DVA. In *Scarnati v. Department of Veteran s Affairs*, the position at issue was in the Veterans Health Administration (VHA), an entity within DVA. The court held that VHA has discretionary authority to appoint health care personnel under 38 U.S.C. § 7401(1) without regard to civil service requirements. Because there is no veterans' preference right applicable to 38 U.S.C. § 7401(1) hiring, a VEOA appeal "for an alleged violation of veterans' preference rights is not available to those applying for § 7401(1) positions."[101] In other words, if there i s no right to be violated, there can be no appeal of a violation of that right. Therefore, to determine whether VEOA jurisdiction applies to a veterans ' preference claim against DVA, it is necessary to determine whether the position's appointment authority is in title 5 or title 38.[102]

Similarly, in *Vores v. Department of the Army*, the Board received a VEOA appeal for an alleged violation of preference rights and the medical position in question was one for which the appointment authority was located in title 38. The Board compared the facts in *Vores* with those in *Scarnati* and noted that the agency in this case was the Department of the Army rather than the Department of Veterans Affairs, and that a different section of title 38 was used in *Vores*. However, because the sections of title 38 used to appoint individuals to the medical positions were "identical in substance" the Board held that preference did not apply to the Army position, and thus the Board lacked VEOA jurisdiction.[103]

Throughout the civil service, certain occupations in title 5 of the U.S Code (such as chaplains or attorneys) are excepted from the rules for competitive examining.[104] When a position in the title 5 excepted service is excepted due to the difficulties inherent in examining for it, agencies must follow the principle of veterans' preference to the extent that it is "administratively feasible."[105] In *Jarrard v. Department of Justice*, the Federal Circuit held that because of the nature of attorney hiring, an agency was not obligated to consult OPM before passing over a veteran for a non -veteran when hiring attorneys, because it was not administratively feasible.[106]

However, most of the other positions in the excepted service will follow different rules for the application of veterans ' preference.[107] For example, when numerical scores are assigned in excepted service examining, then 5- or 10-points may be added, as under competitive examining.[108] As explained in our recent report, *Veteran Hiring in the Civil Service: Practices and Perceptions*, OPM's regulations contain instructions for several different ways in which the referral list may then be ordered.[109] To determine whether a preference right has been violated, it first will be necessary to determine what preference was owed. Parties interested in excepted service positions should be aware that preference can take a variety of forms in the excepted service.

Because VEOA redress applies to any statute or regulation relating to veterans' preference, and veterans' preference permeates a large section of civil service laws and regulations, VEOA appeals can result in litigation in unexpected matters, such as the validity of hiring authorities where the use of one authority may have implications for the disuse of another authority where preference operates.[110]

In *Dean v. Department of Agriculture*, the appellant filed an appeal under VEOA challenging the agency's decision to hire a non -veteran under the Outstanding Scholar hiring authority (a noncompetitive hiring authority in the competitive service) instead of selecting the veteran from a competitive examining certificate where preference applied. In order to determine whether the appellant's rights were violated, the Board examined the validity of the authority that had been used. The Board held that the Outstanding Scholar hiring authority was not valid because the President had not prescribed a rule authorizing Outstanding Scholar to function as an exception to competitive examining nor had he authorized OPM to create such a rule. As a result, the appellant's preference rights had been violated.[111]

In *Dean v. Office of Personnel Management*, the same preference eligible veteran challenged an excepted service hiring authority, the Federal Career Intern Program (FCIP), on the basis that FCIP violated his preference rights. The Board held that FCIP was not valid because it: (1) was inconsistent with the civil service rules that govern placement of positions in the excepted service; and (2) did not require the justification of placement of positions in the excepted service as mandated by statute.[112] The jurisdiction under which the Board reached these conclusions was Mr. Dean's VEOA right to appeal a violation of his preference rights.[113]

Violation of Rights under a Statute or Regulation Relating to Veterans' Preference and Reductions in Force

When VEOA was enacted, it was clear that Congress intended for the redress procedure to apply to both recruitment actions and RIFs.[114] The Board has found that it has jurisdiction over RIF -related VEOA claims. For example, in *Buckheit v. U.S. Postal Service*, the appellant was a preference eligible who asserted in a VEOA claim that the agency had violated his rights in a RIF by retaining non -preference eligibles while reassigning him. The appellant exhausted his remedies before DOL and filed a VEOA appeal with the Board.[115]

The Board noted that 5 C.F.R. part 351 contains the procedures for RIFs, and that an employee's rights under this part are based in part on whether the employee is a preference eligible. The Boar d held that a violation of those regulations may therefore constitute a violation of a regulatory provision relating to veterans' preference. Because the appellant was a preference eligible who exhausted his remedies before DOL and made a nonfrivolous claim that the agency violated his preference rights in a RIF, the Board had jurisdiction over his VEOA appeal. However, on the merits, the Board found that the appellant failed to show that he was denied any preference-related rights to which he was entitle d under part 351 and therefore denied his requested relief.[116]

SECTION FIVE: VEOA ALLEGATIONS OF A VIOLATION OF THE RIGHT TO COMPETE

To establish Board jurisdiction over a right to compete appeal brought under VEOA, an appellant must exhaust his or her administrative remedies before DOL and make nonfrivolous allegations that: (1) the appellant is a veteran within the meaning of 5 U.S.C. § 3304(f)(1);[117] (2) the actions at issue took place on or after the December 10, 2004 enactment date of the VBIA; and (3) the agency denied him or her the opportunity to compete under merit promotion procedures for a vacant position for which the agency accepted applications from individuals outside its own workforce in violation of 5 U.S.C. § 3304(f)(1).[118] Again, to obtain relief, the same elements must be proven by preponderant evidence.

Because allegations involving actions that took place prior to 2004 are unlikely to be decided in the future due to the statutory deadlines to file, we will not discuss that portion of the jurisdictional requirement in this report. However, Appendix C discusses the rare situations in which an exception to the deadlines to file may apply due to equitable tolling.

A Veteran within the Meaning of 5 U.S.C. § 3304(f)(1)

A veteran described in section 3304(f)(1) is a person who has been separated from the armed forces under honorable conditions after 3 years or more of active service.[119] Such individuals "may not be denied the opportunity to compete for vacant positions for which the agency making the announcement will accept applications from individuals outside its own workforce under merit promotion procedures."[120]

Preference eligibles are also entitled to compete for such positions under section 3304(f)(1).[121] Being a veteran and being preference eligible are two separate things, which can, but need not, overlap for the right to compete to apply.[122] The ability to seek redress for a violation of the right to compete under section 3304(f)(1) also applies to both groups. The Board has held that section 3304(f)(1) "stands in some relation to, has a bearing on, concerns, and has a connection with veterans ' preference rights" and is, therefore, a statute "relating to veterans' preference" for which VEOA provides a remedy.[123] Therefore, even if a preference eligible does not meet the definition of veteran under section 3304(f) (such as a service member who served less than 3 years but earned preference in that period or a relative with derived preference),[124] relief may be granted under the provisions discussed in Section Four, involving allegations of a violation of veterans' preference rights.

Agency Denial of the Right to Compete under 5 U.S.C. § 3304(f)(1)

Section 3304 provides for the right to compete for veterans and preference eligibles, but the circumstances under which that section gives a right to compete are limited. There must be one or more "vacant positions for which the agency making the announcement will accept applications from individuals outside its own workforce under merit promotion procedures."[125]

As noted earlier, for most claims of a violation of a veterans' preference right, the jurisdictional question is whether an agency is an employer covered by the statute. For such cases, it does not matter whether the Department of the Army and the Department of the Navy are part of the same agency — only that the hiring agency is covered by the statute. However, for cases involving the right to compete under section 3304(f)(1), the adjudicator must determine: (1) if the hiring entity is an agency covered by the VEOA statute for redress; and (2) if the agency is accepting applications under merit promotion procedures from outside its own workforce.[126] It is the acceptance of such applications that triggers the right to consideration and thus MPSB jurisdiction over claims that the right was violated.[127] Therefore, the definition of the "agency workforce" is critical to the question of whether the right to be considered for the vacancy applies to the situation at issue.

Defining "outside Its Own Workforce" for Right to Compete Cases

To determine if applications are being accepted from outside the workforce, the adjudicator must determine the borders of the agency; only then can he or she determine if applications are being accepted from individuals outside those borders.

For most agencies it is fairly simple to identify the borders of an agency, which means there has not been an opportunity for the Board to address the specific borders of every agency for purposes of VEOA. However, the issue of defining agencies within the Department of Defense (DoD) has arisen in several cases and requires special treatment.

In most cases, "agency" means the parent agency. The example that OPM uses in its *Vet Guide* to describe this concept is that the Internal Revenue Service (IRS) is a part of Department of the Treasury, and therefore the agency for purposes of defining the workforce is the Department of the Treasury. Thus, according to OPM, an IRS office could open a vacancy to employees of both IRS and the Bureau of the Public Debt without moving beyond the agency's workforce.[128]

However, the guidance in the *Vet Guide* becomes a problem when looking at DoD. DoD—and only DoD—has specific case law that states it is not a single agency for purposes of VEOA. [129] (OPM has requested that the Board reconsider its decision in the most recent case on this issue, *Vassallo v. Department of Defense*, 121 M.S.P.R. 70 (2014). The Board has yet to reach a decision in that case. The paragraphs below explain the current state of the law, which may be subject to modifications as case law evolves.)

In *Washburn v. Department of the Air Force*, there was a vacancy in the United States Strategic Command (STRATCOM), a DoD "unified combatant command" that includes elements of the Air Force, Army, and Navy (including the Marine Corps). The agency opened the vacancy to employees of the Air Force and individuals eligible to transfer from other DoD components, such as the Army, Navy, and Defense Finance and Accounting Services (DFAS). The question before the Board was whether this area of consideration meant that the employer was accepting applications from outside its workforce.[130]

The Board concluded that the employing agency was the Air Force, based upon: (1) the extensive history of how DoD was formed in 1949 out of separate agencies; (2) prior holdings outside the VEOA context in which the Board and the Federal Circuit held that DoD's components were separate agencies; (3) the extent to which OPM's regulations defining an agency for "general purposes of recruitment, selection, and placement " distinguished between the military departments; and (4) the agency's own references to the employing agency as "the Department of the Air Force." The Board concluded that by including employees from outside Air Force in its announcement, the agency had created the obligation to consider applications from veterans under 5 U.S.C. § 3304(f).[131]

This holding was reinforced in the Board's decision in *Vassallo v. Department of Defense*, which specifically addressed t he question of OPM guidance on VEOA. In *Vassallo*, the Defense Contract Management Agency (DCMA) announced that a position was open to "current DCMA employees" and "current Department of Defense employees with the Acquisition, Technology, and Logistics Workforce who are outside the Military Components." The question before the Board was whether the inclusion of the individuals from within DoD but outside of DCMA meant that the recruiting office was accepting applications from outside its own workforce.[132]

The Board noted that OPM, in its *Vet Guide*, asserted that DoD was the parent agency for purposes of VEOA, and that if OPM's guidance was correct, then the recruiting office had not moved beyond the agency's workforce. However, the Board found that OPM's *Vet Guide* was not persuasive and reiterated its holding from *Washburn* that the separate components within DOD are different agencies for purposes of the right to compete under VEOA.[133]

What it means to Be Allowed to "Compete"

Being allowed to compete is not the same thing as being selected. Rather, VEOA entitles a preference eligible to have all of his or her experience considered, including work of a similar nature that was performed in the military as well as any related volunteer work.[134] However, "VEOA does not enable veterans to be considered for positions for which they are not qualified."[135] The same minimum qualification requirements used for MPP candidates apply to VEOA applicants.[136]

This includes the requirement that an individual meet certain criteria known as a "positive education requirement." The education requirement is often a certain number of credits in a field or a certain degree.[137] However, OPM guidance specifically recognizes that,

> on rare occasions there may be applicants who may not meet exactly the educational requirements for a particular series, but who, in fact, may be demonstrably well qualified to perform the work in that series because of exceptional experience or a combination of education and experience. In such instances, a more comprehensive evaluation must be made of the applicant's entire background, with full consideration given to both education and experience.[138]

In *Miller v. Federal Deposit Insurance Corporation*, the appellant, a preference eligible, applied for a position that had a positive education requirement. The appellant possessed a Ph.D. in economics, but did not have the required 24 credit hours in education or another field appropriate to the position.[139]

The appellant asserted that while he "may not meet the exact educational requirement for the particular series," he felt that his experience compensated for that lack, as permitted by OPM's policy. However, the agency concluded that he was not qualified.[140]

On appeal, the AJ determined that the agency had properly considered the appellant's education and experience, and denied the appellant's request for relief on those grounds. On petition for review, the appellant asserted that as a preference eligible, he was entitled to have the Board review the quality of the agency's assessment of his background.[141]

The Board held that, "although a preference -eligible is entitled to have a broad range of experiences considered by the agency in reviewing his application for a position, how the agency adjudges and weighs those experiences is beyond the purview of the Board's review in a VEOA appeal." In other words, the Board only reviews whether the agency met its obligation to *consider* the appellant's background, but it has no role in assessing the *conclusions* reached by the agency as a result of that consideration.[142]

Other requirements may also be placed on all applicants, including VEOA applicants. For example, in *Clarke v. Department of the Navy*, the agency announced a vacancy that included, as a selective factor, [143] that:

> [C]andidates must have a minimum of two years of demonstrated professional experience in some combination of selecting, organizing, and providing access to rare books and other special collections materials in an academic or research library. If such experience was gained as part of a set of more diverse responsibilities, the amount of such special collections experience must have cumulated to the equivalent of at least two years of full-time special collections work. [144]

The appellant, a veteran with preference, had more than 20 years of experience working with rare materials, items, and artifacts. However, nothing in his application package indicated that his work cumulated to the equivalent of at least two years of full -time special collections work. The Board determined that the agency had assessed the appellant's background and permitted him to compete, then upheld the agency's decision not to appoint the appellant because he did not have the selective factor.[145]

In *Dale v. Department of Veterans Affairs*, the agency announced a position at both the GS-04 and GS-05 levels. The appellant was referred for the GS -04 position, but not the GS -05. The agency hired a candidate from the GS-05 referral list. On appeal, the appellant did not dispute his lack of qualifications at the GS -05 level, but he asserted that the agency should be required to hire him at the GS -04 level and then train him to become qualified as a GS-05. The Board held that the appellant was only entitled to be considered for the positions for which he qualified, and that the agency met its obligation to give that consideration when it *referred* him at the GS-04 level. The agency was under no obligation to *select* the appellant from the GS-04 list.[146]

As explained in the examples below, in addition to job-related experience, some—but not all—other requirements placed upon MPP candidates can also apply to VEOA applicants.

In *Montee v. Department of the Army*, the area of consideration was all U.S. citizens except those "ordinarily resident" in the United Kingdom (U.K.), where the position in question was located. The agency determined that because the appellant, a preference eligible, was ordinarily resident in the U.K., he could not be considered for the position. The agency explained that the status of forces agreement between the United States and the U.K. prohibited the appointment of such individuals.[147] The Board held that the agency's determination was supported by the evidence. If the appellant was "ordinarily resident" in the U.K., then he was not qualified for the position and therefore not entitled to VEOA consideration.[148]

In contrast, in *Jolley v. Department of Homeland Security*, the agency opened its area of consideration to individuals working at the Federal Law Enforcement Training Center (FLETC) in Glynco, Georgia, regardless of the employing agency. The appellant was employed in Jacksonville, Florida, but applied for the position. The appellant was not referred because he was not in the geographic area of consideration. After an extensive discussion of OPM's *Vet Guide* and its guidance on areas of consideration, the Board held that OPM's guidance could not be interpreted to permit excluding veterans from consideration under 5 U.S.C. § 3304(f) based on an area of consideration's physical restrictions because it would render meaningless the statutory guarantee of consideration.[149]

The lesson to draw from a comparison of *Montee* and *Jolley* is that when an agency seeks to limit the area of consideration in a manner that would exclude candidates who apply under section 3304(f), the type of authority used to create that limit will determine whether section 3304(f) can be overridden.

When an agency assesses a candidate who is a veteran or preference eligible, it is appropriate for the agency to evaluate the individual's past conduct and performance, just as it would for any other candidate.[150] In *Harellson v. U.S. Postal Service*, the appellant was a veteran who had worked for the agency previously and sought reinstatement. The appellant submitted an application for a position and management asked a subject matter expert to assess the appellant's qualifications. The expert determined that there were "problems with the appellant's past performance." The agency then opted to select internal candidates.[151]

On appeal, the Board determined that if the evidence was sufficient to establish that the agency had accepted the application of the appellant, an outside candidate, then it would also establish that the appellant, as a preference eligible, was entitled under section 3304(f) to compete for the position in question.[152] However, the Board found that it was not necessary to determine whether the evidence was sufficient to establish that his application had been accepted, because in assessing the appellant and concluding that there was a history of performance problems, the agency had met the full scope of a section 3304(f) obligation to consider the appellant.[153]

The Board noted that when the right to compete under section 3304(f) requires an agency to consider an application, the agency is not precluded from eliminating a veteran or a preference eligible from further consideration for a position based on his or her qualifications for the position. As the appellant was requesting reinstatement in a position he had previously held, the decision appears to imply that the quality of past performance may be considered a measure of qualifications.[154]

Similarly, in *Smyth v. U.S. Postal Service*, an appellant was removed from further consideration for a position base d upon a work history that included a 5-day suspension for irregular attendance, two deferments of periodic step increases, and two letters of warning related to attendance. The appellant asserted that he had been denied the consideration owed to him. However, the Board held that:

> The appellant has identified no VEOA provision or any other statute or regulation which precluded the agency from finding that he was disqualified from further consideration for the Rural Carrier position because of his prior work history, and we are not aware of any such statute or regulation. Thus, the AJ properly found that the agency 's disqualification of the appellant on this basis did not deny him his rights under the VEOA.[155]

The right to compete under 5 U.S.C. § 3304(f) is statutory, and therefore cannot be superseded by Governmentwide or agency regulations. In *Shapley v. Department of*

Homeland Security, the agency announced that it would accept applications from all U.S. citizens for a position as a Bridge Program Administrator. The appellant, a preference eligible, applied for the position, and his name was placed on a referral list, but that list was never given to the selecting official. Instead, the selecting official was given a list containing the names of two priority consideration candidates and was told that he must make a decision on those candidates before he would be given a list of other candidates.[156]

Priority consideration is permissible under a variety of circumstances, which can be authorized by statute, regulation, or case law.[157] In *Shapley*, the priority candidates were given that status because the agency had improperly denied them consideration for a position on a previous occasion. The Board noted that priority consideration for future vacancies may generally be the proper remedy for individuals who were denied consideration for a position for which they were qualified due to an invalid employment practice and that the agency's actions appeared to comport with OPM's guidance for such situations. However, the Board held that OPM's guidance could not take precedence over a statute, such as 5 U.S.C. § 3304(f). Therefore, when the agency determined that the appellant was qualified to be referred (by placing his name on a referral list) and yet did not refer him to the selecting official, it denied him the opportunity to compete guaranteed by section 3304(f).[158] Although it has been six years since the decision in *Shapley*, OPM's *Delegated Examining Operations Handbook* has not yet been updated to comport with *Shapley*.[159]

What it means to be permitted to compete, and the conditions that an agency may place on candidates, can vary greatly by the specific situation at issue. Agencies and veterans could benefit from clearer guidance, particularly from OPM. While we recognize that OPM has been given extensive responsibilities and limited resources to accomplish those responsibilities, we recommend that OPM make a greater effort to ensure that its regulations, policies, and guidance, including the *Delegated Examining Operations Handbook* and the *Vet Guide*, are regularly checked against new Acts of Congress was well as developments in Federal Circuit and Board case law, and amended as needed. [160] OPM's guidance should be clear, unambiguous, and accurate.

SECTION SIX: VEOA RELIEF

Under VEOA, if an appellant's rights are violated, the appellant is entitled to a reconstruction of the personnel action consistent with law. [161] This means that when the Board finds that an agency has violated an individual's preference eligibility rights or the right of a veteran to compete under 5 U.S.C. § 3304(f), the Board will order the agency to reconstruct the personnel action in question, while following the laws or regulations that were not followed the first time.[162]

To properly reconstruct a selection action, the agency must conduct an *actual* selection process based on the same circumstances surrounding the original faulty selection.[163] A hypothetical process is not sufficient.[164] This means that the agency must take any original selectee out of the position,[165] conduct and evaluate interviews so that they are meaningfully comparable with the original selectee's interview, and fill the same number of vacancies as before.[166]

While an appellant may be entitled to a reconstruction of the selection action in which the laws and regulations are followed, *an appellant is not entitled to a position with the agency and the Board will not order a retroactive appointment as a remedy for a VEOA violation.*[167]

Although an appellant is not automatically entitled to be appointed, if the reconstructed selection process results in the appellant's selection, he or she may be entitled to an award of compensation under VEOA for any loss of wages or benefits that resulted from the agency's violation of his or her rights.[168]

For example, in *Marshall v. Department of Health and Human Services*, the appellant applied for a GS -13 position with the agency. By the time the case reached the Federal Circuit, it was undisputed that the agency had violated the appellant's preference rights during selection and that the appellant would have been selected if not for the violation. However, in the meantime, the appellant had accepted a lower-graded position with the U.S. Coast Guard. The Federal Circuit held that the appellant was entitled to the difference in wages and benefits between the Federal position he held and the position he should have been offered. This entitlement ran from the date of the appointment that had violated his rights to the date that he was either: (1) placed in the position he should have been put in originally; or (2) the date he decline d such a placement. [169]

The VEOA statute provides for an award of lost wages or benefits for an ordinary violation and an additional amount, equal to the award of lost wages or benefits, for a willful violation of the statute.[170] For purposes of VEOA, the term "willful" means that the employer either knew or showed reckless disregard for the matter of whether its conduct was prohibited. [171]

Relief is an important component of a VEOA case. As discussed earlier, an appeal may be dismissed for a failure to state a claim for which relief could be granted.[172] A situation can also evolve in which a case becomes "moot" because there is no relief left for the Board to grant. Mootness can arise at any stage of the proceedings.[173] The dismissal of an appeal as moot amounts to a dismissal for lack of jurisdiction.[174] However, for an appeal to be found moot, the appellant must have received *all* of the relief that he or she could have received if he or she had prevailed on the merits.[175] *Unsatisfactory* relief can render a case moot if there is no more relief to be granted. But, *partial* relief does not create mootness if there is more relief that may be available.[176]

The concept of "dismissal as moot," also called the "mootness doctrine," arises from the constitutional requirement that an Article III court cannot render a decision unless there is a "case or controversy" in which the parties have a recognizable interest in the outcome. It prevents courts from issuing advisory opinions. Because the Board is prohibited from issuing advisory opinions, it recognizes the mootness doctrine, even though the Board is not a court operating under Article III of the U.S. Constitution.[177]

Because mootness is considered a jurisdictional issue in Article III courts, the Board has issued VEOA decisions stating that the Board has found a case moot because no further relief may be granted, and is therefore dismissing the case for *lack of jurisdiction.*[178] We recognize this may be confusing, since the Board has also held that stating a claim for which relief may be granted goes to the merits and *not jurisdiction.*[179] Rather than pondering the relationship between relief and merits or jurisdiction, readers should focus on the central point—the ability of the Board to grant relief is a necessary component for a case to proceed.

SECTION SEVEN: USERRA—COVERED ACTIONS

USERRA provides broad protections to ensure that those who serve in uniform are not discriminated against in employment matters and to eliminate or minimize any disadvantage to their civilian career s resulting from uniformed service.[180] The statute provides that:

> A person who is a member of, applies to be a member of, performs, has performed, applies to perform, or has an obligation to perform service in a uniformed service shall not be denied initial employment, reemployment, retention in employment, promotion, or any benefit of employment by an employer on the basis of that membership, application for membership, performance of service, application for service, or obligation. [181]

Because of other Federal laws pertaining to the employment of veterans, many of these situations can overlap with other appeal rights. For example, an employee (regardless of veterans' status) who is removed, demoted, or suspended for more than 14 days can challenge the underlying action by asserting that the charges are untrue, the penalty is unreasonable, or that procedures were not followed.[182] Similarly, as described in the VEOA sections, a veteran who is not selected may assert that his or her preference rights were denied or that he or she was denied an opportunity to be considered. However, veterans are not usually accorded any preference when seeking promotions, and decisions to grant or deny leave are usually not appealable, so claims related to promotion within the agency or leave use are more likely to stand alone on the alleged USERRA violation.[183]

USERRA cases are typically described as falling under one of two basic categories that will be discussed in this section:

Anti-discrimination: Prohibiting employers from denying employment, promotion, or "any benefit of employment" to anyone based on their uniformed service. It also protects against reprisal for participating in a USERRA-related activity, such as filing a USERRA claim or testifying on behalf of an individual in a USERRA case.[184]

Reemployment: Entitling employees absent from their positions due to uniformed service to prompt reemployment in their former or comparable positions, plus the additional seniority and benefits that they would have had if they had remained continuously employed (called the "escalator principle").[185]

Anti-Discrimination Situations

USERRA anti-discrimination cases brought before the Board can run a wide gamut, but many tend to fall into one of the following categories:

- Adverse actions (such as removals, suspensions, or demotions) in which the appellant alleges the agency acted out of animus towards the person for serving in the military (such as a de sire to remove a person who is frequently absent from work to perform uniformed duty).[186]
- Non-selection decisions (including promotions), where it is alleged that the agency did not want to hire a person who might be absent in the future for military duty (such as individuals in the reserves or National Guard).[187]

- Non-selection decisions based on a desire to avoid veterans' preference rules.[188]
- Denial or improper charging of leave to perform uniformed service duties.[189]

An appellant also may assert discrimination based on the specific nature of the service he or she provided to the military. For example, in *Beck v. Department of the Navy*, the appellant had been an enlisted person in the Navy and asserted that he was passed over for a GS-13 position because the deciding official was "dismissive" of the appellant after learning that he had been an enlisted man and not an officer. The Board held that if there had been discrimination on the basis of the appellant's military rank, then it would qualify as discrimination based on service under USERRA. [190]

However, service-related medical conditions, whether physical or psychological, are unlikely to successfully serve as the basis for a USERRA case. The Board has held that if a medical condition is the result of military service, discrimination on the basis of that medical conditional alone does not support a USERRA claim. The discrimination must be based on the actual service, not on injuries or disabilities incidental to it.[191]

Reemployment Situations

USERRA provides that an employee whose "absence is necessitated by reason of service in the uniformed services " will be entitled to reemployment if: (1) he has given advance notice of such service to his employer; (2) the cumulative absence does not exceed 5 years; and (3) he either reports for employment or requests reemployment after completion of the uniformed service.[192]

As shown in the table below, the time period in which the individual must report for employment or reemployment depends on the length of the period of absence due to military service. Additional time is provided for an individual who is unavailable due to an injury or illness related to uniformed service.[193]

Absence	Obligation
Less than 31 days	Return to work no later than the beginning of the first full regularly scheduled work period on the first full calendar day following the completion of the period of service (provided that this allows 8 hours to rest after returning home from duty).
Between 31 and 180 days	Submit an application for reemployment no later than 14 days after the completion of the period of service.
Over 180 days	Submit an application for reemployment with the employer no later than 90 days after the completion of the period of service.

USERRA reemployment cases brought before the Bo ard can also run a wide gamut, but many allegations tend to fall into one of the following categories:

- That a civilian position was not abandoned and that the appellant is therefore entitled to be reemployed. [194]

- That the appellant would have been in a higher -graded position if not for the service and was therefore not returned to the correct position.[195]
- That the new position is not of a "like status" to the position held prior to a departure for military service. [196]

Below we explain each of these concepts.

Abandonment

Abandonment cases often arise in the context of retirement annuities because of the way in which certain military service may be treated when determining eligibility for a civilian service annuity.[197] However, the issue can arise in any reemployment case, because if an individual has abandoned his or her civilian career, the agency is under no obligation to reemploy the person.[198]

A resignation is but one way to determine if the position has been abandoned.[199] An appellant's actions can lead an employer—and the adjudicator—to infer that the individual has abandoned his civilian job in favor of a career in the military.[200] While not dispositive, a strong indicator can be whether the appellant asked for leave without pay or a separation to perform uniformed service.[201] Similarly, an appellant's expressed intent, such as statements that he is still employed by the agency, can be an important factor in determining abandonment.[202] While USERRA does not have a deadline to file a complaint, the passage of an extensive period of time after the appellant's removal with no challenge by the appellant can also indicate abandonment.[203] The adjudicator must evaluate the totality of the evidence and weigh it in order to determine if abandonment occurred. [204]

The Escalator Principle

Upon return to civilian duty, the individual is entitled to return to the place the person would have been if not for the military service.[205] This is called the "escalator principle" because the individual "does not step back on the seniority escalator at the point he stepped off. He steps back on at the precise point he would have occupied had he kept his position continuously[.]"[206]

In the report accompanying the bill, Congress described the escalator principle's applicability to USERRA as follows:

> [W]hatever position the returning serviceperson would have attained, with reasonable certainty, but for the absence for military service, would be the position guaranteed upon return. This could be the same position or a higher, lower, or lateral (e.g., a transfer) position or even possibly layoff or severance status depending on what has happened to the employment situation in the servicemember's absence.[207]

While the escalator principle is a crucial component of USERRA, it can be difficult to predict what would have occurred if an individual had not left his or her civilian job to perform uniformed service, particularly to the degree of being "reasonably certain." In cases before 2014, the Board repeatedly held that advancement is not reasonably certain if it is dependent on the exercise of "a discriminating managerial choice " and the fitness and ability of the employee.[208] However, in a 2014 decision, *Rassenfoss v. Department of the Treasury*, the Board overruled this line of cases and began using a different test to determine whether the individual was entitled to the escalation that he or she sought.[209] The next few paragraphs discuss an older case, *Leite v. Department of the Army*, followed by a discussion of *Rassenfoss* to highlight the differences in the Board's approach to the question of reasonable certainty.

In *Leite*, the appellant was away on military duty when the agency abolished her GS-13 position and established a GS -14 position for which she competed but was not selected. When she returned from duty, the agency informed the appellant she was entitled to a GS -13 position similar to the position that she had left. The appellant asserted she was entitled to a GS-14 position. Ultimately, the agency placed her in a position in a different pay system that was equivalent to the GS -13 position.[210]

In her USERRA claim, the appellant asserted that other individuals in the organization had been given temporary duties above their pay levels and then promoted into those higher-level positions. She posited that in light of her past exemplary performance it was likely that if not for her military service, she also would have been given greater responsibilities on a temporary basis and then been permanently selected for a temporarily held position. The Board held that while it could not "rule out the possibility" that the appellant might have been promoted if not for her military service, it was not "reasonably certain" that this chain of events would have occurred, and therefore the appellant was not entitled to the promotion under USERRA.[211]

However, in *Rassenfoss v. Department of the Treasury*, the Board expressly overruled the approach used in *Leite*.[212] In *Rassenfoss*, the question was whether the appellant would have received a Quality Step Increase (QSI) for outstanding performance if he had not been away from his civilian work to serve in the military.[213] As stated in Member Robbins' dissenting opinion in *Rassenfoss*, under OPM's regulations, a QSI "shall not be required" but rather may be given "consistent with performance-related criteria in a performance appraisal program."[214] Thus, the awarding of a QSI has traditionally been dependent on management discretion.

In the *Rassenfoss* majority opinion, the Board noted that it had historically distinguished between benefits that are dependent on fitness, ability, or the exercise of managerial discretion and those that are based on seniority, rewards for length of service, or that would have accrued through the mere passage of time. The former category typically did not benefit from the escalator principle because it was too difficult to be reasonably certain whether a discretionary authority would have been exercised.[215]

However, in *Rassenfoss*, the Board also noted that DOL, which has the authority to promulgate pertinent regulations for non -Federal employment, had rejected the discretionary/nondiscretionary management decision distinction undergirding the Board 's approach in earlier cases. Rather, DOL directed employers to adopt a case -by-case approach to determine whether a benefit was reasonably certain to have accrued absent military service.[216] The Board concluded that Congress would not have wanted an outcome in which Federal employees are afforded less protection than state or private sector employees. The Board therefore overruled its earlier holdings that had assumed that discretionary personnel actions inherently fail the reasonable certainty test and instructed that DOL's approach be used instead.[217]

Applying DOL's regulations, the Board explained that relevant factors to consider when assessing whether it is reasonably certain that an employee would have received a discretionary action such as a QSI or promotion can include: (1) the returning employee 's work history; (2) his or her history of merit increases; and (3) the work and pay history of employees in the same or similar position s.[218] The Board remanded *Rassenfoss* to the regional office to further develop the record, particularly the history of others in the same or similar position s as the appellant.[219]

Positions of "like status"

When an individual returns from uniformed service, an agency is obligated to reemploy the appellant in a position of *like status*; however, the new position is not required to have the same duties as the old position.[220] Status means particular attributes of a specific position, including the "rank or responsibility of the position, its duties, working conditions, pay, tenure, and seniority."[221] In comparing two positions, the Board looks beyond the title and grade of the positions involved and compares the scope of actual duties and responsibilities of the new position with those of the former position.[222]

For example, in *Crawford v. Department of the Army*, the Board noted that the appellant's position had been abolished while he was away performing uniformed service, and therefore it was plausible that a position with the exact same duties no longer existed. For the old and new positions, the Board weighed the factors of the duties, pay, tenure, seniority, working conditions, and level of rank and responsibility. The Board found that nearly all of these factors were the same in both positions; only the duties differed. The Board held that despite the difference in duties, under the circumstances the agency had met its obligation to place the appellant in a position of like status to his prior position.[223]

In contrast, in *Nichols v. Department of Veterans Affairs*, when the appellant returned from military service, the agency asserted that, while the appellant's old position had been filled, it had created a "like" position for him. The Federal Circuit held that while the agency's decision to fill the job in the appellant's absence did not alter the appellant's entitlement to his old job, the agency had some discretion to find an equivalent position. However, to be equivalent, the position must be of equal status. The court held that "[i]t goes without saying that when one starts out as the boss, but is placed in a position subordinate to the replacement boss, and other new bosses, there is incontestably a loss of authority, and accordingly a diminished status." Because the new job had less status, it could not be considered equivalent. The agency was ordered to return the appellant to his old job, even though it meant displacing the new incumbent.[224]

In *Heidel v. U.S. Postal Service*, a returning service member was given a position with the same title and grade as his pre -service position. However, in the old position, the appellant performed several tasks, interacted with his coworkers and supervisors, trained new employees, and was exposed to the workplace decision-making process so as to better prepare him to compete to be a supervisor one day. In the new position, the appellant sat alone all day doing one thing, namely, handling and repairing damaged pieces of mail. The Board held that although the two positions were in the same job family and shared the same grade, their duties and responsibilities were not of "like status."[225]

An agency cannot withhold a "like" position based on an assertion that the individual is not initially qualified to perform in the new position. The agency must make "reasonable efforts" to help the person become qualified.[226]

SECTION EIGHT: USERRA—ADJUDICATING CLAIMS

As explained in this section, USERRA differs from VEOA in many respects, including: the roles of DOL and OSC; how to prove a claim; which party has the burden of proof (which differs based on the type of USERRA claim); the right to a hearing; deadlines (or lack thereof) ; and who may be a covered employer. Appendix B contains a table highlighting some of the significant differences between USERRA and VEOA.

Establishing USERRA Jurisdiction

To establish Board jurisdiction over a USERRA discrimination appeal, an appellant must nonfrivolously allege that: (1) he performed duty or has an obligation to perform duty in a uniformed service of the United States; (2) the agency denied him initial employment, retention, promotion, or any benefit of employment; and (3) the denial was due to the performance of duty or obligation to perform duty in the uniformed service. [227]

For USERRA cases in which discrimination is not alleged, the Board typically describes its jurisdiction without phrasing it as a jurisdictional test. For example, in *Welshans v. U.S. Postal Service*, the Board simply stated that, "[u]nder USERRA, the Board has jurisdiction over an appellant's claim that he was denied 'any benefit of employment' on the basis of his membership in the uniformed services."[228] In *O'Bleness v. Department of the Air Force*, a case involving military leave, the Board described the claims being made and then stated that, "[t]he Board's jurisdiction extends to claims such as those raised here[.]"[229]

As with a VEOA claim, a claim under USERRA will be broadly and liberally construed in determining whether it is nonfrivolous. [230] Also in common with a VEOA claim, the weakness of the assertions in support of a USERRA claim is not a basis to dismiss the USERRA appeal for lack of jurisdiction; rather, if the appellant fails to develop his contentions, his USERRA claim will be denied on the merits. [231]

Establishing Merits of a USERRA Case and Burdens of Proof

Under USERRA, there are two crucial differences between proving the merits of a discrimination claim and the merits of a reemployment claim:

1. ***Burden of Proof***: In a *discrimination* case the *appellant* must prove the merits of the case by preponderant evidence. If that burden is met, the agency may avoid relief by showing by preponderant evidence that it would have taken the same action even in the absence of the improper motivation.[232] In a *reemployment* case the *agency* bears the burden of proving, by preponderant evidence, that it met its statutory obligations to reemploy the individual with the appropriate level of career advancement and benefits.[233]
2. ***Motive***: In a *discrimination* case, the appellant *must prove the agency's motivation*; in a *reemployment* rights claim, the individual *does not have to establish the motivation*

for the agency's action or inaction because motive is irrelevant in USERRA reemployment cases.[234]

Establishing a Discrimination Case

A USERRA discrimination case is different from a discrimination case brought under Equal Employment Opportunity Commission procedures. In equal employment opportunity (EEO) discrimination cases, "disparate treatment" and "disparate impact" are two distinct analytical frameworks for establishing discrimination. A disparate treatment claim may succeed only if there is a finding of *intent* to discriminate by the acting party, while a disparate impact claim may succeed if a facially-neutral policy or practice has a disproportionate *effect* on a protected class of people and is not justified by business necessity.[235]

In a USERRA discrimination case, the question is not the effect, but *only the intent*. Therefore, USERRA does not provide a cause of action under the disparate impact theory. While use of an agency policy or practice known to create a disparate impact may be used as evidence of discriminatory intent, the impact alone, in the absence of any discriminatory intent, is not pertinent to a USERRA discrimination case. [236]

Discriminatory motivation in a USERRA case may be reasonably inferred from a variety of factors, including proximity in time between the employee's military activity and the adverse employment action, inconsistencies between the proffered reason and other actions of the employer, an employer's expressed hostility towards members protected by the statute together with knowledge of the employee 's military activity, and disparate treatment of certain employees compared to other employees with similar work records or offenses. In determining whether the employee has proven that his protected status or activity was part of the motivation for the agency's conduct, all record evidence may be considered, including the agency's explanation for the actions taken.[237]

USERRA discrimination cases may refer to hostility towards an individual based on his or her service as "animus," and find that the animus is a motive to discriminate. Discrimination can be found even when animus is not the only motivating factor. The test is often referred to as the "but for" test. Once animus is proven, the adjudicator must ask, if not for the animus, what would have happened? [238]

In USERRA discrimination cases, the question is not whether the official who decided to take the action had animus; rather, it is whether the agency's actions were a *result* of animus, even if that animus was held by someone else or took place at a different point in the process.[239]

In *Staub v. Proctor Hospital*, an individual asserted that two supervisors within the hospital influenced a manager to fire him because the supervisors objected to his absences to perform uniformed service. He did not claim that the deciding manager bore him any animus, but asserted that a corrective action notice was issued by his supervisors out of animus, and that without the notice, the deciding manager would not have later removed him for violating the notice.[240]

The case reached the Supreme Court, where the question was whether an employer could be held liable for employment discrimination under USERRA if an action was based on the discriminatory animus of an employee who influenced, but did not make, the challenged employment decision. (This is known as a "cat's paw" case, a term that comes from a fable in which a monkey convinces a cat to reach into a fire to take roasted chestnuts for them to eat.

While the cat is busy repeatedly singeing his paw with each prize, the monkey eats all of the rewards. In the end, the monkey is fed but the cat has nothing to show for his efforts except a burned paw.)[241]

The Court determined that, "if a supervisor performs an act motivated by antimilitary animus that is *intended* by the supervisor to cause an adverse employment action, and if that act is a proximate cause of the ultimate employment action, then the employer is liable under USERRA."[242]

Proximate cause in this context means that there is a direct relationship between the alleged animus by an official and the alleged employment action. There is no proximate cause if the link is indirect, remote, or completely contingent on other factors.[243]

In *Staub*, the court held that there was evidence that antimilitary animus caused the issuance of a corrective action notice and that non-compliance with that notice caused the removal. It held that a reasonable jury could infer that those with the animus intended the removal and that therefore the hospital could be held liable for a USERRA violation.[244]

This case demonstrates one of many reasons why it is so important for agencies to ensure that all of their employees avoid discriminatory and retaliatory conduct, including but not limited to discrimination based on military service. It is not enough to have deciding officials who respect military service if the system permits antimilitary animus at lower levels that influence the decision-makers. Agencies have a responsibility to keep personnel actions clean of animus at all stages. Otherwise, the "cat's paw" will still get burned, and the agency will still be liable.[245]

Because the intent to discriminate can be challenging to prove, cases often come down to what a witness claims someone else said or did.[246] In such cases, the adjudicator must make a credibility determination. When assessing credibility, an important factor is whether the testimony is supported or contradicted by other evidence.[247]

Witness testimony can be sufficient evidence; however, a witness is more likely to be found credible if there is additional evidence to support that witness's assertions.[248] For this reason, parties may find it useful to keep copies of important documents to produce later, should it become necessary. For agencies, this may include documentation of poor performance or conduct issues unrelated to military service. For appellants, it may include documentation to show that the conduct or performance was approved, to help establish that allegations of performance or conduct issues are a mere pretext for discrimination.

Agency Allegations of Conduct or Performance Issues

Nothing in USERRA requires an agency to disregard misconduct or performance issues.[249] For example, in *Strausbaugh v. Government Printing Office*, the appellant was a probationary employee on a pass during his active military duty status with the U.S. Air Force Reserves. During a hurricane, he requested permission to bring his small child to the agency's facility. The appellant asserted that he had permission, while the supervisor asserted that he expressly and repeatedly denied the appellant's request and that the appellant disobeyed an order to not bring the child. The Board found the agency's witnesses more credible and held that despite the fact that the conduct at issue occurred while the appellant was in an active military status, the reason for the action was his conduct and not antimilitary animus. The appellant's request for relief was therefore denied.[250]

In *McMillan v. Department of Justice*, the appellant was an Army reserve officer as well as a special agent with the Drug Enforcement Administration (DEA) on a tour of duty in

Peru, South America. There was allegedly some conflict between the agency and the appellant arising from the appellant attempting to represent DEA while with the Army and to use Army information in his DEA work. The question was whether the agency's decision to deny the appellant's request for an extension of his civilian tour of duty in Peru was motivated by an antimilitary animus or whether it was a result of the appellant's failure to meet the office's desired goals in terms of seizures, arrests, and informant recruitment. [251]

The AJ determined that the appellant had not shown that the denial of the tour extension was the result of discrimination. On petition for review, the Board held that USERRA should be read to prohibit adverse employment actions based on the content and performance of *any* military assignment, general or specific. Thus, *if the appellant was acting on orders from his military supervisors* when he conflated the two jobs, he could not be punished for it by his civilian supervisors.[252]

However, the Board also noted that USERRA protections are dependent upon an employee's compliance with the reasonable and ordinarily accepted standards of personal conduct and performance expected from all civilian employees. The Board emphasized that its holding should not be read to imply that USERRA prohibits an employer from considering events which occur during a period of service but do not constitute performance of military duty. Nor does USERRA prohibit an employer from taking action against an employee for gratuitous misconduct in the course of performing military duties.[253]

Thus, if the appellant's military orders did not require his actions and his civilian supervisors were opposed to it, his actions could not be protected under USERRA. The Board remanded the case to the AJ to make the necessary credibility determinations regarding precisely what occurred and why.[254]

Department of Labor Role in USERRA Claims

As stated previously, VEOA requires that a complaint be filed with DOL before an appeal may be filed with the Board. However, in a USERRA case, the appellant may file a complaint with DOL or file directly with the Board without seeking assistance from DOL.[255] But, if the appellant opts to file with DOL for a USERRA claim, the appellant must exhaust that remedy before filing a USERRA claim with MSPB.[256]

USERRA also differs from VEOA in that USERRA does not provide for exhaustion of the complaint before DOL as a matter of time; rather, it requires notification from DOL that the Secretary of Labor's efforts did not resolve the appellant's complaint. Thus, if the appellant opts to seek help from DOL, the Board does not acquire jurisdiction over the USERRA claim until the appellant receives the required notification from DOL.[257]

No Deadlines to File USERRA Claims with MSPB, But Laches May Apply

Unlike VEOA, USERRA does not contain a specific time limit to file an appeal. However, the Board has acknowledged that the "doctrine of laches" may apply as a defense to a USERRA claim.[258] Under laches, an unreasonable delay in pursuing a right or a claim can result in the dismissal of the claim by the adjudicating body, even if there is no statutory deadline to file the claim. The idea behind laches is that the passage of time tends to result in the destruction of evidence or loss of witness testimony, putting the defense in an unfair position.[259] The party asserting laches must prove both: (1) an unreasonable delay by the opposing party; and (2) prejudice (meaning that the ability to mount a defense was somehow harmed by the delay).[260]

For example, in *Johnson v. U.S. Postal Service*, the appellant was on a temporary promotion in 2003 when he was called for active duty. While on active duty, he applied to be permanently promoted to the position he temporarily held, but he was not selected. When he returned from military service later in 2003, he was returned to his permanent position, and voluntarily retired within a year. In 2011, the appellant filed a USERRA appeal of his non-selection, asserting that he was not promoted in 2003 because of discrimination regarding his military service. He also asserted that he had just learned of his right to appeal the events of 2003. [261]

The agency moved to dismiss the appeal on the grounds that the officials involved in the 2003 decision had since retired and it could not find its records regarding the action, likely because its policy was to retain such records for only 5 years. [262]

The Board held that if the appellant believed for 8 years that he had been discriminated against, it was unreasonable for him to wait that long without trying to determine what his appeal rights might be. Furthermore, as the appellant had not informed the agency that he felt discriminated against, the agency was not obligated to tell him of his USERRA rights. Thus, the Board found that the delay was unreasonable. [263]

The Board also held that, although the retirement of officials does not alone establish prejudice (particularly if the witness (es) can be located), the combination of the retirements, the deleterious effect of 8 years on memories, and the likelihood that the records had been destroyed in the normal course of business was sufficient to establish prejudice. Accordingly, the appeal was dismissed as barred by the doctrine of laches.[264]

Because USERRA does not have a specific filing deadline, it is possible to file a timely USERRA claim after the deadline to file other claims has passed. As mentioned in the introduction, if an individual has an otherwise appealable action (such as a removal) and asserts that it occurred because of discrimination based on military service, it will be processed as an affirmative defense for the adverse action case. However, if the appellant's adverse action appeal is untimely or not within the Board's adverse action jurisdiction, the Board may still consider his USERRA claim as a separate appeal.[265]

For example, in *Brown v. U.S. Postal Service*, the appellant asserted that his removal was the result of agency actions that were designed to "get rid of him" before he could be called to serve in the Navy. The appellant's adverse action appeal to MSPB was untimely filed without good cause shown for the delay. Nevertheless, the Board noted that the appellant's assertions could constitute a USERRA appeal and that such an appeal would be timely filed.[266]

USERRA's substantive provisions do not apply retroactively, meaning that if a person did not have a particular right prior to USERRA, then the individual cannot assert a violation of the right through USERRA redress proceedings. But, where a governmental action violated a veterans' protection statute *in effect at the time the conduct occurred*, the Board has jurisdiction under USERRA to adjudicate claims arising from that past violation, regardless of whether it occurred before or after USERRA's enactment. This, combined with the lack of a deadline to file, can result in MSPB jurisdiction over events that are several years old,[267] although laches may result in a dismissal of the claim.[268]

Standing to File a USERRA Claim

As explained earlier, to pursue a claim before MSPB, the party must have "standing"—meaning that the law intended that the party should be able to bring the case.[269] Typically, when appearing before MSPB, the party filing the appeal is a person negatively affected by the decision of an employer or potential employer. The person may appear *pro se* (representing himself or herself) or use another person as a representative, such as a union representative or private -sector attorney.[270] However, USERRA provides that OSC may appear on behalf of, and act as attorney for, the person complaining of a violation of his rights under USERRA and explicitly states that OSC may "initiate an action regarding such complaint before the Merit Systems Protection Board."[271]

The ability of OSC to pursue a claim on behalf of an individual under USERRA is an important distinction, because OSC is expressly not permitted to file a complaint for corrective action under VEOA. OSC has the authority to seek corrective action for most PPPs. The VEOA statute created a new PPP, numbered (b)(11), prohibiting a knowing violation of preference rights. Yet, the statute also stated that "[n]ot withstanding any other provision of this title, no authority to or der corrective action shall be available in connection with a prohibited personnel practice described in subsection (b)(11)." VEOA is in title 5, as is OSC's authority to seek corrective actions, while USERRA is in title 38.[272] Thus, the ability of OSC to intercede on an individual 's behalf is dependent upon which statute (VEOA or USERRA) is being used to pursue the claim.

An "Employer" for Purposes of USERRA Jurisdiction

As with VEOA, while USERRA is read broadly, the Board will not have jurisdiction over an employer when the law specifically excludes the employer from the Board's jurisdiction.

The USERRA statute specifically excludes the Board from having jurisdiction over "the Federal Bureau of Investigation, the Central Intelligence Agency, the Defense Intelligence Agency, the National Geospatial-Intelligence Agency, the National Security Agency, the Office of the Director of National Intelligence, and the National Reconnaissance Office[.]"[273]

Other agencies may also be excluded from the Board's USERRA jurisdiction. In *Conyers v. Department of Transportation*, an individual who sought employment as a Supervisory Transportation Security Screener with the TSA filed an appeal with MSPB asserting jurisdiction under several different statutes, including USERRA. The Board held that under the law that created the TSA, Congress specifically excluded TSA screener positions from MSPB's USERRA jurisdiction. The appellant appealed this finding to the Federal Circuit, which reached the same conclusion, that MPSB's jurisdiction is limited to that granted to it by law, and the law specifically excluded the screeners from MSPB's jurisdiction for purposes of USERRA.[274]

USERRA differs from VEOA regarding how the entity being sued is defined. VEOA focuses on the actions of an "agency," which the law does not define, while USERRA is about an "employer," which the law defines in great detail.[275] As explained below, the language used to define employer in the USERRA statute has created a situation where the Board can have USERRA jurisdiction for cases involving individuals who are not paid directly by the Government, even though it lacks jurisdiction over the private sector employer.[276]

Agencies often use contract employees to accomplish work for which the agency is responsible.[277] In *Silva v. Department of Homeland Security*, the appellant was employed by a contractor, performed work for Customs and Border Patrol (CBP) within DHS under the contract, left for military service, was replaced by someone else, returned from military service, and requested a return to his former position serving DHS under the contract between DHS and the private sector company. The contractor did not return the appellant to the position, allegedly at DHS's request.[278]

The Board noted that in the private sector, under USERRA, an employer includes not only the entity that pays an employee's salary or wages, but also anyone to whom an employer has delegated employment-related responsibilities. When the authority over the individual is shared in this manner, both employers share responsibility for compliance with USERRA. The Board recognized the principle that USERRA should be broadly construed and any "interpretive doubt" should be "resolved in the veteran's favor."[279] The Board therefore held that a Federal agency could be considered the employer over a contractor's employee under the right conditions. Because the appellant had made a nonfrivolous allegation that DHS exercised control over his reemployment to such an extent that it should be considered his "employer" under USERRA, and the Board had USERRA jurisdiction over CBP within DHS, the Board held that it had jurisdiction over the appellant's USERRA claim against DHS, even though the appellant's position was not in the civil service. However, the Board lacked jurisdiction over the appellant's claim against the contractor.[280]

The Right to a USERR a Hearing

As explained earlier, a VEOA appellant is not automatically entitled to a hearing regarding either jurisdiction or the merits of a VEOA appeal.[281] In contrast, under USERRA, once an appellant has established Board jurisdiction, he has an unconditional right to a hearing on the merits of his USERRA claim.[282]

However, that right to a hearing attaches only after jurisdiction has been found. For example, in *Downs v. Department of Veterans Affairs*, the appellant was discharged from military service under other than honorable conditions. This deprived the Board of USERRA jurisdiction, even though the appellant made a nonfrivolous allegation under USERRA and therefore met the *general* USERRA jurisdictional test. The Board held that the unconditional right to a hearing does not attach until after jurisdiction has been established, and that since jurisdiction was lacking, a hearing would not be held.[283] This is consistent with the point made by our reviewing court mentioned in the introduction: "When jurisdiction is lacking, the only function remaining to the court is that of announcing the fact and dismissing the cause."[284]

USERRA Relief

USERRA and VEOA have similar provisions instructing the Board on the relief to grant if a violation has been found. Under 5 U.S.C. § 3330c (VEOA), if the Board finds a violation occurred, it will "order the agency to comply with such provisions and award compensation for any loss of w ages or benefits suffered by the individual by reason of the violation involved." Under 38 U.S.C. § 4324 (USERRA), if the Board finds a violation occurred, it will "enter an order requiring the agency or Office [of Personnel Management] to comply with such provisions and to compensate such person for any loss of wages or benefits suffered by such person by reason of such lack of compliance."

As explained earlier, under VEOA, if a candidate's rights were violated with respect to a recruitment action, the proper remedy will usually be to reconstruct the action. The appellant is not entitled to be selected —only to have the process reconstructed with the laws and regulations followed properly.[285] Similarly, in a USERRA case involving non-selection, the fact that a USERRA violation occurred does not automatically require an agency to give the appellant the position. As with VEOA, the action must be reconstructed, and selection and an award for "lost wages"[286] become issues only if the appellant would have gotten t he position in a properly constructed p rocess.[287]

The specific relief granted for a particular USERRA violation will depend on what needs to be remedied (for example, restoration of leave that was denied, reemployment in the position that was previously held, or promotion due to the escalator principle). However, the core principle is the same —to put the appellant where he or she would have been if not for the violation.[288]

Section Nine: Conclusion

The laws for veterans' redress are complicated, especially VEOA because of the way in which it interacts with so many other parts of the civil service. Vague and undefined terms in 5 U.S.C. § 3330a and the statute's applicability to "any statute or regulation relating to veterans' preference" have resulted in an extensive body of case law that may be confusing for the average veteran or preference eligible. It also has resulted in a system with so many rules that OPM has, at times, not kept up with necessary changes. The USERRA statute, while far more extensive, may be easier to use because its terms and provisions are more tightly defined and it has fewer moving parts.

USERRA and VEOA share some common elements, but differ in several important respects. In particular, VEOA requires that an appellant exhaust his or her administrative remedies and adhere to strict deadlines in the absence of an exception known as equitable tolling. In contrast, USERRA does not require an exhaustion of administrative remedies and does not have strict deadlines for filing. VEO A does not have a guaranteed right to a hearing. USERRA has a right to a hearing upon request once jurisdiction is established. Under VEOA, an appellant has the burden of proof on the merits. Under USERRA, the party with the burden of proof depends on whether the claim alleges discrimination or a failure to reemploy.

The complexity of the systems of rights and of redresses for veterans, preference eligibles, and service members create s a burden on the individuals that the laws were meant to help, particularly those who seek to navigate the process without the assistance of a legal expert. While we hope this report will be useful to veterans, preference eligibles, and service members, these individuals could all benefit from a system that requires less ex planation and is easier for agencies and individuals to understand.

A violation of a veteran 's rights—whether adjudicated under USERRA or VEOA—can have serious consequences for a veteran who must wait for the redress procedures in order to get what he or she was entitled to receive— especially if it means a lengthy period of no pay where a salary should have occurred. A violation can also have serious consequences for an innocent bystander who may need to be removed from a position while the personnel action in question is reconstructed. Everyone benefits when employers adhere to the laws and regulations pertaining to veterans and promptly take corrective action in response to any violation of those requirements.

APPENDIX A: DEFINITION OF VETERAN AND RELATED TERMS (5 U.S.C. § 2108)

For the purpose of this title —

(1) "veteran" means an individual who —

(A) served on active duty in the armed forces during a war, in a campaign or expedition for which a campaign badge has been authorized, or during the period beginning April 28, 1952, and ending July 1, 1955;

(B) served on active duty as defined by section 101 (21) of title 38 at any time in the armed forces for a period of more than 180 consecutive days any part of which occurred after January 31, 1955, an d before October 15, 1976, not including service under section 12103 (d) of title 10 pursuant to an enlistment in the Army National Guard or the Air National Guard or as a Reserve for service in the Army Reserve, Navy Reserve, Air Force Reserve, Marine Corps Reserve, or Coast Guard Reserve;

(C) served on active duty as defined by section 101 (21) of title 38 in the armed forces during the period beginning on August 2, 1990, and ending on January 2, 1992; or

(D) served on active duty as defined by section 101 (21) of title 38 at any time in the armed forces for a period of more than 180 consecutive days any part of which occurred during the period beginning on September 11, 2001, and ending on the date prescribed by Presidential proclamation or by law as the last date of Operation Iraqi Freedom;

and, except as provided under section 2108a, who has been discharged or released from active duty in the armed forces under honorable conditions;

(2) "disabled veteran" means an individual who has served on active duty in the armed forces, (except as provided under section 2108a) has been separated therefrom under honorable conditions, and has established the present existence of a service - connected disability or is receiving compensation, disability retirement benefits, or pension because of a public statute administered by the Department of Veterans Affairs or a military department;

(3) "preference eligible " means, except as provided in paragraph (4) of this section or section 2108a (c)—

(A) a veteran as defined by paragraph (1)(A) of this section;

(B) a veteran as defined by paragraph (1)(B), (C), or (D) of this section;
(C) a disabled veteran;
(D) the unmarried widow or widower of a veteran as defined by paragraph (1)(A) of this section;
(E) the wife or husband of a service-connected disabled veteran if the veteran has been unable to qualify for any appointment in the civil service or in the government of the District of Columbia;
(F) the mother of an individual who lost his life under honorable conditions while serving in the armed forces during a period named by paragraph (1)(A) of this section, if—
(i) her husband is totally and permanently disabled;
(ii) she is widowed, divorced, or separated from the father and has not remarried; or
(iii) she has remarried but is widowed, divorced, or legally separated from her husband when preference is claimed;
(G) the mother of a service-connected permanently and totally disabled veteran, if—
(i) her husband is totally and permanently disabled;
(ii) she is widowed, divorced, or separated from the father and has not remarried; or
(iii) she has remarried but is widowed, divorced, or legally separated from her husband when preference is claimed; and
(H) a veteran who was discharged or released from a period of active duty by reason of a sole survivorship discharge (as that term is defined in section 1174 (i) of title 10);

but does not include applicants for, or members of, the Senior Executive Service, the Defense Intelligence Senior Executive Service, the Senior Cryptologic Executive Service, or the Federal Bureau of Investigation and Drug Enforcement Administration Senior Executive Service;

(4) except for the purposes of chapters 43 and 75 of this title, "preference eligible" does not include a retired member of the armed forces unless—
(A) the individual is a disabled veteran; or
(B) the individual retired below the rank of major or its equivalent; and

(5) "retired member of the armed forces" means a member or former member of the armed forces who is entitled, under statute, to retired, retirement, or retainer pay on account of service as a member.

APPENDIX B: COMPARING VEOA AND USERRA

The table below is offered as a quick reference guide to illustrate some similarities and differences between VEOA and USER RA but is not a substitute for consulting pertinent cases, statutes, or regulations. Similarities have a white background; differences have a light colored background.

	VEOA	USERRA
Level of Statutory Detail	The statutory language is relatively brief and occasionally vague, resulting in both the Board and the Federal Circuit defining many of its terms in case law.	The statutory language is extensive, detailed, and often self-explanatory.
Applicability	VEOA applies only to the Federal Government. There is no private sector equivalent.	USERRA rights apply to the private and public sectors, including the Federal Government, but the systems for redress are different.
Defining the Individuals	The individual must be a veteran as described in 5 U.S.C. § 3304(f)(1) or be a preference eligible.[289]	The individual must be a person who is a member of, applies to be a member of, performs, has performed, applies to perform, or has an obligation to perform service in a uniformed service.[290]
Defining the Employer	The employing entity is "an agency," which is not defined in statute.	The employer is a broad category defined in statute.
Scope of MSPB Jurisdiction	MSPB can lack jurisdiction over certain Federal employers.[291]	MSPB can lack jurisdiction over certain Federal employers.[292]
Establishing MSPB Jurisdiction	Jurisdiction can be established through a non-frivolous assertion.[293]	Jurisdiction can be established through a non -frivolous assertion.[294]
Affirmative Defense in an Otherwise Appealable Action	VEOA rights can be raised as an affirmative defense in an action that is otherwise appealable to MSPB.[295]	USERRA rights can be raised as an affirmative defense in an action that is otherwise appealable to MSPB.[296]
Filing with DOL	An individual must (in the absence of equitable tolling) file a complaint with DOL within 60 days after the date of the alleged violation.[297]	An individual has the option to file a complaint with DOL but can seek redress from the Board without first filing a complaint with DOL.[298]
Exhaustion of Remedies at DOL	If DOL has not resolved the complaint after 60 days, an individual may file an appeal with MSPB after notifying DOL of the intent to file with MSPB.[299]	If the individual opted to file a complaint with DOL, the individual must wait for the complaint to be resolved. The passage of time does not enable the individual to file with MPSB. [300]
Deadlines to File	In the absence of equitable tolling, the appellant cannot file: (1) before the 61st day after the date on which the complaint is filed; or (2) later than 15 days after the date on which the individual receives written notification from the Secretary that the matter is closed.[301]	USERRA does not contain a deadline to file, but laches may apply.[302]

(Continued)

	VEOA	USERRA
Burden of Proof	The appellant must prove the merits of the case by preponderant evidence.[303]	In a *discrimination* case, the appellant must prove the merits of the case by preponderant evidence. If that burden is met, the agency may avoid relief by showing by preponderant evidence that it would have taken the same action even in the absence of the improper motivation. [304] In a *reemployment* case, the agency bears the burden of proving, by preponderant evidence, that it met its statutory obligations to reemploy the individual with the appropriate level of career advancement and benefits.[305]
OSC Role	OSC cannot pursue corrective action on the individual 's behalf.[306]	OSC may appear on the appellant's behalf.[307]
Right to a Hearing	No right to a hearing.[308]	Right to a hearing.[309]
Available Remedies	If a violation is found, the agency will be required to comply with the violated provisions and award compensation for any loss of wages or benefits suffered as a result of the violation.[310]	If a violation is found, the agency will be required to comply with the violated provisions and award compensation for any loss of wages or benefits suffered as a result of the violation.[311]

APPENDIX C: EQUITABLE TOLLING

The concept behind equitable tolling is that a party should not be deprived of the ability to pursue a claim because of a statute of limitations if the party, despite diligent efforts, was unaware of the injury.[312] The Supreme Court has extended this concept to suits against the Government, provided that there is not "good reason to believe that Congress did *not* want the equitable tolling doctrine to apply."[313] This is known as the *Irwin* presumption, named for the case in which the Supreme Court established the concept.[314]

In *United States v. Brockamp*, a case involving tax refunds, the Court noted that the language in the statute at issue "sets forth its time limitations in unusually emphatic form." Accordingly, the Court found that the timing requirements in the statute were not subject to equitable tolling —meaning they could not be waived.[315]

The VEOA statute also contains timing requirements for which strong language is used, such as stating that "in no event" may an appeal be brought to MPSB if it is filed too soon or too late.[316] There is also a requirement that a complaint with DOL "must be filed within 60 days."[317] However, as explained below, equitable tolling does apply to VEOA.

In *Kirkendall v. Department of the Army*, the Federal Circuit was presented with a case in which an appellant missed the deadline to file his VEOA complaint with DOL. The question was whether the language in the statute, stating the complaint "must be filed" by a deadline, was intended by Congress to mean "must be filed unless we would usually allow the deadline to be missed for this particular reason;" and whether "in no event" could the appeal deadline be missed was intended to mean "in no event other than events we usually allow when the Government is being sued."[318]

The Federal Circuit held that VEOA was the type of statute for which equitable tolling is appropriate. It particularly noted the canon that veterans' benefits statutes should be construed in the veteran's favor.[319] Therefore, the VEOA deadlines for filing with DOL or with the Board can be waived if the Board finds that the appellant has actively pursued his judicial remedies by filing a defective pleading during the statutory period, or where he has been induced or tricked by his adversary's misconduct into allowing the filing deadline to pass.[320]

APPENDIX D: VETERANS EMPLOYMENT OPPORTUNITIES ACT OF 1998 REDRESS STATUTE (5 U.S.C. § 3330A-C)

5 U.S.C. § 3330a

(a)

(1)

(A) A preference eligible who alleges that an agency has violated such individual's rights under any statute or regulation relating to veterans' preference may file a complaint with the Secretary of Labor.

(B) A veteran described in section 3304 (f)(1) who alleges that an agency has violated such section with respect to such veteran may file a complaint with the Secretary of Labor.

(2)

(A) A complaint under this subsection must be filed within 60 days after the date of the alleged violation.

(B) Such complaint shall be in writing, be in such form as the Secretary may prescribe, specify the agency against which the complaint is filed, and contain a summary of the allegations that form the basis for the complaint.

(3) The Secretary shall, upon request, provide technical assistance to a potential complainant with respect to a complaint under this subsection.

(b)

(1) The Secretary of Labor shall investigate each complaint under subsection (a).

(2) In carrying out any investigation under this subsection, the Secretary's duly authorized representatives shall, at all reasonable times, have reasonable access to, for purposes of examination, and the right to copy and receive, any documents of any person or agency that the Secretary considers relevant to the investigation.

(3) In carrying out any investigation under this subsection, the Secretary may require by subpoena the attendance and testimony of witnesses and the production of

documents relating to any matter under investigation. In case of disobedience of the subpoena or contumacy and on request of the Secretary, the Attorney General may apply to any district court of the United States in whose jurisdiction such disobedience or contumacy occurs for an order enforcing the subpoena.

(4) Upon application, the district courts of the United States shall have jurisdiction to issue writs commanding any person or agency to comply with the subpoena of the Secretary or to comply with any order of the Secretary made pursuant to a lawful investigation under this subsection and the district courts shall have jurisdiction to punish failure to obey a subpoena or other lawful order of the Secretary as a contempt of court.

(c)

(1)

(A) If the Secretary of Labor determines as a result of an investigation under subsection (b) that the action alleged in a complaint under subsection (a) occurred, the Secretary shall attempt to resolve the complaint by making reasonable efforts to ensure that the agency specified in the complaint complies with applicable provisions of statute or regulation relating to veterans' preference.

(B) The Secretary of Labor shall make determinations referred to in subparagraph (A) based on a preponderance of the evidence.

(2) If the efforts of the Secretary under subsection (b) with respect to a complaint under subsection (a) do not result in the resolution of the complaint, the Secretary shall notify the person who submitted the complaint, in writing, of the results of the Secretary's investigation under subsection (b).

(d)

(1) If the Secretary of Labor is unable to resolve a complaint under subsection (a) within 60 days after the date on which it is filed, the complainant may elect to appeal the alleged violation to the Merit Systems Protection Board in accordance with such procedures as the Merit Systems Protection Board shall prescribe, except that in no event may any such appeal be brought —

(A) before the 61st day after the date on which the complaint is filed; or

(B) later than 15 days after the date on which the complainant receives written notification from the Secretary under subsection (c)(2).

(2) An appeal under this subsection may not be brought unless—

(A) the complainant first provides written notification to the Secretary of such complainant's intention to bring such appeal; and

(B) appropriate evidence of compliance with subparagraph (A) is included (in such form and manner as the Merit Systems Protection Board may prescribe) with the notice of appeal under this subsection.

(3) Upon receiving notification under paragraph (2)(A), the Secretary shall not continue to investigate or further attempt to resolve the complaint to which the notification relates.

(e)

(1) This section shall not be construed to prohibit a preference eligible from appealing directly to the Merit Systems Protection Board from any action which

is appealable to the Board under any other law, rule, or regulation, in lieu of administrative redress under this section.

(2) A preference eligible may not pursue redress for an alleged violation described in subsection (a) under this section at the same time the preference eligible pursues redress for such violation under any other law, rule, or regulation.

5 U.S.C. § 3330b

(a) In lieu of continuing the administrative redress procedure provided under section 3330a (d), a preference eligible, or a veteran described by section 3330a (a)(1)(B) with respect to a violation described by such section, may elect, in accordance with this section, to terminate those administrative proceedings and file an action with the appropriate United States district court not later than 60 days after the date of the election.

(b) An election under this section may not be made —

(1) before the 121st day after the date on which the appeal is filed with the Merit Systems Protection Board under section 3330a (d); or

(2) after the Merit Systems Protection Board has issued a judicially reviewable decision on the merits of the appeal.

(c) An election under this section shall be made, in writing, in such form and manner as the Merit Systems Protection Board shall by regulation prescribe. The election shall be effective as of the date on which it is received, and the administrative proceeding to which it relates shall terminate immediately upon the receipt of such election.

5 U.S.C. § 3330c

(a) If the Merit Systems Protection Board (in a proceeding under section 3330a) or a court (in a proceeding under section 3330b) determines that an agency has violated a right described in section 3330a, the Board or court (as the case may be) shall order the agency to comply with such provisions and award compensation for any loss of wages or benefits suffered by the individual by reason of the violation involved. If the Board or court determines that such violation was willful, it shall award an amount equal to backpay as liquidated damages.

(b) A preference eligible who prevails in an action under section 3330a or 33 30b shall be awarded reasonable attorney fees, expert witness fees, and other litigation expenses.

APPENDIX E: VETERANS EMPLOYMENT OPPORTUNITIES ACT OF 1998 OPPORTUNITY TO COMPETE STATUTE (5 U.S.C. § 3304(F))

(1) Preference eligibles or veterans who have been separated from the armed forces under honorable conditions after 3 years or more of active service may not be denied

the opportunity to compete for vacant positions for which the agency making the announcement will accept applications from individuals outside its own workforce under merit promotion procedures.

(2) If selected, a preference eligible or veteran described in paragraph (1) shall receive a career or career-conditional appointment, as appropriate.

(3) This subsection shall not be construe d to confer an entitlement to veterans' preference that is not otherwise required by law.

(4) The area of consideration for all merit promotion announcements which include consideration of individuals of the Federal workforce shall indicate that preference eligibles and veterans who have been separated from the armed forces under honorable conditions after 3 years or more of active service are eligible to apply. The announcements shall be publicized in accordance with section 3327.

(5) The Office of Personnel Management shall prescribe regulations necessary for the administration of this subsection. The regulations shall ensure that an individual who has completed an initial tour of active duty is not excluded from the application of this subsection because of having been released from such tour of duty shortly before completing 3 years of active service, having been honorably released from such duty.

Comparing VEOA and USERRA

The table below is offered as a quick reference guide to illustrate some similarities and differences between VEOA and USERRA but is not a substitute for consulting pertinent cases, statutes, or regulations. Similarities have a white background; differences have a light colored background.

	VEOA	USERRA
Level of Statutory Detail	The statutory language is relatively brief and occasionally vague, resulting in both the Board and the Federal Circuit defining many of its terms in case law.	The statutory language is extensive, detailed, and often self-explanatory.
Applicability	VEOA applies only to the Federal Government. There is no private sector equivalent.	USERRA rights apply to the private and public sectors, including the Federal Government, but the systems for redress are different.
Defining the Individuals	The individual must be a veteran as described in 5 U.S.C. § 3304(f) (1) or be a preference eligible.[1]	The individual must be a person who is a member of, applies to be a member of, performs, has performed, applies to perform, or has an obligation to perform service in a uniformed service.[2]
Defining the Employer	The employing entity is "an agency, " which is not defined in statute.	The employer is a broad category defined in statute.
Scope of MSPB Jurisdiction	MSPB can lack jurisdiction over certain Federal employers.[3]	MSPB can lack jurisdiction over certain Federal employers.[4]
Establishing MSPB Jurisdiction	Jurisdiction can be established through a non-frivolous assertion.[5]	Jurisdiction can be established through a non-frivolous assertion.[6]

	VEOA	USERRA
Affirmative Defense in an Otherwise Appealable Action	VEOA rights can be raised as an affirmative defense in an action that is otherwise appealable to MSPB.[7]	USERRA rights can be raised as an affirmative defense in an action that is otherwise appealable to MSPB.[8]
Filing with DOL	An individual must (in the absence of equitable tolling) file a complaint with DOL within 60 days after the date of the alleged violation.[9]	An individual has the option to file a complaint with DOL but can seek redress from the Board without first filing a complaint with DOL.[10]
Exhaustion of Remedies at DOL	If DOL has not resolved the complaint after 60 days, an individual may file an appeal with MSPB after notifying DOL of the intent to file with MSPB.[11]	If the individual opted to file a complaint with DOL, the individual must wait for the complaint to be resolved. The passage of time does not enable the individual to file with MPSB.[12]
Deadlines to File	In the absence of equitable tolling, the appellant cannot file: (1) before the 61st day after the date on which the complaint is filed; or (2) later than 15 days after the date on which the individual receives written notification from the Secretary that the matter is closed.[13]	USERRA does not contain a deadline to file, but laches may apply.[14]
Burden of Proof	The appellant must prove the merits of the case by preponderant evidence.[15]	In a *discrimination* case, the appellant must prove the merits of the case by preponderant evidence. If that burden is met, the agency may avoid relief by showing by preponderant evidence that it would have taken the same action even in the absence of the improper motivation.[16] In a *reemployment* case, the agency bears the burden of proving, by preponderant evidence, that it met its statutory obligations to reemploy the individual with the appropriate level of career advancement and benefits.[17]
OSC Role	OSC cannot pursue corrective action on the individual's behalf. [18]	OSC may appear on the appellant's behalf. [19]
Right to a Hearing	No right to a hearing. [20]	Right to a hearing. [21]
Available Remedies	If a violation is found, the agency will be required to comply with the violated provisions and award compensation for any loss of wages or benefits suffered as a result of the violation.[22]	If a violation is found, the agency will be required to comply with the violated provisions and award compensation for any loss of wages or benefits suffered as a result of the violation. [23]

[1] 5 U.S.C. § 3330a(a)(1).

[2] 38 U.S.C. § 4311(a). *See Lourens v. Merit Systems Protection Board*, 193 F.3d 1369, 1371 (Fed. Cir. 1999) (holding that the Board did not have USERRA jurisdiction over claims by a widow with

derived preference eligibility when the widow had not been a member of —or applicant to —a uniformed service).

[3] *Morse v. Merit Systems Protection Board*, 621 F.3d 1346, 1348 -51 (Fed. Cir. 2010) (holding that the Board lacks jurisdiction over VEOA appeals from TSA applicants); *see Belhumeur v. Department of Transportation*, 104 M.S.P.R. 408, 8 (2007) (holding that the Board lacks jurisdiction over VEOA appeals from FAA employees and applicants).

[4] *Conyers v. Merit Systems Protection Board*, 388 F.3d 1380, 1381 -83 (Fed. Cir. 2004); *see Spain v. Department of Homeland Security*, 99 M.S.P.R. 529, 8-9 (2005) (applying *Conyers* to find that the Board lacked USERRA jurisdiction over termination and failure to reemploy claims). *But see Quinlan v. Department of Homeland Security*, 118 M.S.P.R. 362, 8 (2012) (finding that MSP Bhas jurisdiction over TSA reductions in grade under the language of 49 U.S.C. § 40122(g)(3)); *Aquino v. Department of Homeland Security*, 121 M.S.P.R. 35, 12 (2014) (explaining that MSPB has jurisdiction over TSA whistle blower claims under the Whistle blower Protection Enhancement Act of 2012).

[5] *Lazaro v. Department of Veterans Affairs*, 666 F.3d 1316, 1319 (Fed. Cir. 2 012); *Becker v. Department of Veterans Affairs*, 115 M.S.P.R. 409, 5 (2010).

[6] *Mims v. Social Security Administration*, 120 M.S.P.R. 213, 22 (2013); *Williams v. Department of the Air Force*, 97 M.S.P.R. 252, 10 (2004).

[7] *Aguilar v. U.S. Postal Service,* 102 M.S.P.R. 102, 8 (2006).

[8] *Aguilar v. U.S. Postal Service,* 102 M.S.P.R. 102, 8 (2006).

[9] *See Kirkendall v. Department of the Army*, 479 F.3d 830, 844 (Fed. Cir. 2007) (holding that 5 U.S.C. §§ 3330a (a)(1)(A) and 3330a(d)(1)(B) are subject to equitable tolling); 5 U.S.C. § 3330a(a)(2)(A).

[10] *Gossage v. Department of Labor*, 118 M.S.P.R. 455, 8 (2012); *Graham v. Commodity Futures Trading Commission*, 105 M.S.P.R. 392, 5 (2007).

[11] *Burroughs v. Department of the Army*, 116 M.S.P.R. 292, 8, 10 (2011); 5 U.S.C. § 3330a(d).

[12] *Gossage v. Department of Labor*, 118 M.S.P.R. 455, 8 (2012); *Graham v. Commodity Futures Trading Commission*, 105 M.S.P.R. 392, 5 (2007).

[13] 5 U.S.C. § 3330a(d)(1).

[14] *See Garcia v. Department of State*, 101 M.S.P.R. 172, 14 -17 (2006).

[15] *Lis v. U.S. Postal Service*, 113 M.S.P.R. 415, 11 (2010).

[16] *Burroughs v. Department of the Army*, 120 M.S.P.R. 392, 5 (2013); *Strausbaugh v. Government Printing Office*, 117 M.S.P.R. 566, 11 (2012).

[17] *Clavin v. U.S. Postal Service*, 99 M.S.P.R. 619, 6 (2005) (explaining that the standard for reemployment cases is derived from 5 U.S.C. § 7701(c)(2)(B)). *See* 5 U.S.C. § 7701(c)(2)(B) (stating that an agency must prove its case by preponderant evidence).

18 *See* 5 U.S.C. §§ 2302(b)(11), 2302(e)(2), 1214.

19 *Silva v. Department of Homeland Security*, 112 M.S.P.R. 362, 15, 19 (2009) (quoting 38 U.S.C. § 4324(a)(2)(A)).

20 *Compare Burroughs v. Department of the Army*, 115 M.S.P.R. 656, 8 (2011) (finding no entitlement to VEOA hearing), *with Kirkendall v. Department of the Army*, 479 F.3d 830, 844 -46 (Fed. Cir. 2007) (finding that the Boar cannot exercise discretion but rather must grant a USERRA hearing if one is requested).

[21] *Compare Burroughs v. Department of the Army*, 115 M.S.P.R. 656, 8 (2011) (finding no entitlement to VEOA hearing), *with Kirkendall v. Department of the Army*, 479 F.3d 830, 844 -46 (Fed. Cir. 2007) (finding that the Board cannot exercise discretion but rather must grant a USERRA hearing if one is requested).

[22] 5 U.S.C. § 3330c.

[23] 38 U.S.C. § 4324.

End Notes

[1] President Franklin D. Roosevelt, Letter to Re presentative Ramspeck (1944) (c ited in *Mitchell v. Cohen*, 333 U.S. 411, 419, n.12 (1948)).

[2] *See* U.S. Merit Systems Prtection Board, *Veteran Hiring in the Civil Service: Practices and Perceptions* (2014), available at www.mspb.gov/ studies.

[3] The Veterans' Benefits Improvement Act of 2004 (VBIA) (Pub.L. No. 108 -454) modified 5 U.S.C. §§ 3330a and 3330b, which contain provisions initially codified by VEOA. For a discussion of the effect of the VBIA on VEOA, *see Sty slinger v. Department of the Army*, 105 M.S.P.R. 223, 22 -30 (2007). For convenience, the statutory provisions established directly by VEOA, or in any amendment to statute s established by VEOA, are typically referred to as VEOA.

[4] *See Hilton v. S ullivan*, 334 U.S. 323, 336-37 (1948) (explaining the history and scope of the retention provisions for veterans).

[5] *Mitchell v. Cohen*, 333 U.S. 411, 418 -20 (1948).

[6] "Veterans' preference rights are defined by the Veterans' Preference Act of 1944 ("VPA"), Pub. L. No. 78–359, 58 Stat. 387 (codified at 5 U.S.C. §§ 2108, 3309 –3320), and its attendant regulations, *see* 5 C.F.R. §§ 302.101 –302.403 (2005). " *Patterson v. Department of the Interior*, 424 F.3d 1151, 1155 (Fed. Cir. 2005). "The legal basis for veterans' preference is the Veterans' Preference Ac t of 1944, as amended." U.S. Office of Personnel Management, *Guide to Processing Personnel Actions*, Chapter 7-3.

[7] Veterans Employment Opportunities Act of 1998, S. Rep. 105-340, at 15 (1998) (citing testimony by the Government Accountability Office (GAO) (then called the General Accounting Office)).

[8] Veterans Employment Opportunities Act of 1998, S. Rep. 105 -340, at 15 (1998).

[9] 5 U.S.C. § 3330a.

[10] 5 U.S.C. §§ 3304(f), 3330a.

[11] VEOA also added a new prohibited personnel practice (PPP), codified at 5 U.S.C. § 2302(b)(11), which prohibits an official involved in a personnel action from knowingly acting or knowingly failing to act if such action or lack of action violates a veterans' preference requirement.

[12] A Federal employee who believes his employer has violated USERRA may seek corrective action by filing a complaint with the Secretary of Labor through the Veterans' Employment and Training Services (VETS), or by filing an appeal directly with the Board. *Wible v. Department of the Army*, 120 M.S.P.R. 333, 12 (2013). As explained in Section Eight, *USERRA —Adjudicating Claims*, when a USERRA appellant opts to use the services of DOL, the individual must then exhaust that avenue for redress before filing an appeal with MSP B.

[13] 38 U.S.C. § 4311(a).

[14] 38 U.S.C. § 4313.

[15] *Schmittling v. Department of the Army*, 219 F.3d 1332, 1337 (Fed. Cir. 2000); *King v. Reid*, 59 F.3d 1215, 1217 (Fed. Cir. 1995).

[16] *Schmittling v. Department of the Army*, 219 F.3d 1332, 1337 (Fed. Cir. 2000) (citing *Spruill v. Merit Systems Protection Board*, 978 F.2d 679, 686 (Fed. Cir. 1992)).

[17] *Schmittling v. Department of the Army*, 219 F.3d 1332, 1337 (Fed. Cir. 2000).

[18] *Chertkov v. Office of Personnel Management*, 52 F.3d 961, 966 (Fed. Cir. 1995) (internal punctuation and citations omitted).

[19] *See, e.g., Scott v. Department of the Air Force*, 113 M.S.P.R. 434, 5 (2010) (re opening an appeal on the Board's own motion to dismiss the case for lack of jurisdiction). Case law refers to this type of motion as "*suasponte*"—meaning it was done by an adjudicator y body on its own accord without a request from a party.

[20] For one PPP, 5 U.S.C. § 2302(b)(11), OSC does not have the authority to seek corrective action. *See* 5 U.S.C. § 2302(e)(2). Section 2302(b)(11) is the PP P relating to knowing violations of veterans' preference rights. As explained in this report, individuals who believe their preference rights have been violated can seek redress under VEOA, thereby obtaining corrective action if the merits of the case are proven.

[21] *See Speker v. Office of Personnel Management*, 45 M.S.P.R. 380, 385 (1990) (explaining that a statutory deadline cannot be waived except in rare circumstances).

[22] *See* 5 C.F.R. § 1201.12 (explaining that the Board may r evoke, amend, or waive any of its regulations and a judge may, for good cause shown, waive a Board regulation unless a statute requires application of the regulation).

[23] *Compare* 5 U.S.C. § 3330a (d)(1)(B) (15 days), *with* 5 C.F.R. § 1201.22 (30 days).

[24] The Board has held that a VEOA claim should be liberally construed and an allegation, in general terms, that an appellant's veterans' preference rights were violated is sufficient to meet the requirement of a nonfrivolous allegation establishing Board jurisdiction. *Searcy v. Department of Agriculture*, 115 M.S.P.R. 260, 11 (2010); *Loggins v. U.S. Postal Service*, 112 M.S.P.R. 471, 14 (2009).

[25] *Lazaro v. Department of Veterans Affairs*, 666 F.3d 1316, 1319 (Fed. Cir. 2012) (VEOA preference rights); *Becker v. Department of Veterans Affairs*, 115 M.S.P.R. 409, 5 (2010) (VEOA veterans' right to compete); *Gossage v. Department of Labo*, 118 M.S.P.R. 455, 10 (2012) (USERRA rights).

[26] *Beyers v. Department of State*, 120 M.S.P.R. 573, 6 (2014) (VEOA); *Burroughs v. Department of the Army*, 120 M.S.P.R. 392, 5 (2013) (USERRA). The Board may consider unrebutted sworn statements as competent evidence of the matter s asserted in the statement. *Melendez v. Department of Veterans Affairs*, 73 M.S.P.R. 1, 4 (1996).

[27] *Compare Lis v. U.S. Postal Service*, 113 M.S.P.R. 415, 11 (2010) (the appellant must prove the VEOA case), *with Clavin v. U.S. Postal Service*, 99 M.S.P.R. 619, 6 (2005) (the agency has the burden of proof in a USERRA reemployment case, while there is a shifting burden for a USERRA dis crimination case).

[28] *Goldberg v. Department of Homeland Security*, 99 M.S.P.R. 660, 10, n.2 (2005).

[29] *See, e.g., Elliott v. Department of the Air Force*, 102 M.S.P.R. 364, 8-9 (2006) (explaining that the Board had jurisdiction because the appellant made the required nonfrivolous allegations, but that relief must be denied because the evidence showed his preference rights were not violated).

[30] *Nahoney v. U.S. Postal Service,* 112 M.S.P.R. 93, 16 (2009); *Aguilar v. U.S. Postal Service,* 102 M.S.P.R. 102, 8 (2006). An affirmative defense is when an employee claims that an action should not be sustained because: (1) there was a harmful error in the agency's procedures for taking the action; (2) the decision was based on a PP P (such as whistle blower retaliation); or (3) the decision was otherwise not in accordance with the law. 5 U.S.C. § 7701(c)(2).

Affirmative defenses involving veterans' rights are relatively rare. For example, of the 5 C.F.R. Part 752 cases closed by MSP B between FY 2008 and F Y 2013, less than 2 percent involved an affirmative defense under USERRA and less than 2 percent involved an affirmative defense under VEOA.

[31] *Nahoney v. U.S. Postal Service,* 112 M.S.P.R. 93, 16 (2009); *Aguilar v. U.S. Postal Service,* 102 M.S.P.R. 102, 8 (2006).

[32] 5 U.S.C. § 1204(a)(3).

[33] Between F Y 2008 and F Y 2013, the Board closed 2,766 cases involving a USERRA claim and 1,625 cases involving a VEOA claim. Of these, only 195 cases involved both a USERRA and a VEOA claim.

[34] 5 U.S.C. § 1204(h).

[35] A mandatory decision is one that is binding on the Board, such as a decision by the Federal Circuit or the Supreme Court. Decisions by other courts may inform deliberations by the Board and those decisions may be followed if the Board finds their logic persuasive. However, such holdings are not binding and the Board may hold differently if it see s fit. *See Fairall v. Veterans Administration*, 33 M.S.P.R. 33, 39, *aff'd*, 844 F.2d 775 (Fed. Cir. 1987).

[36] 38 U.S.C. § 4303(4)-(6).

[37] *Compare* 38 U.S.C. § 4323 (private and state employer s), *with* 38 U.S.C. § 4324 (Federal executive agencies).

[38] 5 U.S.C. § 3330a (a)(1)(A). The Board has held that 5 U.S.C. § 3330a does not define the term "relating to veterans ' preference " and that, among other things, veterans' preference app lies to section 3304(b), which require s an examination before an individual may enter the competitive service. *Dean v. Department of Agriculture*, 104 M.S.P.R. 1, 8-10 (2006). *See also Willingham v. Department of the Navy*, 118 M.S.P.R. 21, 8 (2012) (holding that veterans' preference for purposes of VEOA redress could be found in an agency regulation).

[39] 5 U.S.C. §§ 3330a (a)(1)(B); 3304(f)(1). A copy of a section of the VEOA redress statute is in Appendix D.

[40] *See Searcy v. Department of Agriculture*, 115 M.S.P.R. 260, 11 (2010) (burden for jurisdiction); *Beyers v. Department of State*, 120 M.S.P.R. 573, 6 (2014) (preponderant evidence is required to prove the merits of a VEOA claim).

[41] *See Haasz v. Department of Veterans Affairs*, 108 M.S.P.R. 349, 8-11 (2008); *Cruz v. Department of Homeland Security*, 98 M.S.P.R. 492, 6 (2005).

[42] *See Alford v. Department of Defense*, 113 M.S.P.R. 263, 11 -12, 14 (2010) (holding that the AJ should not have dismissed the case for lack of jurisdiction but rather should have dismissed it for failure to state a claim for which relief may be granted).

[43] *Compare Burroughs v. Department of the Army*, 115 M.S.P.R. 656, 8 (2011) (finding no entitlement to a VEOA hearing), *with Kirkendall v. Department of the Army*, 479 F.3d 830, 844-46 (Fed. Cir. 2007) (enbanc) (finding that the Boar d cannot exercise discretion, but rather must grant a USERRA hearing if one is requested).

[44] 5 C.F.R. § 1208.23.

[45] *Burroughs v. Department of the Army*, 115 M.S.P.R. 656, 8 (2011).

[46] *Lazaro v. Department of Veterans Affairs*, 666 F.3d 1316, 1319 (Fed. Cir. 2012); *Campion v. Merit Systems Protection Board*, 326 F.3d 1210, 1213, 1215 (Fed. Cir. 2003). *See* 5 U.S.C. § 3330a.

[47] 5 U.S.C. § 3304(f)(1) states that if an agency uses merit promotion procedures for a vacancy and accepts applicants from outside its own workforce, the agency must also consider applications from "preference eligibles or veterans who have been separated from the armed forces under honorable conditions after 3 years or more of active service. "

[48] *Becker v. Department of Veterans Affairs*, 115 M.S.P.R. 409, 5 (2010); *Styslinger v. Department of the Army*, 105 M.S.P.R. 223, 31 (2007).

[49] *Lis v. U.S. Postal Service*, 113 M.S.P.R. 415, 11 (2010).

[50] *See, e.g., Gonzalez v. Department of Transportation*, 109 M.S.P.R. 250, 16 (2008) (explaining in the context of a whistle blowing appeal that exhaustion of remedies before OSC is not required to raise whistle blower retaliation as an affirmative defense in an otherwise appealable action).

[51] *Woodford v. Ngo*, 548 U.S. 81, 88-89 (2006) (internal punctuation and citations omitted).

[52] *Woodford v. Ngo*, 548 U.S. 81, 89 (2006).

[53] *Woodford v. Ngo*, 548 U.S. 81, 89 (2006).

[54] *Woodford v. Ngo*, 548 U.S. 81, 89 (2006). In *Ngo*, the Court noted that the record created when exhausting administrative remedies may be useful for "judicial consideration." The Board is a quasi - judicial agency operating under administrative law. However, the record established when an appellant exhausts his or her administrative remedies with DOL may be helpful to the Board when adjudicating an appeal as well as assisting its reviewing court when reviewing the Board 's decision.

[55] *Burroughs v. Department of the Army*, 115 M.S.P.R. 656, 9 (2011) (quoting 5 U.S.C. § 3330a(a)(2)(B); 5 C.F.R. § 1208.23(a)(4)).

[56] *Burroughs v. Department of the Army*, 115 M.S.P.R. 656, 10 (2011) (explaining that although the Board uses a liberal pleading standard for allegations of veterans ' preference violations in a VEOA appeal, evidence of the exhaustion requirement is mandatory under the statute and is not subject to the same liberal construction).

[57] 5 U.S.C. § 3330a(a)(2)(A).

[58] *Hayes v. Department of the Army*, 111 M.S.P.R. 41, 10 (2009) (quoting *Irwin v. Department of Veterans Affairs*, 498 U.S. 89, 96 (1990); *Garcia v. Department of Agriculture*, 110 M.S.P.R. 371, 6 (2009). *See also Irwin v. Department of Veterans Affairs*, 498 U.S. 89, 96 (1990) (explaining that equitable relief is granted "sparingly" and does not apply "where the claimant failed to exercise due diligence in preserving his legal rights.")

[59] *Kirkendall v. Department of the Army*, 479 F.3d 830, 844 (Fed. Cir. 2007) (holding that 5 U.S.C. §§ 3330a(a)(1)(A) and 3330a(d)(1)(B) are subject to equitable tolling).

[60] *Thompson v. Department of the Army*, 112 M.S.P.R. 153, 14 (2009) (explaining that "simply calling" DOL doe s not satisfy the requirement, unless DOL —through a failure to perform its obligations —caused the appellant to miss the opportunity to file in writing); 5 U.S.C. § 3330a(d)(1). *See Sears v. Department of the Navy*, 86 M.S.P.R. 76, 7 (2000) (holding that the Board cannot have jurisdiction in a VEOA case if the appellant fails to file a complaint with DOL).

[61] 5 U.S.C. § 3330a(b)(1). A knowing violation of veterans' preference is a PPP under 5 U.S.C. § 2302(b)(11), but OSC's authority to seek corrective action is different for (b)(11) than it is for the other PPPs. 5 U.S.C. § 2302(e)(2). Under a memorandum of understanding between OSC and DOL, "[i]f OSC receives an allegation of a violation of veterans' preference under section 2302(b)(11) of title 5, OSC will advise the complainant that it doe s not have the authority to seek corrective action for alleged violations of § 2302(b)(11) and will refer the individual to VETS to seek redress under VEOA." Memorandum of Understanding Between Veterans ' Employment and Training Service, United States Department of Labor and the United States Office Of Special Counsel, at 3, available at https:// osc.gov/resources/ osc_d11.pdf.

[62] *Burroughs v. Department of the Army*, 115 M.S.P.R. 656, 10 (2011). Because Mr. Bur roughs has multiple Board cases that are instructive, his cases in this report include the full citation in the text to distinguish between the m. For an explanation of pass-over procedures, preference points, and the right to compete, please see our report

Veteran Hiring in the Civil Service: Practices and Perceptions, available at www.mspb.gov/ studies.

[63] *Burroughs v. Department of the Army*, 115 M.S.P.R. 656, 10 (2011).

[64] The statute instructs DOL to make its determinations based upon a preponderance of the evidence. *See* 5 U.S.C. § 3330a(c).

[65] 5 U.S.C. § 3330a(c)(2).

[66] *Gingery v. Department of the Treasury*, 110 M.S.P.R. 83, 4-8, 20 (2008).

[67] *Morris v. Department of the Army*, 113 M.S.P.R. 304, 10 (2010).

[68] *Styslinger v. Department of the Army*, 105 M.S.P.R. 223, 15 (2007). The appellant must give DOL 60 days in which to attempt to re solve the complaint before the appellant may seek redress by filing an appeal with MSP B. 5 U.S.C. § 3330a(d).

[69] 5 U.S.C. § 3330a(d).

[70] *Burroughs v. Department of the Army*, 116 M.S.P.R. 292, 8, 10 (2011).

[71] *Kirkendall v. Department of the Army*, 479 F.3d 830, 843 -44 (2007) (holding that 5 U.S.C. §§ 3330a(a)(1)(A) and 3330a(d)(1)(B) are subject to equitable tolling).

[72] 5 U.S.C. § 3330a(d).

[73] *See Irwin v. Department of Veterans Affairs*, 498 U.S. 89, 96 (1990).

[74] 5 U.S.C. § 3330b. In F Y 2009-2013, only three case s were closed at MSPB as a result of notice that the appellant intended to file an appeal in a district court. We cannot know the reasoning of individual appellants, but one possible explanation why district courts are not used f or more VEOA appeals may be that, by law, there is a fee to file a civil action with the district court, whereas there are no fees for filing with the Boar d. *See* 28 U.S.C. § 1914.

[75] *See Hill v. Potte*, 48 F. App'x 198, 199 (6th Cir. 2002); *Hunt v. Department of the Army*, 30 F. App'x 567, 568 (6th Cir. 2002); *Daniels v. Department of Veterans Affairs*, 2014 WL 1651967, at *2 (N. Dist. Ga. 2014); *King v. Tobyhanna Army Depot*, 2013 WL 2896841, 17 (Middle Dist. Pa. 2013).

[76] 5 U.S.C. § 3330b.

[77] 5 U.S.C. § 3330b. *See, e.g., Conyers v. Rossides*, 558 F.3d 137, 149 (2nd Cir. 2009) (noting that filing notice with the Board is a prerequisite to bringing a claim under 5 U.S.C. § 3330b); *Williams v. General Services Administration*, 2011 WL 1344173, at *6 (Middle Dist. Fl. 2011) (holding that the district court had jurisdiction because the appellant timely filed with the court after notifying the Board of its intent to do so).

[78] 5 U.S.C. § 3330b.

[79] *See James v. Federal Energy Regulatory Commission*, 747 F.2d 1581, 1582 -83 (Fed. Cir. 1984); 5 C.F.R. § 1201.113.

[80] 5 C.F.R. § 1201.113.

[81] *James v. Federal Energy Regulatory Commission*, 747 F.2d 1581, 1582 -83 (Fed. Cir. 1984).

[82] *Lazaro v. Department of Veterans Affairs*, 666 F.3d 1316, 1319 (Fed. Cir. 2012); *Campion v. Merit Systems Protection Board*, 326 F.3d 1210, 1213, 1215 (Fed. Cir. 2003). *See* 5 U.S.C. § 3330a.

[83] *Wilks v. Department of the Army*, 91 M.S.P.R. 70, 11 (2002) (describing the issue as one of standing).

[84] *Wilks v. Department of the Army*, 91 M.S.P.R. 70, 11 (2 002). An excerpt from 5 U.S.C. § 2108 is in Appendix A. Title 5 is the section of the law that addresses the civil service and VEOA redress is in title 5. Title 10 is the section of law that addresses the Armed Force s.

[85] *Willingham v. Department of the Navy*, 118 M.S.P.R. 21, 7-8 (2012).

[86] *Willingham v. Department of the Navy*, 118 M.S.P.R. 21, 8 (2012).

[87] *Willingham v. Department of the Navy*, 118 M.S.P.R. 21, 10 (2012).

[88] 10 U.S.C. § 1587(a)(1) (de scribing NAF I employees). GAO has noted that there is no official definition or commonly understood opinion of what constitutes a NAF I. Government Accountability Office, GAO-08-978SP, Appropriations Law —Vol. III, Chapter 15 at 226 -27 (Sept. 2008).

[89] Civil service employees, whether in the competitive or excepted service, are protected from reprisal for whistle blowing activities under 5 U.S.C. § 2302(a)(2)(B) and (b)(8). However, protections from whistle blowing reprisal for NAF I employees are codified at 10 U.S.C. § 1587, and the Secretary of Defense has the authority to prescribe regulations to carry out that section. 10 U.S.C. § 1587(e). With respect to workplace injuries, civil service employees are covered by the Federal Employee s Compensation Act, while NAF I employees are covered by the Longshoremen's and Harbor Worker s ' Compensation Act. *Lewis v. Department of the Air Force*, 31 M.S.P.R. 328, 331 n1 (1986). *Compare* 5 U.S.C. § 8101(1), *with* 5 U.S.C. § 8171(a).

[90] 5 U.S.C. § 2105(c). *See generally* title 5 of the U.S. Code.

[91] *Willingham v. Department of the Navy*, 118 M.S.P.R. 21, 14, 18 (2012).

[92] *Sedgwick v. World Bank*, 106 M.S.P.R. 662, 9 (2007).

[93] *See, e.g., Jolley v. Department of Homeland Security*, 105 M.S.P.R. 104, 5 -7 (2007) (finding that VEOA applies to a DHS Federal Law Enforcement Training Center (FL ETC)); *Cruz v. Department of Homeland Security*, 98 M.S.P.R. 492, 7 (2005) (finding jurisdiction in a VEOA appeal involving the Coast Guard).

[94] *Morse v. Merit Systems Protection Board*, 621 F.3d 1346, 1347 -48 (Fed. Cir. 2010).

[95] *Morse v. Merit Systems Protection Board*, 621 F.3d 1346, 1348 -51 (Fed. Cir. 2010); *see Belhumeur v. Department of Transportation*, 104 M.S.P.R. 408, 8 (2007) (holding that the Board lacks jurisdiction over VEOA appeals from FAA employees and applicants).

[96] *Morse v. Merit Systems Protection Board*, 621 F.3d 1346, 1351 (Fed. Cir. 2010) (quoting *Barnhart v. Sigmon Coal Co.*, 534 U.S. 438, 461 (2002)).

[97] *See Willingham v. Department of the Navy*, 118 M.S.P.R. 21, 8 (2012); *Wilks v. D epartment of the Army*, 91 M.S.P.R. 70, 11 (2002).

[98] The position need not be permanent for the right to compete to apply. In *Modeste v. Department of Veterans Affairs*, 121 M.S.P.R. 254, 7-12 (2014), the Board held the statute clearly provides a preference eligible or veteran with the right to compete for vacant positions without qualification as to the duration of those positions.

[99] *See* U.S. Merit Systems Protection Board, *Veteran Hiring in the Civil Service: Practices and Perceptions* (2014), available at www.mspb.gov/ studies.

[100] *See, e.g., Lazaro v. Department of Veterans Affairs*, 666 F.3d 1316, 1319 (Fed. Cir. 2012) (explaining in a VEOA preference rights appeal that the only issue in dispute was whether DVA 's actions violated a statute or regulation related to veterans' preference); *Olson v. Department of Veterans Affairs*, 100 M.S.P.R. 322, 9 (2005) (finding in a VEOA appeal "that the agency violated the appellant 's rights under a statute relating to veterans' preference").

[101] *Scarnati v. Department of Veterans Affairs*, 344 F.3d 1246, 1249 (Fed. Cir. 2003).

[102] Earlier, we explained that the type of appointment authority was not pertinent to whether the individual had preference. *See Willingham v. Department of the Navy*, 118 M.S.P.R. 21, 8 (2012); *Wilks v. Department of the Army*, 91 M.S.P.R. 70, 11 (2002). However, whether the person has preference is a separate question from whether the position is one to which preference applies.

[103] *Vores v. Department of the Army*, 109 M.S.P.R. 191, 22 –23 (2008).
[104] 5 C.F.R. § 213.3102.
[105] *Jarrard v. Department of Justice*, 669 F.3d 1320, 1323 (Fed. Cir. 2012). *See* 5 C.F.R. § 302.101(c) (when a position is in the excepted service, "each agency shall follow the principle of veteran preference as far as administratively feasible"); *see also* 5 U.S.C. § 3320 (selection "for appointment to each vacancy in the excepted service in the executive branch" shall be "from the qualified applicants in the same manner and under the same conditions required for the competitive service by sections 3308 - 3318 of this title ").
[106] *Jarrard v. Department of Justice*, 669 F.3d 1320, 1324 -26 (Fed. Cir. 2012). *See also Asatov v. Agency for International Development*, 119 M.S.P.R. 692, 8-9 (2013) (holding that the position of Foreign Service Junior Executive Officer is covered by 22 U.S.C. § 3941, which is outside the title 5 competitive service rules, and therefore only requires that an agency use veterans ' preference as "an affirmative factor " in selection).
[107] *See, e.g., Williams v. Department of the Air Force*, 97 M.S.P.R. 252, 8-9 (2004) (explaining veterans' preference ranking order under the Veterans Recruitment Appointment (VRA) authority); 38 U.S.C. § 4214(b)(1)(C) (granting a preference in VRA appointments to veterans entitled to disability compensation); 5 U.S.C. § 3320 ("The nominating or appointing authority shall select for appointment to each vacancy in the excepted service in the executive branch and in the government of the District of Columbia from the qualified applicants in the same manner and under the same conditions required for the competitive service by sections 3308 –3318 of this title. ") *See also* 5 C.F.R. Part 302 (containing rules for veterans' preference in the excepted service).
[108] 5 C.F.R. § 302.201.
[109] 5 C.F.R. § 302.304.
[110] An agency may choose from among different valid hiring authorities, eve n if that choice happens to be less beneficial for veterans. *See Joseph v. Federal Trade Commission*, 505 F.3d 1380, 1384 -85 (Fed. Cir. 2007) (explaining that an agency did not violate veterans ' preference when it used parallel procedures and opted to select from the merit promotion list rather than appoint a veteran from the competitive examining certificate).
[111] *Dean v. Department of Agriculture*, 99 M.S.P.R. 533, 2, 8, 22, 31-33, 38 (2005).
[112] *Dean v. Office of Personnel Management*, 115 M.S.P.R. 157, 22 (2010).
[113] *Dean v. Office of Personnel Management*, 115 M.S.P.R. 157, 13, 25 (2010).
[114] *See* Veterans Employment Opportunities Ac t of 1998, S. Rep. 105 -340, at 15 (1998) (stating that, "while veterans as a group appear to be faring well in Federal employment, individual case s reveal that there is a pressing need for a uniform redress mechanism for the enforcement of veterans' preference laws in both hiring and reductions-in-force decisions").
[115] *Buckheit v. U.S. Postal Service*, 107 M.S.P.R. 52, 5, 10 (2007).
[116] *Buckheit v. U.S. Postal Service*, 107 M.S.P.R. 52, 11-13, 15 (2007). *See also Burger v. U.S. Postal Service*, 88 M.S.P.R. 579, 12 (2001) (noting that an appellant had raised assertions related to a RIF for which the Board could potentially have VEOA jurisdiction and ordering the AJ to determine if a VEOA claim had been asserted).
[117] 5 U.S.C. § 3304(f)(1) is a law that states that if an agency uses merit promotion procedures for a vacancy, and accepts applicants from outside its own workforce, then the agency must also consider applications from "preference eligibles or veterans who have been separated from the armed force s under honorable conditions after 3 years or more of active service. "
[118] *Becker v. Department of Veterans Affairs*, 115 M.S.P.R. 409, 5 (2010); *Styslinger v. Department of the Army*, 105 M.S.P.R. 223, 31 (2007).
[119] *Styslinger v. Department of the Army*, 105 M.S.P.R. 223, 22 (2007).
[120] 5 U.S.C. § 3304(f)(1).
[121] 5 U.S.C. § 3304(f)(1).
[122] *See, e.g., Washburn v. Department of the Air Force*, 119 M.S.P.R. 265, 5 n.1 (2013) (explaining that although the appellant may not be preference eligible because he retired at the rank of Major, *see* 5 U.S.C. § 2108(4)(B), he is nevertheless covered as a "veteran" because he separated from the armed forces under honorable conditions after 3 years or more of active service).
[123] *Walker v. Department of the Army*, 104 M.S.P.R. 96, 16 (2006).
[124] Preference may granted "to the widow/ widower or mother of a deceased veteran or to the spouse or mother of a disabled veteran. It is called 'derived preference' because it is derived from the military service of someone else —a veteran who is not using it for preference. When the disabled veteran does u se the service for preference, then the spouse or mother is no longer entitled to preference." OPM's *Guide to Processing Personnel Actions*, Glossary, at 35 -10.
[125] 5 U.S.C. § 3304(f)(1).
[126] *Brandt v. Department of the Air Force*, 103 M.S.P.R. 671, 12-13 (2006).
[127] A case may potentially be made that an agency has violated the section 3304(f)(1) right to compete if the agency is required to accept applications under merit promotion procedures but has circumvented that requirement, thereby circumventing the requirement to consider certain veterans and preference eligibles with those merit promotion candidates. *See Morris v. Department of the Army*, 113 M.S.P.R. 304, 15 -18 (2010) (remanding a

case to determine whether the agency was required to u se merit promotion procedures to fill a job for which it used the VRA hiring authority).

[128] U.S. Office of Personnel Management, *Vet Guide*, available at http://www.opm.gov/policy - data-over sight/veterans-services/vet-guide/.

[129] The Board has held that the different components of DoD constitute separate agencies for other purpose s as well, such as the requirement that a probationary period be completed in the same agency. *See Francis v. Department of the Navy*, 53 M.S.P.R. 545, 551 (1992) (holding that civilian service in the Department of the Army cannot be credited toward s completing a probationary period in the Department of the Navy). The Federal Circuit explicitly endorsed this finding in *Pervez v. Department of the Navy*, 193 F.3d 1371, 1373 -74 (Fed. Cir. 1999), in which it cited *Francis* when holding that the fact that Army and Navy "also are part of the Department of Defense is not inconsistent with their treatment as separate agencies for personnel purposes").

[130] *Washburn v. Department of the Air Force*, 119 M.S.P.R. 265, 6 (2013).

[131] *Washburn v. Department of the Air Force*, 119 M.S.P.R. 265, 7-11 (2013).

[132] *Vassallo v. Department of Defense*, 121 M.S.P.R. 70, 2-6 (2014).

[133] *Vassallo v. Department of Defense*, 121 M.S.P.R. 70, 7-11 (2014).

[134] *Lazaro v. Department of Veterans Affairs*, 666 F.3d 1316, 1318 -19 (Fed. Cir. 2012); 5 U.S.C. § 3311; 5 C.F.R. § 302.302(d). The Board has not yet had occasion to look at the question of consideration of a non-preference eligible's complete background.

[135] *Lazaro v. Department of Veterans Affairs*, 666 F.3d 1316, 1319 (Fed. Cir. 2012).

[136] *See Burroughs v. Department of the Army*, 115 M.S.P.R. 656, 13 (2011) (holding that OPM's minimum educational requirements for "scientific, technical, or professional" positions apply to VEOA applicants); *Ramsey v. Office of Personnel Management*, 87 M.S.P.R. 98, 9 (2000) (holding that VEOA did not exempt covered veterans from meeting minimum qualification standards in order to compete for vacant positions under merit promotion procedures).

[137] *See* U.S. Office of Personnel Management, General Schedule Qualification Standards, available at http:// www.opm.gov/policy-data-oversight/classification-qualifications/general-schedule-qualification-standards/#url=Group-Standards (explaining that to qualify for a professional or scientific position, the individual typically must have a 4 -year degree or a "c or e of educational credit " such as 24 semester hours in the field). *See also* U.S. Office of Personnel Management, Classification Appeal Decision No. C -1910-12-01, Dec. 28, 2000, at 1 (explaining the positive education requirement).

[138] U.S. Office of Personnel Management, General Schedule Qualification Policies, available at http://www.opm.gov/polic y -data-oversight/classification -qualifications/general - schedule-qualification-policies/ #url=General -Policies.

[139] *Miller v. Federal Deposit Insurance Corporation*, 121 M.S.P.R. 88, 2-3 (2014).

[140] *Miller v. Federal Deposit Insurance Corporation*, 121 M.S.P.R. 88, 2-3 (2014).

[141] *Miller v. Federal Deposit Insurance Corporation*, 121 M.S.P.R. 88, 4-5 (2014).

[142] *Miller v. Federal Deposit Insurance Corporation*, 121 M.S.P.R. 88, 9 (2014).

[143] Selective factors are knowledge, skills, abilities, or special qualifications that are required of candidates, in addition to the minimum requirements in an OP M qualification standard, but are determined to be essential to perform the duties and responsibilities of a particular position. *See* U.S. Merit Systems Protection Board, *Issues of Merit*, "Selecting with Selective Factors" (Jan. 2008), available at www.mspb.gov/ studies.

[144] *Clarke v. Department of the Navy,* 94 M.S.P.R. 604, 8 (2003).

[145] *Clarke v. Department of the Navy,* 94 M.S.P.R. 604, 8-9 (2003). *See also Beyers v. Department of State*, 120 M.S.P.R. 573 9 (2014) (explaining in a denial of preference rights case that because the appellant failed a suitability determination, and suitability was a requirement of the position, the agency did not err in withdrawing a tentative job offer.)

[146] *Dale v. Department of Veterans Affair*, 102 M.S.P.R. 646, 11-13 (2006).

[147] *Montee v. Department of the Army*, 110 M.S.P.R. 271, 6, 10 (2008). The Board remanded the case to the field office for the AJ to deter mine if the appellant was in fact "ordinarily resident."

[148] *Montee v. Department of the Army*, 110 M.S.P.R. 271, 10 (2008).

[149] *Jolley v. Department of Homeland Security*, 105 M.S.P.R. 104, 2, 7-8, 12-16, n.2 (2007).

[150] *See, e.g.,* U.S. Office of Personnel Management, *Delegated Examining Operations Handbook*, at 160 (stating that a "selecting official may object to an eligible on the basis of negligence or misconduct in previous service/employment with the same or another agency/employer.")

[151] *Harellson v. U.S. Postal Service*, 113 M.S.P.R. 534, 2, 9 -10 (2010).

[152] *Harellson v. U.S. Postal Service*, 113 M.S.P.R. 534, 11 (2010).

[153] *Harellson v. U.S. Postal Service*, 113 M.S.P.R. 534, 11 (2010).

[154] *Harellson v. U.S. Postal Service*, 113 M.S.P.R. 534, 2, 10-11 (2010).

[155] *Smyth v. U.S. Postal Service*, 89 M.S.P.R. 219, 3, 7 (2001).

[156] *Shapley v. Department of Homeland Security*, 110 M.S.P.R. 31, 3, 8, 10-11 (2008).

[157] For example, when an employee fully recovers from an injury after more than one year from the date of commencement of compensation, the employing agency must make all reasonable efforts to place, and accord

priority to placing, the employee in his former or equivalent position. *See Welby v. Department of Agriculture*, 101 M.S.P.R. 17, 13 (2006); 5 U.S.C. § 8151(b)(2); 5 C.F.R. § 353.301(b). In another context, an applicant who is improperly rated ineligible f or a particular position may be entitled to priority consideration for future vacancies. *Baxter v. Office of Personnel Management*, 44 M.S.P.R. 125, 133 (1990). Priority consideration is also a concept frequently used in settlement agreements which the Board enforces. *See, e.g., Outlaw v. Department of the Army*, 99 M.S.P.R. 302, 2, 12 –13 (2005).

[158] *Shapley v. Department of Homeland Security*, 110 M.S.P.R. 31, 14-17 (2008).

[159] U.S. Office of Personnel Management, *Delegated Examining Operations Handbook*, at 81-82, 170-71, available at http://www.opm.gov/ policy -data-oversight/ hiring-authoritie s/competitive -hiring/de o_handbook.pdf. (According to O PM's website, the Hand book has not been updated since May 2007.)

[160] In a 2006 report, the Board noted that the Federal Circuit had declared in 1999 that, "to the extent that OPM's regulations are contrary to the proposition that an individual is an "employee" if he or she meets the requirements of either 5 U.S.C. § 7511(a)(1)(C)(i) or (ii), they are invalid[,] " and OPM had not yet fixed its regulations to comport with the court 's decision. U.S. Merit Systems Protection Board, *Navigating the Probationary Period After Van Wersch and McCormick*, at 18 -19, available at www.mspb.gov/studies ; *see Van Wersch v. Department of Health and Human Services*, 197 F.3d 1144, 1151, n.7 (Fed. Cir. 1999). OP M amended its regulations shortly after that report was issued. *See* 72 Fed. Reg. 23772, May 1, 2007.

[161] *Lodge v. Department of the Treasury*, 109 M.S.P.R. 614, 7 (2008) (veterans' preference); *Washburn v. Department of the Air Force*, 119 M.S.P.R. 265, 14 (2013) (right to compete). The Board has yet to find a veterans' preference violation in a RIF case brought under VEOA, perhaps because selection actions are far more common than RIF actions, and thus there have not been as many VEOA RIF appeals.

[162] *Lodge v. Department of the Treasury*, 109 M.S.P.R. 614, 7 (2008) (veterans' preference); *Washburn v. Department of the Air Force*, 119 M.S.P.R. 265, 14 (2013) (right to compete).

[163] *Washburn v. Department of the Air Force*, 119 M.S.P.R. 265, 14 (2013); *Phillips v. Department of the Navy*, 114 M.S.P.R. 19, 15 –19 (2010).

[164] *Weed v. Social Security Administration*, 110 M.S.P.R. 468, 14 (2009).

[165] The Board has held that while the selectee must be re moved from the position, there is no requirement that the selectee be removed from Federal service as a whole. *See Modeste v. Department of Veterans Affairs*, 121 M.S.P.R. 254, 14 (2014); *Weed v. Social Security Administration*, 110 M.S.P.R. 468, 13 (2009).

[166] *Russell v. Department of Health and Human Services*, 120 M.S.P.R. 42, 13 (2013).

[167] *See Gonzalez v. Department of Homeland Security*, 110 M.S.P.R. 567, 6 (2009); *Lodge v. Department of the Treasury*, 109 M.S.P.R. 614, 7 (2008). However, "[w]he n an agency violates a veteran's preference rights during selection in the competitive service and when it is undisputed that the agency would have selected the veteran for the position sought but for the violation, [5 U.S.C.] § 3330c requires the agency to offer the same—or, as near as possible, a substantially equivalent —position to the veteran." *Marshall v. Department of Health and Human Services*, 587 F.3d 1310, 1318 (Fed. Cir. 2009).

[168] *See Shapley v. Department of Homeland Security*, 110 M.S.P.R. 31, 18 (2008); 5 U.S.C. § 3330c(a).

[169] *Marshall v. Department of Health and Human Services*, 587 F.3d 1310, 1312, 1317 -18 (F ed. Cir. 2009).

[170] *Williams v. Department of the Air Force*, 116 M.S.P.R. 245, 11 (2011). An award for "lost wages " in the context of a VEOA appeal doe s not have the same meaning as the term of art "back pay " under the Back Pay Act, because VEOA appeals are not governed by the Back Pay Act. *Williams v. Department of the Air Force*, 116 M.S.P.R. 245, 8, n.4 (2011).

[171] *Williams v. Department of the Air Force*, 108 M.S.P.R. 567, 12 (2008).

[172] *See Haasz v. Department of Veterans Affairs*, 108 M.S.P.R. 349, 8-11 (2008); *Cruz v. Department of Homeland Security*, 98 M.S.P.R. 492, 6 (2005).

[173] *Washburn v. Department of the Air Force*, 119 M.S.P.R. 265, 12 (2013).

[174] *Haskins v. Department of the Navy*, 106 M.S.P.R. 616, 17 (2007).

[175] *Haskins v. Department of the Navy*, 106 M.S.P.R. 616, 17 (2007). *See, e.g., Wheeler v. Department of Defense*, 113 M.S.P.R. 376, 18 (2010) (dismissing a VEOA appeal as moot because the appellant had already obtained all the relief he could have obtained from the Board if he had prevailed in his appeal).

[176] *Wheeler v. Department of Defense*, 113 M.S.P.R. 376, 12 (2010); *see Modeste v. Department of Veterans Affairs*, 121 M.S.P.R. 254, 13 (2014) (holding that the appeal could not be rendered moot because the appellant had not yet received all of the relief to which he may have been entitled).

[177] *Wheeler v. Department of Defense*, 113 M.S.P.R. 376, 11 (2010). An "Article III court" refers to the judiciary as it is established in Article III of the U.S. Constitution. MSPB is an administrative body in the executive branch of the Government, although its decisions are reviewable by an Article III court —the Federal Circuit.

[178] *See, e.g., Wheeler v. Department of Defense*, 113 M.S.P.R. 376, 18 (2010) (dismissing a VEOA appeal as moot because the appellant had already obtained all the relief he could have obtained from the Board if his appeal had prevailed).

[179] *Compare Wheeler v. Department of Defense*, 113 M.S.P.R. 376, 18 (2010) (dismissing VEOA case for lack of jurisdiction because there was no *further* effectual relief that could be gr anted and thus the case was moot), *with Alford v. Department of Defense*, 113 M.S.P.R. 263 11 -12 (2010) (holding that the AJ should not have

dismissed the VEOA case for lack of jurisdiction but rather should have dismissed it for failure to state a claim for which relief may be granted).

[180] 38 U.S.C. § 4301. This report does not contain a copy of the USERRA statute because of its length. A copy of the statute can be found on DO L's website at http://www.dol.gov/vets/u sc/vpl/u sc38.htm.

[181] 38 U.S.C. § 4311(a); *but see Lourens v. Merit Systems Protection Board*, 193 F.3d 1369, 1371 (Fed. Cir. 1999) (holding that the Board did not have USERRA jurisdiction over claims by a widow with derived preference eligibility when the widow had not been a member of —or applicant to —a uniformed service).

[182] USERRA can provide MSP B jurisdiction over suspensions that are too brief to meet the requirements for MSP B's ad verse action jurisdiction (14 days or less). *See, e.g., Johnson v. U.S. Postal Service*, 85 M.S.P.R. 1, 11 (1999), in which the Board found USERRA jurisdiction over a 7 -day suspension when the appellant alleged that he was denied l eave and instead was charged with absence without leave (AWOL) for period s during which he served on Reserve duty, leading to a suspension for AWOL.

[183] *See Hamner v. Department of Housing and Urban Development*, 93 M.S.P.R. 84, 20 (2002) (explaining that veterans are not usually accorded any preference when seeking promotions). *But see Holloway v. Department of Interior*, 82 M.S.P.R. 435, 15 (1999) (holding that the Board had jurisdiction over a Whistle blower Protection Act claim that the appellant was denied leave in retaliation for perceived whistle blowing activity).

[184] 38 U.S.C. § 4311.

[185] 38 U.S.C. §§ 4312-18.

[186] *See, e.g., Erickson v. U.S. Postal Service*, 571 F.3d 1364, 1368 -69 (Fed. Cir. 2009) (holding that the agency could not re move the appellant for excessive u se of military leave).

[187] *See, e.g., Becwar v. Department of Labor*, 115 M.S.P.R. 689, 6-7 (2011) (finding jurisdiction over the appellant's assertions that the agency's decision not to promote her was motivated by the agency's discontent with her absence s from work for military duty); *Isabella v. Department of State*, 106 M.S.P.R. 333, 9-10 (2007) (finding jurisdiction over the appellant's claim that the agency was willing to process his application when it thought he had separated from the military, but stopped processing when it learned he was still a reservist).

[188] *See, e.g., Williams v. Department of the Navy*, 94 M.S.P.R. 206, 8 (2003) (finding jurisdiction over the appellant's assertion that the agency did not want to hire veterans because they have a higher retention standing in a RIF).

[189] While military leave case s have become less common, several years ago there was a misunderstanding that caused some individuals to be charged annual or other leave for periods that should have been covered by military leave. This error by agencies was appealable under USERRA and led to a multitude of cases to seek correction of leave records. These cases are known as *Butterbaugh* cases, after the lead case identifying the error. *Butterbaugh v. Department of Justice,* 336 F.3d 1332, 1333 –34 (Fed. Cir. 2003); *see Duncan v. Department of the Air Force*, 115 M.S.P.R. 275, 6 (2010).

[190] *Beck v. Department of the Navy*, 120 M.S.P.R. 504, 5, 9-10 (2014).

[191] *McBride v. U.S. Postal Service*, 78 M.S.P.R. 411, 415 (1998) (holding that the fact that the appellant incurred a back injury while performing military service was incidental to her claim of disability discrimination). *See also Holmes v. Department of Justice*, 498 F. App'x 993, 995 (Fed. Cir. 2013) (Table) (agreeing with the holding of *McBride*). *But see Davison v. Department of Veterans Affairs*, 115 M.S.P.R. 640, 14-15 (2011) (finding that a case could be brought under USERRA when the appellant asserted the discrimination was based on his u se of leave without pay for a medical condition where such leave was only available to service members).

[192] *Silva v. Department of Homeland Security*, 112 M.S.P.R. 362, 12 (2009); *see* 38 U.S.C. § 4312(a), (e). Advanced notice of departure for service is not require d if it is impossible, unreasonable, or precluded by military necessity. 38 U.S.C. § 4312(b).

[193] 38 U.S.C. § 4312(e).

[194] *See, e.g., Kiszka v. Office of Personnel Management*, 372 F.3d 1301, 1307 -08 (Fed. Cir. 2004) (finding that a resignation is not require d for the adjudicator to find that an appellant abandoned his civilian career in favor of a military career and therefore was not entitled to reemployment).

[195] *See, e.g., Leite v. Department of the Army*, 109 M.S.P.R. 229, 2-4 (2008) (alleging that the appellant would have been promoted in her civilian position during the period in which she was away in military service).

[196] *See, e.g., Crawford v. Department of the Army*, 117 M.S.P.R. 38, 2, 8, 22-23, 26 (2011).

[197] *See, e.g., Lindsley v. Office of Personnel Management*, 96 M.S.P.R. 259, 8, 19 (2004) (holding that the appellant was not entitled to have his military time credited towards a civil service annuity because he had abandoned his civilian career).

[198] *Corkery v. Office of Personnel Management*, 94 M.S.P.R. 118, 15 (2003).

[199] *See Woodman v. Office of Personnel Management*, 258 F.3d 1372, 1378 -79 (Fed. Cir. 2001) (holding that the lack of a resignation by the appellant is not determinative of whether he abandoned his civilian career for one in the military).

[200] *See Erickson v. U.S. Postal Service*, 636 F.3d 1353, 1356 -57 (Fed. Cir. 2011) (discussing *Woodman v. Office of Personnel Management*, 258 F.3d 1372 (Fed. Cir. 2001)).

[201] *See Erickson v. U.S. Postal Service*, 636 F.3d 1353, 1356 -57 (Fed. Cir. 2011) (discussing *Moravec v. Office of Personnel Management*, 393 F.3d 1263 (Fed. Cir. 2004) and *Dowling v. Office of Personnel Management*, 393 F.3d 1260 (Fed. Cir. 2004)).

[202] *See Erickson v. U.S. Postal Service*, 636 F.3d 1353, 1359 (Fed. Cir. 2011) (finding pertinent the appellant's unrebutted testimony that he had not resigned because he believed he was still employed by the agency).

[203] *See Erickson v. U.S. Postal Service*, 636 F.3d 1353, 1358 -59 (Fed. Cir. 2011) (finding that the appellant's failure to contest his removal for a period of six years was an indication of abandonment, although it was not dispositive).

[204] *See Erickson v. U.S. Postal Service*, 636 F.3d 1353, 1356 -59 (Fed. Cir. 2011) (weighing several factor s before concluding that there was not sufficient evidence of abandonment).

[205] *Leite v. Department of the Army*, 109 M.S.P.R. 229, 10 (2008).

[206] *Fishgold v. Sullivan Drydock & Repair Corp.*, 328 U.S. 275, 284 -85 (1946).

[207] H. Re p. 103-65, at 30-31 (1994 U.S.C.C.A.N. 2463 -64) (internal citations omitted).

[208] *See West v. Department of the Air Force*, 117 M.S.P.R. 24, 8 (2011); *Leite v. Department of the Army*, 109 M.S.P.R. 229, 10 (2008).

[209] *Rassenfoss v. Department of the Treasury*, 121 M.S.P.R. 512, 13 (2014).

[210] *Leite v. Department of the Army*, 109 M.S.P.R. 229, 2-4 (2008).

[211] *Leite v. Department of the Army*, 109 M.S.P.R. 229, 12-14 (2008). *See also West v. Department of the Air Force*, 117 M.S.P.R. 24 9 (2011) (holding that there is no basis for requiring an agency to consider an absent employee for promotion as though she had the experience and skills she might have obtained if she had continued her civilian employment).

[212] *Rassenfoss v. Department of the Treasury*, 121 M.S.P.R. 512, 13 (2014).

[213] *Rassenfoss v. Department of the Treasury*, 121 M.S.P.R. 512, 3 (2014).

[214] *Rassenfoss v. Department of the Treasury*, 121 M.S.P.R. 512, 523 (2014) (Member Robbins, dissenting).

[215] *Rassenfoss v. Department of the Treasury*, 121 M.S.P.R. 512, 12 (2014).

[216] *Rassenfoss v. Department of the Treasury*, 121 M .S.P.R. 512, 12-13 (2014).

[217] *Rassenfoss v. Department of the Treasury*, 121 M.S.P.R. 512, 13 (2014). The Board noted that OPM has the authority to promulgate USERRA regulations for Federal employment and stated that such regulations should be read i n a manner "consistent with" those issued by DOL.

[218] *Rassenfoss v. Department of the Treasury*, 121 M.S.P.R. 512, 13 (2014).

[219] *Rassenfoss v. Department of the Treasury*, 121 M.S.P.R. 512, 17 (2014).

[220] *Crawford v. Department of the Army*, 117 M.S.P.R. 38, 10, 22 (2011); 38 U.S.C. § 4313(a)(2).

[221] *Crawford v. Department of the Army*, 117 M.S.P.R. 38, 10 (2011) (quoting 5 C.F.R. § 353.102).

[222] *Crawford v. Department of the Army*, 117 M.S.P.R. 38, 19 (2011).

[223] *Crawford v. Department of the Army*, 117 M.S.P.R. 38, 2, 8, 22 -23, 26 (2011).

[224] *Nichols v. Department of Veterans Affairs*, 11 F.3d 160, 163 -64 (Fed. Cir. 1993). *Nichols* was adjudicated prior to the enactment of USERRA. However, because the concept of "like status " was a part of the law prior to U SERRA, the Federal Circuit has continued to apply *Nichols* to more recent case s, such as *Crawford v. Department of the Army*, 718 F.3d 1361, 1366 (Fed. Cir. 2013).

[225] *Heidel v. U.S. Postal Service,* 69 M.S.P.R. 511, 513, 518 (1996).

[226] *Crawford v. Department of the Army*, 117 M.S.P.R. 38, 11 (2011).

[227] *Mims v. Social Security Administration*, 120 M.S.P.R. 213, 22 (2013); *Williams v. Department of the Air Force*, 97 M.S.P.R. 252, 10 (2004). While the jurisdictional standard doe s not mention the nature of an appellant's discharge, the Board has held that to have standing, the individual cannot be a person who has left uniformed service under other than honorable conditions. "[S]tanding is a jurisdictional requirement that must be met before the jurisdictional test [ ] is ever applied." Thu s, the Board will not find USERRA jurisdiction for an individual who was discharged under other than honorable conditions. *Downs v. Department of Veterans Affairs*, 110 M.S.P.R. 139, 16 (2008).

[228] *Welshans v. U.S. Postal Service*, 107 M.S.P.R. 110, 4 (2007).

[229] *O'Bleness v. Department of the Air Force*, 106 M.S.P.R. 457, 9 (2007).

[230] *Mims v. Social Security Administration*, 120 M.S.P.R. 213, 22 (2013).

[231] *Swidecki v. Department of Commerce*, 113 M.S.P.R. 168, 6 (2010); *Randall v. Department of Justice*, 105 M.S.P.R. 524, 5 (2007). As explained earlier, preponderance of the evidence means that the evidence shows that a contested fact is more likely to be true than untrue. 5 C.F.R. § 1201.56(c)(2).

[232] *Burroughs v. Department of the Army*, 120 M.S.P.R. 392, 5 (2013); *Strausbaugh v. Government Printing Office*, 117 M.S.P.R. 566, 11 (2012); *see* 38 U.S.C. § 4311(c).

[233] *Clavin v. U.S. Postal Service*, 99 M.S.P.R. 619, 6 (2005) (explaining that the standard for reemployment cases is derived from 5 U.S.C. § 7701(c)(2)(B)). *See* 5 U.S.C. § 7701(c)(2)(B) (stating that an agency must prove its case by preponderant evidence).

[234] *Wyatt v. U.S. Postal Service*, 101 M.S.P.R. 28, 12 (2006); *Clavin v. U.S. Postal Service*, 99 M.S.P.R. 619, 5-6 (2005).

[235] *Harellson v. U.S. Postal Service*, 115 M.S.P.R. 378, 12 (2011).

[236] *Harellson v. U.S. Postal Service*, 115 M.S.P.R. 378, 20-21 (2011).

[237] *McMillan v. Department of Justice*, 120 M.S.P.R. 1, 20 (2013) (quoting extensively from *Sheehan v. Department of the Navy*, 240 F.3d 1009, 1014 (Fed. Cir. 2001)).

[238] *Sheehan v. Department of the Navy*, 240 F.3d 1009, 1013 (Fed. Cir. 2001).

[239] *Staub v. Proctor Hospital*, 131 S. Ct. 1186, 1193 -94 (2011).

[240] *Staub v. Proctor Hospital*, 131 S. Ct. 1186, 1189 -90 (2011). Although *Staub* involved a private sector employer, as noted earlier, decisions of the Supreme Court and Federal Circuit are binding on the Board. Decisions of other courts interpreting USERRA provisions may be followed at the Board's discretion, if the Board find s them persuasive.

[241] *Staub v. Proctor Hospital*, 131 S. Ct. 1186, 1190, n.1 (2011). A copy of the fable, "The Monkey and the Cat" is available at http://www.gu tenberg.org/ files/25357/25357 -h/25357 -h.htm#Page_140.

[242] *Staub v. Proctor Hospital*, 131 S. Ct. 1186, 1194 (2011) (emphasis in original).

[243] *Staub v. Proctor Hospital*, 131 S. Ct. 1186, 1192 (2011).

[244] *Staub v. Proctor Hospital*, 131 S. Ct. 1186, 1194 (2011).

[245] *See also Aquino v. Department of Homeland Security*, 121 M.S.P.R. 35, 23 (2014) (applying the cat 's paw approach to whistle blower cases in which the decision-maker may lack a retaliatory animus but the official is influenced by someone seeking to retaliate for whistleblower activity).

[246] *See, e.g., Williams v. Department of the Navy*, 94 M.S.P.R. 206, 2 (2003) (in which the appellant alleged that he was told that the hiring agency did not want to hire veterans); *Pruitt v. Department of Veterans Affairs*, 97 M.S.P.R. 495, 497 -98 (2004) (Separate Op., Chairman McPhie) (explaining that the appellant alleged that an agency personnel officer told her that the selecting official did not want to hire a veteran).

[247] To resolve credibility issues, an administrative judge must identify the factual questions in dispute, summarize the evidence on each disputed question, state which version he believes, and explain in detail why he found the chosen version more credible, considering such factors as: (1) the witness 's opportunity and capacity to observe the event or act in question; (2) the witness 's character; (3) any prior in consistent statement by the witness; (4) a witness 's bias, or lack of bias; (5) the contradiction of the witness's version of events by other evidence or its consistency with other evidence; (6) the inherent improbability of the witness 's version of events; and (7) the witness 's demeanor. These are known as the "*Hillen* factors." *See Hillen v. Department of the Army*, 35 M.S.P.R. 453, 458 (1987).

[248] *Compare Duncan v. Department of the Air Force*, 674 F.3d 1359, 1364 (Fed. Cir. 2012) (finding that the Board could find that the appellant's testimony was insufficient to establish that the agency improperly charged him military leave when the appellant failed to produce pay records to support his claims), *with Tierney v. Department of Justice*, 717 F.3d 1374, 1377 -79 (Fed. Cir. 2013) (finding that the Board could not overrule the AJ's de termination that a witness was credible when the witness's statements were supported by pay records).

[249] *See, e.g., Strausbaugh v. Government Printing Office*, 117 M.S.P.R. 566 (conduct -based action); *McMillan v. Department of Justice*, 120 M.S.P.R. 1 (2013) (performance -based action).

[250] *Strausbaugh v. Government Printing Office*, 117 M.S.P.R. 566, 3-7, 12, 15 (2012). *See also Swidecki v. Department of Commerce*, 113 M.S.P.R. 168, 8-10 (2010) (remanding the case for a decision on the merits as to whether the agency re moved the appellant from consideration for a position due to antimilitary discrimination or if it was because he failed a background check due to criminal conduct).

[251] *McMillan v. Department of Justice*, 120 M.S.P.R. 1, 2-9 (2013).

[252] *McMillan v. Department of Justice*, 120 M.S.P.R. 1, 11, 16-18 (2013).

[253] *McMillan v. Department of Justice*, 120 M.S.P.R. 1, 17 (2013).

[254] *McMillan v. Department of Justice*, 120 M.S.P.R. 1, 2-9, 11, 16 -18 (2013).

[255] DOL and OSC have "inter related statutory obligations" under USERRA. In the past, they have addressed this situation through the use of a memorandum of understanding. Individuals interested in using either agency to pursue a USERRA claim may benefit from checking to see which agency they should contact as such agreements can change. *See, e.g.,* Memorandum of Understanding Between Veterans 'Employment and Training Service, United States Department of Labor and the United States Office of Special Counsel, at 6, available at available at https://osc.gov/resources/ osc_d1 1.pdf (explaining that "[t]he provisions [of the agreement] may be reviewed and modified or terminated when it is determined, by either agency that such review and modification or termination is in [the] interest of efficient enforcement of the law or law s involved").

[256] *Gossage v. Department of Labor*, 118 M.S.P.R. 455, 8 (2012); *Graham v. Commodity Futures Trading Commission*, 105 M.S.P.R. 392, 5 (2007).

[257] *Gossage v. Department of Labor*, 118 M.S.P.R. 455, 8 (2012); *Graham v. Commodity Futures Trading Commission*, 105 M.S.P.R. 392, 5 (2007).

[258] *See Garcia v. Department of State*, 101 M.S.P.R. 172, 14 -17 (2006).

[259] *Jones v. Perkins*, 76 F. 82, 85 (Mich., E. Dist., 1896).

[260] *Pueschel v. Department of Transportation*, 113 M.S.P.R. 422, 6 (2010).

[261] *Johnson v. U.S. Postal Service*, 121 M.S.P.R. 101, 2-3 (2014).

[262] *Johnson v. U.S. Postal Service*, 121 M.S.P.R. 101, 4 (2014).

[263] *Johnson v. U.S. Postal Service*, 121 M.S.P.R. 101, 5-7 (2014).

[264] *Johnson v. U.S. Postal Service*, 121 M.S.P.R. 101, 8-9 (2014).

[265] *See Brown v. U.S. Postal Service*, 106 M.S.P.R. 12, 19 (2007); *Holmes v. Department of Justice*, 92 M.S.P.R. 377, 11-12 (2007).

[266] *Brown v. U.S. Postal Service*, 106 M.S.P.R. 12, 9, 18-19 (2007).

[267] *See, e.g., Machulas v. Department of the Air Force*, 109 M.S.P.R. 165, 7 (2008) (finding that the Board could have jurisdiction over military leave issue s from 15 years earlier).

[268] *See, e.g., Johnson v. U.S. Postal Service*, 121 M.S.P.R. 101, 8-9 (2014) (dismissing the appellant's claim as barred by the doctrine of laches).

[269] *Wilks v. Department of the Army*, 91 M.S.P.R. 70, 11 (2002) (de scribing the issue as one of standing).

[270] A party may choose any representative as long as that person is willing and available to serve. 5 C.F.R. § 1201.31(b).

[271] *Silva v. Department of Homeland Security*, 112 M.S.P.R. 362, 7 (2009) (quoting 38 U.S.C. § 4324(a)(2)(A)).

[272] *See* 5 U.S.C. §§ 2302(b)(11), 2302(e)(2), 1214; 38 U.S.C. § 4301 *et seq.*

[273] 38 U.S.C. § 4303(5); 5 U.S.C. § 2302(a)(2)(C)(ii). *See Erlendson v. Justice*, 121 M.S.P.R. 441, 6 (2014); (finding that the Board lacked jurisdiction over the appellant's USERRA complaint against the Federal Bureau of Investigation); *Alford v. Department of Defense*, 113 M.S.P.R. 263, 15 (2010) (finding that an employee of the Defense Intelligence Agency cannot file a USERRA appeal with the Board).

[274] *Conyers v. Merit Systems Protection Board*, 388 F.3d 1380, 1381 -83 (Fed. Cir. 2004) (explaining why the undersecretary has "greater flexibility regarding screener positions than he or she may have with respect to other classes of employees"); *see Spain v. Department of Homeland Security*, 99 M.S.P.R. 529, 8-9 (2005) (applying *Conyers* to find that the Board lacked USERRA jurisdiction over termination and failure to reemploy claim s). *But see Quinlan v. Department of Homeland Security*, 118 M.S.P.R. 362, 8 (2012) (finding that MSP B has jurisdiction over TSA reductions in grade under the language of 49 U.S.C. § 40122(g)(3)); *Aquino v. Department of Homeland Security*, 121 M.S.P.R. 3 5, 12 (2014) (explaining that MSP B has jurisdiction over TSA whistleblower claims under the Whistle blower Protection Enhancement Act of 2012). TSA began as a part of the Department of Transportation and later became a part of the Department of Homeland Security. Thus, TSA case s may be found under either name, depending on when the suit occurred.

[275] *Compare* 5 U.S.C. § 3330(a)(1) (not defining "agency"), *with* 38 U.S.C. § 4303(4) (explaining that an "employer" includes an entity that has control over employment opportunities).

[276] The Board has not yet been presented with a case where an individual asserts a VEOA claim against a private sector contractor, and therefore cannot state what might occur under such a case.

[277] In 2011, it was estimated that the Government spent approximately $320 billion on contracts for services. Ron Nixon, "Government Pays More in Contracts, Study Finds," New York Times, Se p. 12, 2011, available at http:// www.nytimes.com/2011/09/ 13/us/13contractor. html.

[278] *Silva v. Department of Homeland Security*, 112 M.S.P.R. 362, 2 (2009).

[279] *Silva v. Department of Homeland Security*, 112 M.S.P.R. 362, 10, 13-14 (2009) (quoting *Kirkendall v. Department of the Army*, 479 F.3d 830, 846 (Fed. Cir. 2007)).

[280] *Silva v. Department of Homeland Security*, 112 M.S.P.R. 362, 15, 19 (2009).

[281] *Compare Burroughs v. Department of the Army*, 115 M.S.P.R. 656, 8 (2011) (finding no entitlement to VEOA hearing), *with Kirkendall v. Department of the Army*, 479 F.3d 830, 844 -46 (Fed. Cir. 2007) (finding that the Board cannot exercise discretion but rather must grant a USERRA hearing if one is requested).

[282] *Gossage v. Department of Labor*, 118 M.S.P.R. 455, 10 (2012).

[283] *Downs v. Department of Veterans Affairs*, 110 M.S.P.R. 139, 17 18 (2008).

[284] *Chertkov v. Office of Personnel Management*, 52 F.3d 961, 966 (Fed. Cir. 1995) (internal punctuation and citations omitted).

[285] *See Gonzalez v. Department of Homeland Security*, 110 M.S.P.R. 567, 6 (200 9); *Lodge v. Department of the Treasury*, 109 M.S.P.R. 614, 7 (2008).

[286] Lost wages under USERRA are different from back pay under the Back Pay Act (which applies to many other Board decisions). Under USERRA, a service member is expected to exercise reasonable diligence to mitigate economic damage s suffered as a result of an employer's violation of USERRA. Therefore, an award of lost wage s and benefits must be offset by the amount the appellant should have reasonably earned during the relevant period. In contrast, the Back Pay Act doe s not require that a back pay award be offset by what an employee should have reasonably earned during the relevant period; rather, 5 U.S.C. § 5596 requires only that an award of back pay be offset by amounts actually earned by the employee through other employment during the period at issue. *Erickson v. U.S. Postal Service*, 120 M.S.P.R. 468, 17, n.6 (2013).

[287] *See Grandberry v. Department of Homeland Security*, 406 F. App'x 472, 475 (Fed. Cir. 2010).

[288] *See, e.g., Tully v. Department of Justice*, 481 F.3d 1367, 1369 (Fed. Cir. 2007) (explaining that a basic principle of USERRA is that service member employees receive benefits equal to, but not more favorable than, those generally available to all employees of the employer).

[289] 5 U.S.C. § 3330a(a)(1).

[290] 38 U.S.C. § 4311(a). *See Lourens v. Merit Systems Protection Board*, 193 F.3d 1369, 1371 (Fed. Cir. 1999) (holding that the Board did not have USERRA jurisdiction over claims by a widow with derived preference eligibility when the widow had not been a member of —or applicant to —a uniformed service).

[291] *Morse v. Merit Systems Protection Board*, 621 F.3d 1346, 1348 -51 (Fed. Cir. 2010) (holding that the Board lacks jurisdiction over VEOA appeals from TSA applicants); *see Belhumeur v. Department of Transportation*, 104 M.S.P.R. 408, 8 (2007) (holding that the Board lacks jurisdiction over VEOA appeals from F AA employee s and applicants).

[292] *Conyers v. Merit Systems Protection Board*, 388 F.3d 1380, 1381 -83 (Fed. Cir. 2004); *see Spain v. Department of Homeland Security*, 99 M.S.P.R. 529, 8-9 (2005) (applying *Conyers* to find that the Board lacked USERRA jurisdiction over termination and failure to reemploy claims). *But see Quinlan v. Department of Homeland Security*, 118 M.S.P.R. 362, 8 (2012) (finding that MSPB has jurisdiction over TSA reductions in grade under the language of 49 U.S.C. § 40122(g)(3)); *Aquino v. Department of Homeland Security*, 121 M.S.P.R. 35, 12 (2014) (explaining that MSPB has jurisdiction over TSA whistle blower claims under the Whistle blower Protection Enhancement Act of 2012).

[293] *Lazaro v. Department of Veterans Affairs*, 666 F.3d 1316, 1319 (Fed. Cir. 2012); *Becker v. Department of Veterans Affairs*, 115 M.S.P.R. 409, 5 (2010).

[294] *Mims v. Social Security Administration*, 120 M.S.P.R. 213, 22 (2013); *Williams v. Department of the Air Force*, 97 M.S.P.R. 252, 10 (2004).

[295] *Aguilar v. U.S. Postal Service,* 102 M.S.P.R. 102, 8 (2006).

[296] *Aguilar v. U.S. Postal Service,* 102 M.S.P.R. 102, 8 (2006).

[297] *See Kirkendall v. Department of the Army*, 479 F.3d 830, 844 (Fed. Cir. 2007) (holding that 5 U.S.C. §§ 3330a(a)(1)(A) and 3330a (d)(1)(B) are subject to equitable tolling); 5 U.S.C. § 3330a(a)(2)(A).

[298] *Gossage v. Department of Labor*, 118 M.S.P.R. 455, 8 (2012); *Graham v. Commodity Futures Trading Commission*, 105 M.S.P.R. 392, 5 (2007).

[299] *Burroughs v. Department of the Army*, 116 M.S.P.R. 292, 8, 10 (2011); 5 U.S.C. § 3330a(d).

[300] *Gossage v. Department of Labor*, 118 M.S.P.R. 455, 8 (2012); *Graham v. Commodity Futures Trading Commission*, 105 M.S.P.R. 392, 5 (2007).

[301] 5 U.S.C. § 3330a(d)(1).

[302] *See Garcia v. Department of State*, 101 M.S.P.R. 172, 14 -17 (2006).

[303] *Lisv. U.S. Postal Service*, 113 M.S.P.R. 415, 11 (2010).

[304] *Burroughs v. Department of the Army*, 120 M.S.P.R. 392, 5 (2013); *Strausbaugh v. Government Printing Office*, 117 M.S.P.R. 566, 11 (2012).

[305] *Clavin v. U.S. Postal Service*, 99 M.S.P.R. 619, 6 (2005) (explaining that the standard for reemployment cases is derived from 5 U.S.C. § 7701(c)(2)(B)). *See* 5 U.S.C. § 7701(c)(2)(B) (stating that a n agency must prove its case by preponderant evidence).

[306] *See* 5 U.S.C. §§ 2302(b)(11), 2302(e)(2), 1214.

[307] *Silva v. Department of Homeland Security*, 112 M.S.P.R. 362, 15, 19 (2009) (quoting 38 U.S.C. § 4324(a)(2)(A)).

[308] *Compare Burroughs v. Department of the Army*, 115 M.S.P.R. 656, 8 (2011) (finding no entitlement to VEOA hearing), *with Kirkendall v. Department of the Army*, 479 F.3d 830, 844 -46 (Fed. Cir. 2007) (finding that the Board cannot exercise discretion but rather must grant a USERRA hearing if one is requested).

[309] *Compare Burroughs v. Department of the Army*, 115 M.S.P.R. 656, 8 (2011) (finding no entitlement to VEOA hearing), *with Kirkendall v. Department of the Army*, 479 F.3d 830, 844 -46 (Fed. Cir. 2007) (finding that the Board cannot exercise discretion but rather must grant a USERRA hearing if one is requested).

[310] 5 U.S.C. § 3330c.

[311] 38 U.S.C. § 4324.

[312] *Black's Law Dictionary*, 9th e d. (2009).

[313] *United States v. Brockamp*, 519 U.S. 347, 350 (1997) (emphasis in original, punctuation modified).

[314] *See Kirkendall v. Department of the Army*, 479 F.3d 830, 836 (Fed. Cir. 2007) (explaining that the court must be guided by the presumption established in *Irwin v. Department of Veterans Affairs*, 498 U.S. 89 (1990)).

[315] *United States v. Brockamp*, 519 U.S. 347, 350, 354 (1997).

[316] 5 U.S.C. § 3330a(d); *see Kirkendall v. Department of the Army*, 479 F.3d 830, 838 (Fed. Cir. 2007) (describing this language as "certainly strong").

[317] 5 U.S.C. § 3330a(a)(2)(a).

[318] *Kirkendall v. Department of the Army*, 479 F.3d 830, 838 -41 (Fed. Cir. 2007).

[319] *Kirkendall v. Department of the Army*, 479 F.3d 830, 843 -44 (Fed. Cir. 2007).

[320] *Roesel v. Peace Corps*, 111 M.S.P.R. 366, 8 (2009).

INDEX

#

A

B

C

N

O

P

Q

R

S

T

U

V

W